Negotiating Critical Literacies in Classrooms

Negotiating Critical
Literacies in Classrooms

Edited by

Barbara Comber
Anne Simpson

Centre for Studies in Literacy, Policy and Learning Cultures
University of South Australia

LAWRENCE ERLBAUM ASSOCIATES, PUBLISHERS
2001   Mahwah, New Jersey   London

LC
149
.N39
2001
ERC

Lawrence Erlbaum Associates, Inc., Publishers
10 Industrial Avenue
Mahwah, NJ 07430

Cover design by Kathryn Houghtaling Lacey

Library of Congress Cataloging-in-Publication Data

Negotiating critical literacies in classrooms / edited by Barbara Comber and
    Anne Simpson.
p. cm.
Includes bibliographical references and index.
ISBN 0-8058-3793-0 (cloth: alk. paper)—ISBN 0-8058-3794-9 (pbk: alk.
paper)
1. Literacy—Social aspects 2. Critical pedagogy.
I. Comber, Barbara.   II. Simpson, Anne, 1944—
LC149.N39   2001
370.11'5—dc21   00-064652
                                                      CIP

Books published by Lawrence Erlbaum Associates are printed on
acid-free paper, and their bindings are chosen for strength and durability.

Printed in the United States of America
10 9 8 7 6 5 4 3 2

Contents

Part II: Exploring Critical Literacies in Primary Schooling: Unresolved Questions

Part III: Critical Literacies and Questions of Identity

Preface

As educators in diverse communities research ways of giving students access to powerful literate practices (Comber, 1994; Lankshear, 1994), so the topic of critical literacy appears more and more often in professional journals and national and international conferences. Although critical literacy has a long history (Freire, 1970; Willinsky, 1993) what counts as powerful or critical literacies is a matter for debate and local negotiation (Lankshear & McLaren, 1993; Luke & Freebody, 1997).

Despite the growing interest in critical literacies, there remain relatively few theorised accounts of enacted classroom practices in different institutional and geographic sites (for exceptions see Fairclough, 1992; Muspratt, Luke, & Freebody, 1997). This collection proposes to bring together accounts of a number of educators who have sought to make a difference in the lives of their students through literacy education—from university classrooms in the United States, England, and South Africa, to multicultural primary school classrooms in rural India and Canada, to policy and curriculum development in Singapore and Australia. In each case the writers have worked with particular theories and political commitments in negotiating and constructing local versions of critical literacies. Moreover, they have remained open to the sometimes unanticipated effects of enacted theories in specific political and cultural contexts. The belief that there are no generic universal critical or empowering literacies or pedagogies (Kamler & Comber, 1996; Luke, 1996), but rather that these literacies must be worked out in specific locations, is the overarching theme that unites this collection.

History has shown that different pedagogical orientations, even those that make claims for emancipatory effects, have differential consequences for different groups of students in different locations (Cochran-Smith, 1995; Edelsky, 1991; Ellsworth, 1992). With regard to literacy education, critical researchers have demonstrated that assumptions held by White middle-class progressivists about the empowering effects of naturalistic approaches are unfounded (Delpit, 1988; Freebody, Ludwig, & Gunn, 1995; Lensmire, 1994; Luke, 1993; Walton, 1993; Willis, 1995). Evidence suggests that race, ethnicity, language, poverty, location and gender impact on students' educational success and the ways in which they participate in the authorised discursive practices available in educational institutions. As the writers of these chapters reveal, it is not possible to work with any simple formula, and each group of students' specific cultural and political histories impact what is needed and what is possible.

The authors of the chapters represented here write as teachers. The literacy classrooms they explore include the early years of schooling, primary and secondary education through to community and university sites. Each of the chapters represents the results of extended periods of research on classroom practice. The writers take different theoretical starting points. For example, several writers draw on a critical language-awareness approach (Clarence-Fincham, chap. 15; Cruddas & Watson, chap. 12; Janks, chap. 9; Stein, chap. 10; Wallace, chap. 13) and another group focuses on the ways in which students use the classroom space of literacy lessons to pursue their own social and political agendas (Cheah, chap. 5; Dyson, chap. 1; Sahni, chap. 2; Vasquez, chap. 4). A number of other writers start with a commitment to examining the textual construction of gender (Bell, chap. 14; O'Brien, chap. 3; Mellor & Patterson, chap. 8; Martino, chap. 11). Hence the collection acknowledges that there is no one generic critical literacy, in theory or in practice. Rather there is a range of theories that are productive starting points for educators working on social justice agendas through the literacy curriculum.

The book is organized around different levels of education, but there are clearly overlapping themes across the chapters, including identity formation and textual practices, politicizing curriculum and textbook production, and changing the power relationships in classroom talk around text.

The collection is divided into four main sections:

- Critical from the Start: Examining Relations of Power in Textual Practices,

- Exploring Critical Literacies in Primary Schooling: Unresolved Questions,

- Critical Literacies and Questions of Identity, and

- Tertiary Education as a Site for Critical Literacies.

CRITICAL FROM THE START: EXAMINING RELATIONSHIPS
OF POWER IN TEXTUAL PRACTICES

We begin with those chapters that explore the early years of schooling. It is sometimes assumed that critical literacies occur within a developmental hierarchy, after students have achieved automaticity with decoding, meaning making, and functional uses of texts. However contributors in this section demonstrate how critical literacies can incorporate textual material from the everyday worlds of young children, including the media and peer and home traditions, in addition to authorized school texts.

Dyson (chap. 1) argues that theorists of critical pedagogy sometimes ignore children's social worlds. Dyson draws on her observations in a multiracial, urban primary school in San Francisco's East Bay to consider the dynamics of children exploring socio-political issues in the literacy classroom. In particular Dyson shows how play around the texts of popular culture—"children's semiotic materials"—can create spaces for critical reflection on power. Sahni (chap. 2) also explores questions concerning children's purposes through discussions of children in a Grade 2 class in rural India. Like Dyson, Sahni retheorizes connections between literacy and power in "children's terms." She contends that empowerment needs to be understood as relational and therefore must be examined in specific contexts rather than in broad political terms.

O'Brien (chap. 3) reports on her extended classroom research as an early years teacher with 5- to 8-year-old children in a suburban classroom in South Australia. O'Brien's explicit project was to examine the ways in which texts construct gendered identities. She begins by explaining the theoretical frame she brought to her teaching and research, and then describes how she and her class critically read a range of texts, including informational texts, children's literature, everyday texts, and texts associated with popular culture. O'Brien concludes by discussing some unanticipated problems and contradictions with her "critical enterprise."

The context for the chapter by Vasquez (chap. 4) is a multiracial class of 4- and 5-year-olds in Toronto. Vasquez began with the belief that children will raise cultural questions about their everyday lives that could be used as the basis for conversations that would generate a critical curriculum. She uses Harste's concept of an *audit trail* as a public display of her notes and artifacts to allow others to trace the development of her thinking, which foregrounds a critical approach to social justice issues such as race and gender in the curriculum.

EXPLORING CRITICAL LITERACIES IN PRIMARY SCHOOLING:
UNRESOLVED QUESTIONS

In this section, five educators concerned with primary schooling consider negotiating critical literacies in their very different classroom contexts. Cheah (chap. 5) examines what might count as critical literacy for children learning English as a second language in Singapore. She points out that in Singapore the move to participatory language practices is revolutionary when compared with traditional "top–down, teacher-dominated and examination driven" pedagogies. A case study of the ways in which one teacher negotiated official curriculum demands and incorporated new literacy practices is provided. What might constitute *critical* rather than *functional* literacy for non-native speakers of English is one of the issues that an appreciation and acknowledgment of local context foregrounds.

A different perspective is offered by Lin (chap. 6) who presents a fine grained analysis of a videotaped lesson in a school located in a working-class residential area in Hong Kong. Her analysis shows how these limited English speaking Cantonese school children subverted an English reading lesson. She examines how they artfully and playfully contested the school reading curriculum with their own preferred narrative practices that were illegitimate in the school.

Bigelow (chap. 7) focuses on an important new site for critical practices: curriculum software produced for use in schools. He presents his analysis of a popular educational computer game, The Oregon Trail CD-ROM and shows how it marginalizes the experiences of women, African Americans and Native Americans, and is contemptuous of the earth. The choice-posing structure of the game fails to alert individual players to the social or ecological consequences of their decisions. The author suggests a series of questions for teachers to ask of educational CD-ROMs and outlines a number of classroom activities to begin to develop a more critical computer literacy.

Finally in this section, Mellor and Patterson (chap. 8) reconsider the nature and effects of critical reading practices. Through an examination of their own countersexist curriculum materials and their use in upper primary Western Australian classrooms, they question the extent to which critical literacy requires fundamental shifts in personal thinking, ethical and ideological positions, and to what extent might it be helpful to think about critical reading as learned practices that foster alternative normative positions.

CRITICAL LITERACIES AND QUESTIONS OF IDENTITY

Working with adolescents and young adults poses particular questions and issues for literacy educators, as Janks (chap. 9) found when she trialed her Critical Language Awareness Series in secondary schools in Johannesburg. Janks begins by contextualizing the development of the series within the political and cultural history of South Africa. The major part of chapter details the responses of teachers and students to the materials. Janks explores the possibilities, challenges, insights, frustrations, fears, and excitement generated by the use of the series. Also located in the high school setting of Johannesburg is the work of Stein (chap. 10). Stein writes about a multilingual storytelling project with high school students in a Black township. She demonstrates how students combined African oral storytelling, contemporary film, and television performance genres for their own purposes.

Gender plays a crucial role in adolescent literacy practices and therefore in the negotiation of critical literacies in high schools. Martino (chap. 11) describes his research on masculinity and critical reading practices with adolescent boys in a Western Australian high school. Starting with an explication of his theoretical position on masculinity, Martino then moves to examine boys' different responses to texts that open up different positions for them as gendered subjects.

In South Africa, Black writers have historically been excluded from publishing, but with the dismantling of apartheid, the situation is rapidly changing. However as Cruddas and Watson (chap. 12) discuss, there are still tensions between the language and the content of the material being produced, particularly that produced specifically for teaching adult literacy. The project they describe was designed to allow Black writers to "reposition themselves and to challenge the dominance of the English language and literacy traditions."

TERTIARY EDUCATION AS A SITE FOR CRITICAL LITERACIES

This section focuses on higher education and how university and professional development sites mediate critical literacies. Wallace (chap. 13) explores how critical interpretations of texts can be negotiated in a culturally diverse group of adult second language learners. She focuses on specific spoken interactions around written texts and the circumstances in which interpretations might diverge or converge toward consensus. One factor that may condition the nature and range of responses is the role of the teacher in adjudicating or legitimating responses. She explores whether teachers can differentiate between control and power and asks, "How might the teacher maintain the former while avoiding the latter in her role as equal participant in consensual talk?" The chapter discusses the role of the teacher as facilitative or obstructive in the development of critical debate around texts.

Bell's (chap. 14) chapter explains how he has used film to attempt to make critical theory and critical literacies more accessible to student teachers. He reports some of the difficulties faced by the students in developing critical literate practices around the selected films and presents an evaluation of the project from his and the students' points of view.

Clarence-Fincham (chap. 15) considers the impact of university discourse on students who come to the university with English as a second language. She delivers a critical literacy course for first-year students that encourages them to examine how they are positioned by university discourses and at the same time provides some of the academic strategies required for university success. The course engages students and their tutors in deconstructing both the university institutional context as well as the language practices within it.

Wooldridge (chap. 16) was involved in a collaborative action research project with secondary school teachers exploring the meaning and potential of critical literacy in their schools. Taking the view that critical literacy contributes to the ways schools can become sites for social justice, Wooldridge and her colleagues probed the tensions and ambiguities involved in designing and implementing a critical orientation to curriculum and literacy pedagogy. In this chapter she addresses the difficulties teachers anticipated in confronting the political nature of their work within a state education system that emphasized standards and outcomes.

In each of these accounts educators explain how they have taken a body of theory and worked with and on it in classrooms. Their rich portrayals and narratives of classroom realities illustrate the unanticipated effects of pedagogies that emerge in specific contexts. Experiences from the classrooms have led them to revise theories that are central to critical literacy, including constructs such as *empowerment*, *resistance*, and *multiple readings*. This collection documents what occurs when educators confront the difficult ethical and political issues which evolve in particular classroom situations.

REFERENCES

Cochran-Smith, M. (1995). Uncertain allies: Understanding the boundaries of race and teaching. *Harvard Educational Review, 65*(4), 541–561.

Comber, B. (1994). Critical literacy: An introduction to Australian debates and perspectives. *Journal of Curriculum Studies, 26*(6), 655–668.

Delpit, L. (1988). The silenced dialogue: Power and pedagogy in educating other people's children. *Harvard Educational Review, 58*(3), 280–298.

Edelsky, C. (1991). *With literacy and justice for all: Rethinking the social in language and education.* New York: Falmer.

Ellsworth, E. (1992). Why doesn't this feel empowering? Working through the repressive myths of critical pedagogy. In C. Luke & J. Gore (Eds.), *Feminisms and critical pedagogy* (pp. 90–119). New York: Routledge & Kegan Paul.

Fairclough, N. (Ed.). (1992). *Critical language awareness.* London: Longman.

Freebody, P., Ludwig, C., & Gunn, S. (1995). *Everyday literacy practices in and out of schools in low socio-economic urban communities.* Brisbane, Australia: Griffith University.

Freire, P. (1970). *Pedagogy of the oppressed.* New York: Herder & Herder.

Kamler, B., & Comber, B. (1996). Critical literacy: Not generic—not developmental—not another orthodoxy. *Changing Education: A Journal for Teachers and Administrators, 3*(1), 1–2, 4–5.

Lankshear, C. (1994). *Critical literacy (Occasional paper no. 3).* Canberra, Australia: Australian Curriculum Studies Association.

Lankshear, C., & McLaren, L. (1993). *Critical literacy: Politics, praxis and the postmodern.* Albany, NY: SUNY Albany.

Lensmire, T. (1994). Writing workshop as carnival: Reflections on an alternative learning environment. *Harvard Educational Review, 64*(4), 371–391.

Luke, A. (1993). Stories of social regulation: The micro politics of classroom narrative. In B. Green (Ed.), *The insistence of the letter: Literacy studies and curriculum theorizing* (pp. 137–155). London: Falmer.

Luke, A. (1996). When literacy might (not) make a difference: Life trajectories and cultural capital. In C. Baker, J. Cook-Gumperz, & A. Luke (Eds.), *Cross cultural perspectives on literacy learning.* Mahwah, NJ: Lawrence Erlbaum Associates.

Luke, A., & Freebody, P. (1997). Critical literacy and the question of normativity: An introduction in classroom narrative. In S. Muspratt, A. Luke, & P. Freebody (Eds.), *Constructing critical literacies* (pp. 1–18). Creskill, NJ: Hampton.

Muspratt, S., Luke, A., & Freebody, P. (Eds.). (1997). *Constructing critical literacies.* Creskill, NJ: Hampton.

Walton, C. (1993). Literacy in Aboriginal contexts: Re-examining pedagogy. In A. Luke & P. Gilbert (Eds.), *Literacy in contexts: Australian issues and perspectives* (pp. 39–45). St. Leonards, Australia: Allen & Unwin.

Willinsky, J. (1993). Lessons from the literacy before schooling 1800–1850. In B. Green (Ed.), *The insistence of the letter: Literacy studies and curriculum theorizing* (pp. 58–74). London: Falmer.

Willis, A. (1995). School literacy experiences: How culturally narrow are they? *Discourse, 16*(2), 219–235.

List of Contributors

James Bell is a lecturer in the Context Section of the School of Education, Murdoch University, Western Australia. His professional interests include sociological and philosophical perspectives in education with a particular interest in critical theory and popular culture, postmodern critiques of schooling, and relistening to silenced voices and social change. His PhD thesis was *Democratic Faith: In Search of a More Accessible Critical Pedagogy for Teachers in Their Classrooms* (1995). His most recent work includes the CD-ROM WEB program *Changing Outcomes: A Meeting Needs Approach to Course Design in Universities* (2000; with Annette Patterson).

Bill Bigelow teaches at Franklin High School in Portland, Oregon. He is an editor of the journal *Rethinking Schools*, and is the author and/or editor of several curricula, including *Strangers in Their Own Country: A curriculum on South Africa* (1985) and (with Norman Diamond) *The Power in Our Hands: A Curriculum on the History of Work and Workers in the United States* (1988). He coedited *Rethinking Columbus: Teaching about the 500th anniversary of Columbus's Arrival in the Americas* (1991; 2nd edition, 1998) and *Rethinking our Classrooms: Teaching for Equity and Justice* (1994). His research interests include the production and reproduction of inequality in public schools; and critical, antiracist, multicultural teaching experiences.

Yin Mee Cheah is an educational consultant who has more than 20 years experience as a teacher and teacher educator in Singapore. Her latest publication is a co-edited book on *Language Instructional Issues in Asian*

Classrooms (1999) published by the International Development in Asia Committee (IDAC) and distributed by the International Reading Association (IRA). Her research interests are in language and literacy education and teacher education.

Jenny Clarence-Fincham is a senior lecturer in the Department of Applied Language Studies at the University of Natal, Pietermaritzburg, South Africa. Her professional interests include critical linguistics and literacy, genre analysis, language acquisition, English as second language (ESL) methodology, curriculum, and academic development. She is the author of *Language Power and Voices of a University: The Role of Critical Linguistics in Curriculum Development* (1992) and with F. Jackson, *A Critical Reflection on the Use of Reaction Papers as a Means of Academic Development in a Postgraduate Course* (1993). Her recently completed doctoral thesis is entitled: "Voices in a university: A critical exploration of black students' responses to institutional discourse."

Barbara Comber is an associate professor at the Centre for Studies in Literacy, Policy and Learning Cultures at the University of South Australia. Her professional interests include developing literacy pedagogies for diverse and disadvantaged student communities, critical literacies, teachers' work, the relationships between literacy and social justice, and historical changes in the construction of literacy curriculum. Publications include *Critical Literacies: An Introduction to Australian Debates and Perspectives* (1994), *Classroom Explorations in Critical Literacy* (1993) and *Negotiating Critical Literacies in Classrooms* (2001).

Leora Cruddas is currently working in an inner city London borough with a commitment to inclusive education as an officer for the Local Education Authority.

Anne Haas Dyson is Professor of Language, Literacy, and Culture in the School of Education at the University of California, Berkeley and a recent recipient of UC-Berkeley's Distinguished Teaching Award. A former teacher of young children, she studies the social lives and literacy learning of schoolchildren. Among her publications are *The Need for Story: Cultural Diversity in Classroom and Community* (co-edited with Celia Genishi), *Social Worlds of Children Learning to Write in an Urban Primary School*, which was awarded NCTE's David Russell Award for Distinguished Research, and *Writing Superheroes: Contemporary Childhood, Popular Culture, and Classroom Literacy*.

Hilary Janks is an associate professor and head of the Division of Applied English Language Studies at the University of the Witwatersrand, Johannesburg, South Africa. Her professional interests include English teacher education, English curriculum and critical discourse analysis. She is the editor of the *Critical Language Awareness* Series workbooks, which make theories about the relation between language, ideology and power accessible to students in schools.

Angel M.Y. Lin is an assistant professor at the Department of English, City University of Hong Kong. Her professional interests include literacy development, school ethnography and critical cultural studies. She has authored research reports: *Teaching in Two Tongues: Language alternation in foreign language classrooms* (1990); *Intrinsic Motivation and Second Language Attainment* (1991); and research articles: *Bilingualism or Linguistic Segregation? Symbolic domination, resistance and code switching in Hong Kong schools* (1996); *Understanding the Issue of the Medium of Instruction in Hong Kong: What research approaches do we need?* (1996).

Wayne Martino lectures in the School of Education at Murdoch University in Perth, Western Australia. He has published two textbooks which deal with critical literary perspectives on teaching texts—*From the Margins* and *Gendered Fictions* with Bronwyn Mellor. He has just completed two books: *Boys Stuff: Boys Talk about What Really Matters,* and *What About the Boys: Issues of Masculinity in Schools,"* with Bob Meyenn. Currently he is working on another book with Maria Pallotta-Chiarolli entitled *"So What's A Boy?"*

Bronwyn Mellor is Editorial Director of Chalkface Press and author of several books in the NCTE Chalkface Series on critical literacy. She is currently working on a new book with Brian Moon on writing in the literature classroom. Dr. Mellor is the author of scholarly articles addressing her primary areas of research which include English and literature education and reading practices.

Jennifer O'Brien is a research assistant at the Language and Literacy Research Centre, University of South Australia. Her research interests include critical literacy and popular culture in early years classrooms. Recent publications include *Critical Literacies and Cultural Studies* (1996) with Allan Luke and Barbara Comber and *Key Literacy Planning: Planning and Programming for Literacy Equity* (1995) with Tony Hole.

Annette Patterson teaches sociology and literacy education courses at James Cook University, School of Education, Townsville, Queensland, Australia. Her research interests include histories of literacy education, and English and literature education. Her most recent book, *Questions of English*, (London & New York: Routledge) co-authored with Robin Peel and Jeanne Gerlach, explores the use of English pedagogy for civic and moral formation in three countries. She has co-authored with Bronwyn Mellor and Marnie O'Neill, three books for secondary schools in the NCTE Chalkface Series (Urbana, Illinois) on critical literacy and literature education.

Urvashi Sahni is a founder principal of an experimental elementary school in Lucknow called Study Hall, and is also Project Director of a USAID funded Action Research project on improving girls' education in India. She works with teachers in primary schools in villages in Uttar Pradesh, India, helping them examine their classroom practice for gender biases. She is also involved in developing and implementing other in-service training modules to help teachers gain a better understanding of language development in children and sensitizing teachers to more child-responsive and participatory ways of transacting the curriculum. Recent publications include *A Teacher's Manual for First Grade Teachers*.

Anne Simpson was until recently, a senior lecturer in Literacy and Language Education at the University of South Australia. Her professional and research interests include literature for children and adolescents, reading programs, gender issues in literature and literacy, and critical reading practices. She has also conducted research in the area of visual literacy in the classroom. Recent publications include *Critical Questions: Whose questions?* (1996); *Fiction and Facts: Girls' and Boys' Reading Practices* (1996) and *There's More Than Tomato Day to Come: Shared Reading and the Teacher-Librarian* (1996). She is now working as an educational consultant.

Pippa Stein is a senior lecturer in the Department of Applied English Language Studies at the University of the Witwatersrand, Johannesburg, South Africa. Her research interests are in the area of literacies including multiliteracies and early literacy. She has published in the *Harvard Educational Review, the TESOL Quarterly* and with the New London Group Multiliteracies Project. She is co-author of *Communicating Today,* an English textbook series for South African multilingual, multicultural classrooms.

Vivian Vasquez is an assistant professor in the School of Education at American University. Her research interests include critical literacy in practice, language curricula and cultural literacy. Her work has appeared in various publications including *The Reading Teacher, Language Arts, Primary Voices, Reading,* and *Indirections*, and has been presented at international conferences in England, Australia, the United States, and Canada.

Vivian is a past board member of the Whole Language Umbrella Conference and is chair of the Elementary Section Steering Committee.

Catherine Wallace is Senior Lecturer in Education in the academic group Languages in Education at the Institute of Education, University of London. Her research interests are in the area of language and literacy, critical linguistics and sociolinguistics. Publications include: *Learning to Read in a Multicultural Society: The Social Context of Second Language Literacy* (Prentice Hall, 1988) and *Reading* (Oxford University Press, 1992).

Patricia Watson is a lecturer in the Applied English Language Studies at the University of Witwatersrand, Johannesburg, South Africa. Her professional interests include classroom based research; the development of popular education media; language, ideology, and power; and the impact of new information technologies for learning in cyberspace. Publications include: *The Politics of Popular Visual Literature: Electing Images with the Community* (1994) and *Comics and Rural Development* (1994); *Voices from the Classroom: The Relationship between a New Science Teacher's Pedagogic Beliefs and Classroom Practice* (1995) and *Dynamising Authorship: Creating Readers with Readers* (1996).

Nathalie Wooldridge is English coordinator at Marryatville High School in South Australia. She is a former curriculum officer, Literacy R-12 for the South Australian Department for Education and Children's Services. Current areas of professional interest include literacy in different areas of study and school structures and practices that impact on literacy teaching. Recent publications include *Planning for Early Assistance* (1995); *Social Justice and Literacy* with Robert Hattam (1995) and *Critical Literacy: Against Consent* with Robert Hattam and Lyn Kerkham (1994).

I

Critical From the Start:
Examining Relations of
Power in Textual Practices

1

Relational Sense and Textual Sense in a U.S. Urban Classroom: The Contested Case of Emily, Girl Friend of a Ninja

Anne Haas Dyson
University of California, Berkeley

Emily is a Euro-American girl, a preteen, blonde, and quite pretty. Emily does not say much, and she is almost always polite, but she does have some spunk. She has a crush on Rocky, her good-looking, brown-haired neighbor boy, and vice versa; sometimes, however, she is quite disgusted with his tendency to be a macho "show off." Mainly Emily and Rocky smile at each other and inquire about each other's well-being. Whenever Rocky so much as glances at Emily, his brothers Colt and TumTum enjoy chanting "Rock-y loves, Em-i-ly," to Rocky's dismay. Rocky's grandfather is teaching him and his brothers the ancient martial arts of the ninjas (which will come in handy against Grandfather's former student and nemesis, the evil Snyder).

Emily is not real, in the strict sense of the word because she is a character in a movie marketed to children: *Three Ninjas* (Chang, 1992). Despite her young age, she is now, by all accounts, a has-been, no longer a part of

3

the social and narrative life of the school children I observe in the San Francisco East Bay. Even in the original movie, Emily was only a very minor figure. She had few lines—approximately 23, averaging 4.5 words; and she asked a lot of questions: "Hi. You guys ready?" "Rocky, are you alright?" "Rocky, is that you?" But, at one time, in one classroom, Emily played a starring role; that role was a mediational one—she was used by the children to further their social and textual ends, and so I shall use her here.

Given that this is a book on critical literacy, I anticipate that readers would now expect me to explain how the children's teacher, Kristin, had the children interrogate this movie as a kind of text. That text, with its passive female and active males, its emphasis on the joy and glory of kicking (targeting others only when absolutely necessary) no doubt suggests a fertile textual field for critical uprooting. But this is not what happened, at least not in any simple sense.

Although many of the children were quite familiar with Emily, at first Kristin did not even know who she was. Kristin learned of Emily only because of the classroom literacy practices she initiated, practices that led the children to bring Emily, and other figures from their social lives as children, into the official school world. In fact, this chapter's thesis is that Emily became a useful mediational tool for children's critical reflections in part because of that rootedness in the children's unofficial (child-governed) social world, as well as the official world of school literacy practices. Through those practices, Emily was dialogized, to use a key concept of the language theorist Bakhtin (1981); that is, she was rendered a reflexive symbol whom the children could use both to reflect on and, through writing, to take action within their worlds.

In this chapter, I present narrative examples that illustrate this dialogizing process, and I discuss the local conditions that furthered it, including not only the classroom's literacy practices but also the diversity of its child members and the participatory ethic of its culture. (A more thorough consideration is available in Dyson [1997b]). I begin, however, with a brief explanation of the theoretical underpinnings of this view of children's literacy and its link to their social worlds.

RELATIONAL SENSE, NARRATIVE SENSE, AND THE (RE-) CONSTRUCTION OF SELVES AND OTHERS

It is within the comfort of familiar relations and interactional rhythms with family members that children begin to speak (Bruner, 1983). From those others, children take words—symbols—to name the people, objects, and actions that energize their shared worlds (e.g., mama, daddy, and vacuum. These words are important in an example to follow.) Those given and taken words will always taste of the situational and relational contexts in which they were learned (Bakhtin, 1981). So, as children participate in the recurrent activities or practices of everyday life, they also learn, often quite tacitly, about appropriate relationships between boys and girls, adults, and children, between people of varied physical demeanors and material possessions (Goodnow, Miller, & Kessel, 1995).

In part, critical literacy involves participating in activities or practices in which we use language, oral and written, to reflect on given words and, most importantly, on their familiar relational backdrops (Freire, 1970; Weiler, 1991). At any age, critical literacy is always a personal as well as a political (power-related) matter because it entails reconsidering one's own experience (Williamson, 1981/1982). And critical literacy is always a local as well as a societal matter because it is something we do in response to others' words and actions, including their voiced views on the social world.

Consider, for example, the following family exchange about relationships between mothers, fathers, and vacuum cleaners, reformatted but taken from Dunn's (1988) study of British families:

Megan, 36 months, is arguing with her older brother over who has the right to play with a toy vacuum cleaner. It is Megan's vacuum cleaner, but David has just fixed it. The children plead their case to their mother:

David:　(to Mother) I wanted to do it. Because I fixed it up. And made it work.

Mother:　(to David) Well, you'll have to wait your turn.
　　　...
　　　(to Megan) Are you going to let David have a turn?

Megan:　I have to do it. Ladies do it.

Mother:　Yes, ladies do it. Yes, and men do it sometimes. Daddy sometimes does the hoovering, doesn't he?

Megan:　But I do sometimes.

Mother:　Yes, but Daddy does it sometimes so you let David do it.
　　　(p. 57)

As Dunn makes vividly clear, children's language knowledge and their social ideas, including their consciousness of social categories and possible roles and relationships, emerge from their ongoing participation in relationships that matter to them. Even within Megan's intimate family world, ideological differences emerged. "Ladies do it", Megan had said, voicing the dominant ideology (i.e., societal assumption) about gender relations and appropriate work. But this authoritative statement (Bakhtin, 1981) did not remain unchallenged.

Precisely because of their shared family world, both Megan and her older brother knew the procedures—the family practice—for seeking redress. In their quest for the vacuum, Megan and David addressed their appeals to their mother, justifying their claims to her in a more elaborate way than they did with each other. They articulated their assumptions: investment should yield reward, appropriate tools should go to appropriate persons, the appropriate person for hoovering is a lady.

In the process, then, of seeking identities as powerful people in the family and, more particularly, as people who get to hoover, ideological gaps opened up. In the context of a family practice, these gaps provided all concerned dialogic space within which to give clarifications and (in Mother's case) reasoned orders, and to generate social change in the family's world (i.e., in their management of the toy vacuum).

Such social change for the better is the ultimate goal of critical literacy. Ladies and Daddies have more possibilities than Megan had imagined, and, so, she will have to make some room for David, and, we might hope, David will make some space for her in desirable things that "Daddies do" and "Ladies don't." (We do not know, of course, what happened when Mother, and Dunn, went away ... if Megan had been "internally persuaded" (Bakhtin, 1981, p. 346) or if she had just temporarily acquiesced to a higher power).

As with Megan and David, in diverse cultures, young children's knowledge about rules, roles, and obligations is mediated by their dramatic play and stories (Dunn, 1988; Konner, 1991). Increasingly in the United States, children's play and storytelling makes use of the repertoire of common characters and plots provided by the popular media (Seiter, 1993; Sutton-Smith, Mechling, Johnson, & McMahon, 1995; Tucker, 1995). At the same time, however, those characters and plots are apt to reverberate differently for children who vary, not only in gender, but also in race, ethnicity, class, and other significant social categories that influence children's daily lives. Children with such diverse sociocultural backgrounds can be found in U.S. classrooms like Kristin's.

None of Kristin's young students would have been surprised, I suspect, if an adult did not like a story about ninjas. In her school, some teachers even banned such media stories from their classrooms, and some children reported that their parents found these stories too violent. The children's critical engagement with Emily—their consideration of the relational background within which she (and they) were embedded—emerged within, and was channeled by, the official school world's practices. But their engagement was fueled and given substance by the unofficial world of peer relations—by the children's desires to play certain roles (although, certainly, not the 'hooverer') and by their concern for fairness. The classroom writing practices gave children a means for seeking both access and redress—and that redress included a redressing, so to speak—a rewriting—of a meek figure named Emily.

THE CLASSROOM SITE OF EMILY'S ADVENTURES

The writing and rewriting of Emily was documented during the course of an ethnographic study in Kristin's urban school; the study focused on 7- to 9-year-old urban school children's use of popular culture, especially superhero stories, in their unofficial social play and their official school writing. (For methodological details, including data analysis procedures, see Dyson, 1997b). Like many inner city schools in densely populated urban areas, the school was high poverty (i.e., more than half of a school's families qualify for the federal school lunch program) and, in addition, populated primarily by children of color. However, the school also served a substantial percentage of White students who came primarily from a middle-class community surrounding the school (31%).

Out on the playground, the children tended to play in social circles marked by the interplay of gender, race, and social class (the boys, with their team games, being less segregated than the girls). In the classroom, however, the children were more apt to interact with others who experienced the social world quite differently. The social structures that organized this interaction were set in place by Kristin, in her role as teacher. She started a free writing period, which included an Author's Theatre activity; in that activity, child authors chose classmates to act out their written stories; after the performance, the class responded with comments and questions.

A Euro-American woman in her late 20s, Kristin became the teacher of 28 second graders in March and then kept her class through their third grade year. I knew Kristin because she had earned her Master's degree at the University of California, where I teach. I had gone to Kristin's classroom for a brief visit but had become fascinated by the ninjas and other popular characters that dominated her daily composing period. And so, shortly after she had arrived in the school, I began observing, and I also returned for 6 months in the third grade, observing 2 to 5 hours per week throughout the entire project. Although I came to know all her children, I had focal children who provided me reference points in the classroom drama, one of whom figures into this chapter, Tina; like the other focal children, she was knowledgeable about the media and active in the peer world.

I also had to become knowledgeable about the media. With the help of my assistants, I studied the children's products and, also, all the movies, video games, and television shows the children referenced, in order to figure out how the children were appropriating and transforming human relationships. Among such relationships were parents and children; spouses and lovers; friends or peers; good guys and bad guys; and perpetrators, victims, and rescuers. In studying my field notes, I described the social goals that energized the children's composing (e.g., affiliating with others, resisting them, negotiating with them) and also the sorts of ideological tensions that their texts could generate.

In this chapter, I aim to illustrate how the classroom composing practices helped generate and, in addition, provided a means of addressing ideological tensions among children. To this end, I am asking one basic question of my data: Who is Emily? I address this question by first introducing the major way in which Emily initially figured into human relationships in and out of the children's texts and then by presenting three different Emilys, that is, Emilys who figured differently into a written story's human relationships because she was figuring differently into the social relationships of the classroom community.

THE DIALOGIZATION OF EMILY: EMILY AS GIRL FRIEND

Ladies hoover and guys battle evil, according to the traditional storylines. Thus, it was not surprising that, in the second grade, Emily's prospects for textual action seemed bleak. Five of the 11 boys wrote at least one *Three Ninjas* story (although no second grade girl did). But these boys rarely mentioned Emily in their brief texts: Ninja stories feature good guys and bad guys, not boy friends and girl friends.

Nonetheless, Emily was very much a part of the unofficial social talk during official composing, and, in this talk, the boys used Emily much as Rocky's brothers Colt and TumTum did. For the boys, Emily's dominant meaning was the passive but cute girl friend, and, as such, she was useful for peer group fun. Any reference to Emily—and, especially, any attempt by a composer to cast a part for Emily—generated group chanting by the surrounding boys: "Rocky loves Em-i-ly. Rocky loves Em-i-ly." The chanting was a kind of bonding ritual and an occasion to exercise control over the embarrassed boy and girl who had been offered, or had asked for, the roles of Rocky or Emily. Rocky was a great fighter and karate was fun, but the potential for romantic meaning made even the strongest warriors run.

Given her romantic meaning, most boys never even considered including Emily in their stories. In fact, the absence of Emily could be a point of reassurance for potential male actors in the Rocky role. Nyem, for example, said to a reluctant Patrick, "It ain't no girl gonna be in it. Emily ain't gonna be in it." If the role of Emily was considered, however, the potential actress discussed was either Sarah or Melissa, both of whom resembled Emily in certain ways (fair-skinned, light haired, slim, well-dressed, friendly).

For the girls who wanted roles in ninja stories, Emily also symbolized the cute girl friend. But her social role or meaning was different. For the girls, Emily meant access. There were many boy parts in ninja stories, but just this one girl part. The desiring girls assumed the presence of Emily when any boy began a ninjas story, and, moreover, they campaigned for the part (i.e., they requested the role of Emily, without asking *if* Emily was going to be in the story). So, for girls, as well as for boys, social authority or power was gained primarily by referencing the original story (i.e., the girls assumed the boys' obligation to include Emily because the original story includes Emily).

Still, it was among the girls, especially the girls of color, that the boys' composed ninja stories generated ideological tensions. Tina's friend Johnetta, both children of color, was quite blunt about her feelings. "What you got against girls?" she asked Michael, a well-known superhero fan. And when Lawrence claimed that only White girls could play another media miss, April of *Teenage Mutant Ninja Turtles* (Dawson, Fields, & Chan, 1990), because April was White in the movie, Holly, Lettrice, Johnetta, and Aloyse (all children of color) raised their voices in protest. The conflict led to an explicit classroom rule that anyone could play any role, without regard to sex or race.

So, in the second grade, Emily generated issues of access, not of her own representational stuff (i.e., her identity). The girls acted on their access issues by protesting Emily's absence, her limited role, or the chosen actress, but not by writing their own Emily. However, this would change in the third grade, when the female admirers of ninja stories began to write poor Emily a place in the action.

EMILY EMERGES FROM THE SHADOWS
(ONLY TO BE PUT IN THE CLOSET): EMILY AS VICTIM

In the third grade, Emily continued to make her presence felt. She retained her meaning as girl friend, and her social power to make the boys run away. But the boys were no longer the only ones writing stories featuring superheroes. In the third grade, 5 of the 10 girls (primarily working-class girls) wrote about superheroes on occasion too. (For a discussion of class-related patterns of child media use, see Dyson, 1996.) When they wrote these stories, the girls featured female characters, and, like the boys, they used those characters' roles for peer affiliation. For example,

Tina's best friend, Makeda, wrote the first piece featuring Emily, and she promised that starring role to Tina.

However, although Makeda made Emily a star, she did not make her a superhero. She made her a victim, just as Emily is in the film's scenes that feature her. In one scene, Emily is the victim of school bullies who take her bike, and, in the other, of the evil Snyder's bullies, who temporarily hold her hostage. Thus, Emily acquired a larger piece of the textual action by becoming central to the plot and, also, by becoming a victim. (For a discussion of girls' use of the victim role as a major means for exciting adventure play, see Walkerdine, 1990.)

To illustrate, the following is an excerpt from the first of several variations Makeda wrote of her basic ninja story:

> Once upon a time there was three boys. Their name was Rocky, TumTum, and Colt. And there was a girl named Emily. And Rocky was in love with her. And she was walking down the street. And then some bad guys came to get Emily. And she said, "Help me," she said. And then she called their names. "Rocky, TumTum, and Colt," she called. And they came to save [her]....
>
> Chapter 2
>
> And they came to get her. And she was not locked in the closet. And they said, "Can you hear me?" Rocky said. She said, "I can hear you," and she got out of the closet. End [In the film, another female character—the boys' babysitter—is put in a closet by the bullies; spelling and punctuation corrected for ease of reading.]

Although her story details were not identical to those of the film, Makeda maintained Emily's victim role. Nonetheless, Makeda did make one authorial change that generated objections to her Author's Theater presentation: she eliminated all fighting and, thus, for some children, she eliminated the desirable action. The former bad guy Thomas complained:

> Thomas: Why we didn't get to fight Rocky, TumTum, and Colt?
>
> Makeda: Because it [the fighting group of actors] gets too much out of hand.

Although the class continued to discuss the necessity of fighting (with body and with words) to the story, there was absolutely no objection to—or discussion of—Emily's actions. Emily, after all, had had quite a bit to do and to say, and all of her actions were appropriate for a lady.

EMILY TAKES CHARGE: EMILY AS SUPERHERO

Although the third-grade girls sometimes wrote superhero stories, they wrote mainly rescue stories (e.g., Lena's Superman saved Lois Lane, and, as just seen, Makeda's Rocky, TumTum, and Colt rescued Emily). In January, even Tina, who had written second-grade texts featuring female X-men superheroes, wrote a story in which Batman saved "us girls." She told Kristin that she was not going to write any more "boyish" X-men stories.

But Tina was not of one mind on the issue of "us girls," and neither were many others in the class. During a class meeting, she sparked an intense discussion with her complaint that "in every story the boys always have to win. And that's really not fair to the girls.... The boys are always doing things for the girls, and it seems like the girls are weak." This was an ideologically charged complaint, not about access to a given story, but about the representational stuff of the story itself and, moreover, about the responsibility of the authors (i.e., about whether or not authors were being fair in their stories). Thus, it was not surprising (although certainly it was not predictable) when Tina saw new possibilities in Emily.

In the original *Three Ninjas* movie, Emily has a moment of physical glory, when she follows up TumTum's swats to an adolescent bad guy with a swift kick and a punch of her own ("Way to go, Emily!" says Colt). But it is only a brief episode in a movie in which she is mainly a smitten girl and an easy target for bullies, a victim to be rescued. In Kristin's class, Emily finally had an opportunity to be tough when Tina wrote a ninjas story (in March). And in that story, the usual gender relationships were inverted: Emily became the rescuer:

> Once there was a girl named Emily. She was tough. Her and her boy friend was eating pizza. They love to eat pizza. So one day they were going to school. They love school. Emily's mother walks them to school. She was nice. She love little kids. Kids love her. Then they went into the room. Bad boys, they love to beat up kids.... School is over now. Rocky, Emily, TumTum and Colt. Colt was going away. Emily found him. The bad boys had him. Emily can whip some butt. So she did. So they all ran away. She is tough, I said. So they walk home again. The end. [Spelling and punctuation corrected for ease of reading.]

Emily was Tina's mediational material, her means of participating in—and resisting the dominant ideology of—the community dialogue about gender. Unfortunately, though, Emily as superhero was not able to generate a public response. Tina, who missed a great deal of school, did not bring her to Author's Theater. However, she did bring her next Emily story, and the resulting event suggested that Emily, Tina, and the community as a whole had, at long last, gained some agency, some responsibility for choosing actions from an expanded range of possibilities.

EMILY GAINS DIALOGIC POWERS (AND BECOMES SUBJECT TO SOCIAL CRITICISM): EMILY AS MEANING POTENTIAL

Tina's next Emily story was a horror story (meant to be both funny and scary) about a scientist, his wife, and a crazed bat. It featured a grown-up Emily, marked as pretty and married, with no specific occupation. Her husband was Batman ("like in the cartoon," as Tina explained), but this Batman did not save "us girls"; he studied bats. Moreover, Batman was victimized by girls and avenged by a man-obsessed female bat named Bebe. The original *Bebe*, whose name rhymes with Tina's given name, was a girl in a chapter book the class had read, *The Sideways Stories* (Sachar, 1985).

Both Tina's actors and her audience enjoyed her story. Seemingly pleased with their response, Tina incorporated her actor's improvizations into her oral presentation, exaggerating Batman's fear and Bebe's ferocious love. The ever faithful Emily moved further into the background, as she waited at home for her man, and the more active characters took over:

> Tina takes her place in the front of the rug and calls her actors. Edward is to be the scientist, Makeda the wife, and Rhonda the baby bat Bebe. Tina begins to read with great expressiveness:

> Tina: Once there was a man that studied bats. He loved to study bats. He was married ... ['O::h', says the audience.] "Her name was Emily."

> Edward: Just like "Three Ninjas!" (Tina grins very widely.)

> Tina: She was *pretty*. So her husband went to the lab and was studying a bat named Bebe. (Tina stops reading and begins improvising but, at this point, stays very close to her text.)

> Rhonda: I'm Bebe. I'm a bat. (Class laughs enthusiastically. Edward, apparently responding to the class's playful mood, gasps,

> runs off to the far corner of the rug, and stands shaking. Tina then responds to his actions, improvising her next line.)

Tina: He was afraid of her. She lo::ved him.... Whoever messed with him she would kill them. One day the man went back home. He told his wife about the bad day he had.

Edward: I had a bad day! That bat is messed up. She tried to kill me, man! (The audience laughs. Edward may have misunderstood Tina's text, since his improvisation suggests that the bat was trying to kill him, which was not the case. However, Tina once again picks up on Edward's improvization.)

Tina: He went back to the lab. And the bat killed him. And he died. The End (audience laughter)

In the fun of a performance, Tina's relieved Emily, dutiful Batman, and vigilant Bebe had become caricatures (the female vampire, the nerdy scientist, the little woman at home). But it was, nonetheless, a performance in a literacy event in a classroom community in which appropriated heroes—whatever their cultural source—were potentially subject to critical reflection. In the discussion following Tina's performance, the mood of the class shifted, and they began to wonder about the inner lives of the characters and their responses to their life circumstances. A number of children audibly wondered about Emily and, more importantly, about Tina's decisions about Emily. Indeed, the first questioner was Emily herself (Makeda), who asked about the motivation of her husband's killer:

Makeda: Why did Rhonda—no, the bat have to kill um my husband?
...

Tina: Cause he poked her, and she didn't like it. And so she just killed him.
...

Lettrice: How come you didn't tell that thing you told, that he poked Rhonda?

Tina does not respond to this inquiry about the representation of her story but calls on Jonathan, who has his hand up.

Jonathan: I think you should tell how they [Emily and Batman] met.

Tina: The next chapter is where they met.

Jonathan: But if there's a next chapter—the guy died, so he couldn't tell that part.

Tina: I know. I'm telling it without him.

Kristin: Could you tell a flashback? Have you ever seen a flashback?

Many assents in the audience, and Tina recalls another horror story:

Tina: Like Jason, yeah Jason. The girl had a flashback to when she was a little girl and she didn't know her father.
            ...

Lena: ... Makeda [Emily] could've like um write her story about her husband and then start crying [because she was having a flashback].
            ...

Kristin: In the beginning of the story, you [Tina] said that Bebe the bat was protecting the man from other people ... And then, all of a sudden, she killed him. And I wondered, how did she change from loving him ...?

Tina: And so—he didn't like her. And so he—when he was studying her, and she had rabies in her, and when he was studying her, he poked her, and she didn't like that ...
            ...

As the discussion continues, Kristin asks if Tina's characters 'had a purpose in life':

Jonathan: Well, [Batman's] might've been to study bats ... to figure out which bats to avoid ...

Lynn: Well, one for the bat might've been—two purposes, to either be studied and to be sort of an example for other bats on how to be studied and, also, to um—fall in love with [Batman] and to kill him.

Kristin: So maybe to kill him had some larger purpose?

Lynn: And [Batman's]—[Batman's] wife um, Emily, Emily's pur-
            pose might have been—maybe she didn't follow her pur-
            pose. And it might've been that she should've gotten there
            and saved him some way.

Tina had liberated the characters from their usual plots, where actions and motivations were assumed (to get one's bike back, to defeat the bad guys, to marry the desired). But the characters' lives continued to be reinterpreted by Tina and others—in the fun of a performance and the serious consideration of the group as a whole. Some community members requested more explicit textual representations; others suggested possibilities that challenged Emily's silence and her passive relationship to her husband and to Bebe.

In Halliday's (1978) sense, a text did indeed seem to represent "meaning potential," a "choice ... from the total set of options ..." (p. 189). As for Emily, it seems fair to say that she had been novelized, taken from the absoluteness of her place among the ninjas and brought into "a certain semantic openendedness, a living contact with unfinished, still-evolving contemporary reality (the open-ended present)," in which another version, another rewriting, is always a possibility (Bakhtin, 1981, p. 5). At least, in this classroom community, it was now possible—it was not ideologically out of the question (or out of the text)—for an Emily to whip some butt, so to speak. And with new possibilities come new responsibilities (for author and for Emily). Perhaps, thought Lynn, Emily missed her chance.

ON CHILDREN'S AND TEACHERS' AUTHORIAL AGENCY

"Who's Emily?" I imagine that, for most of my readers, this question would be interpreted as a basic request for Emily's identity. But, in the social world of Kristin's children, this question meant, "Who gets to be Emily?," a variant of a familiar playground question. Emily's identity was taken for granted. As with Megan and David, the ch ildren were concerned about participation, about access (i.e., "Who gets to be the hooverer?").

In the context of the composing period and of Author's Theater, the "who gets to be" question (i.e., who, if anyone, has the right to imagine themselves in a ninjas tale) gave rise to the children's articulations of what it means to be Emily: Emily is a boy's girl friend, on the sidelines of the action, or a victim of the bad guys. When those textual relations were played out in the children's social world, they were no longer so readily taken for granted, especially by the girls. The resulting ideological differences revealed gaps, dialogic space, in which children could consider new ways of authoring Emily's relationships and, thus, new ways of authoring their own.

Alternative stories did not eliminate or even change the community status quo, nor did they signal a permanent change in any one child's way of participating in the community. Tina, for all her irritation about weak female characters, left Emily on the sidelines when Batman and Bebe were generating great fun. Still, alternative stories did change the community. When taken-for-granted human relationships had been publicly questioned, they could no longer, in fact, be taken for granted. Emily, for example, did not necessarily have to leave Batman in the lurch (or in the lab, as the case may be).

In any community, whether of children or adults, the evolution of such a dialogic process—a process of articulating and reimagining the taken for granted—would seem to require, first, appropriate social structures, locally defined. Certainly Kristin's children were aided by her social organization of writing time: the provision for child choice of material, for individuals' opportunities for peer sharing and performance, and for class discussions of shared texts, all of which potentially support children's exercise of authorial agency.

Second, the dialogic process would also seem to need some voicing of different perspectives, which, in Kristin's room, was aided by the sociocultural diversity of her students. To move beyond the taken-for-granted, to become more conscious of ideological choices and of the social consequences of words, we all benefit from interaction with those differently positioned in the social world.

However, neither social organization nor social membership in and of themselves can account for critical reflection and for the appropriation of authorial agency. The pedagogical values undergirding the community also seem key, values that might be summarized as a participatory ethic, the third important factor. In Kristin's room that ethic was most visible in the public forum created through Author's Theater. That forum was not simply a kind of whole-class conference (Graves, 1983) in which the community responded to or helped individuals and their writing. Individuals' contributions were also responses to the community, their means of participating in, and helping develop, community life (a dialogic complication consistent with recent shifts in developmental theories about child communication, see, e.g., Goodnow et al., 1995).

In this forum, Kristin's role was to monitor the proceedings, summarize points of connection and difference, supply clarifying assertions, and, in addition, maintain the children's focus on authorial agency (i.e., on writing decisions). When social or relational sense was linked with textual sense (i.e., with details of characters and plots, with qualities of genre), a community dialogue, mediated by stories, evolved.

In U.S. schools, there is an urgent need for teachers themselves to participate in evolving school communities (Dyson, 1997a). In her school, Kristin felt isolated, unable to discuss her own goals and experiences with colleagues. Moreover, to administrators, children (especially urban children "at risk" of low-achievement test scores) engaged in dramatising and talking (especially about the popular media) could seem a scandalous waste of time.

And yet, to Kristin and to me, all that dramatising and talking about symbols drenched with children's relationships seemed so powerful. Surely that activity furthered children's skill in interpreting, analysing, comparing and contrasting texts, as well as their skill in writing more elaborate texts (Dyson, 1997a, 1997b). But most important in the context of this book, it provided children with a participatory forum. Emily was a transitory symbol, but the cultural tensions at the heart of her classroom life were not—the children grappled with gender roles, beauty and race, and physical strength and power. Moreover, those tensions were evident in the responses of individual children, who did not have simplistic, unified selves. It is, to draw once again on Bakhtin (1981), precisely play with appealing but contradictory voices that allows us all to escape ideological bullies, intellectual kidnappers, and too slick cultural heroes and, thus, to remain open to new ways to tell our common tales.

REFERENCES

Bakhtin, M. (1981). Discourse in the novel. In C. Emerson & M. Holquist (Eds.), *The dialogic imagination: Four essay by M. Bakhtin* (pp. 259–422). Austin, TX: University of Texas.

Bruner, J. S. (1983). *Child's talk.* New York: Norton.

Chang, M. (Producer), & Turteltaub, J. (Director). (1992). *Three ninjas* [Film]. Burbank, CA: Touchstone Pictures.

Dawson, J., Fields, S., & Chan, D. (Producers), & Barron, S. (Director). (1990). *Teenage mutant ninja turtles* [Film]. (Available from Limelight Productions, Burbank, CA).

Dunn, J. (1988). *The beginnings of social understanding.* Cambridge, MA: Harvard.

Dyson, A. H. (1996). Cultural constellations and childhood identities: On Greek gods, cartoon heroes, and the social lives of schoolchildren. *Harvard Educational Review, 66*(3), 471–495.

Dyson, A. H. (1997a). *What differences does difference make? Teacher reflection on diversity, literacy, and the urban primary school.* Urbana, IL: National Council of Teachers of English.

Dyson, A. H. (1997b). *Writing superheroes: Contemporary childhood, popular culture, and classroom literacy.* New York: Teachers College Press.

Freire, P. (1970). *Pedagogy of the oppressed.* New York: Herder & Herder.

Goodnow, J. J., Miller, P., & Kessel, F. (1995). *New directions for child development, no. 67: Cultural practices as contexts for development.* San Francisco: Jossey-Bass.

Graves, D. H. (1983). *Writing: Teachers and children at work.* Portsmouth, NH: Heinemann.

Halliday, M. (1978). *Language as a social semiotic.* London: Edward Arnold.

Konner, M. (1991). *Childhood.* Boston: Little, Brown & Co.

Sachar, L. (1985). *The sideways stories.* New York: Avon.

Seiter, E. (1993). *Sold separately: Children and parents in consumer culture.* New Brunswick, NJ: Rutgers.

Sutton-Smith, B., Mechling, J., Johnson, T. W., & McMahon, F. R. (Eds.). (1995). *Children's folklore: A source book.* New York: Garland.

Tucker, E. (1995). Tales and legends. In B. Sutton-Smith, J. Mechling, T. W. Johnson, & F. R. McMahon (Eds.), *Children's folklore* (pp. 193–211). New York: Garland.

Walkerdine, V. (1990). *Schoolgirl fictions.* London: Verso.

Weiler, K. (1991). Freire and a feminist pedagogy of difference. *Harvard Educational Review, 61*(4), 449–474.

Williamson, J. (1981/1982). How does girl number twenty understand ideology. *Screen Education, 40,* 80–87.

2

Children Appropriating Literacy: Empowerment Pedagogy From Young Children's Perspective

Urvashi Sahni
Studyhall Educational Foundation, India

This chapter is based on a micro-ethnographic study conducted in a second grade classroom of a rural primary school in North India. It describes and analyzes the means through which children appropriate literacy; the purpose that drove their development as writers; and the ways in which, as they enacted their purposes in this context, they grew as persons or were empowered. The term *appropriation* is used in this context to mean "making one's own." To appropriate literacy is to add to one's symbolic repertoire aiding one in interpretive, constructive, creative interaction with the world and others in it. Appropriation is also used in the Marxian sense of appropriating a power-commodity or a set of practices controlled by dominant classes or cultures.

Empowerment has been conceived largely in political terms by critical educators like Freire, Giroux, Lankshear, and others. In this chapter, I suggest that this conception of empowerment and critical pedagogy is more appropriate for adults than for children. The main thrust of this chapter is a presentation of a reconstructed definition of empowerment and power in children's terms. This case study centers on classroom life in general and four focal children in particular. In this chapter, I refer to only two of the children.

The school in which the study was conducted is a typical government-run primary school in Jannaki bagh, a small village in Lucknow district. Jannaki bagh Primary School (JPS) was established in 1956. The total enrollment in its five grades numbers 236 boys and girls, taught by five teachers, all of them women; the principal is a man. All of children come from a very low socioeconomic background. The majority of their parents work as farm laborers, some of them renting land to work. According to information provided by the village head-man, 60% to 85% of the population falls below the poverty line. Literacy figures are low, with only 22% of the entire population having had any education. JPS is situated on the road side, just off the highway. There are two rooms in which classes four and five are housed, while the other three classes are conducted in the open, unpaved ground in front of these rooms, under two large trees. The seating arrangement is flexible, depending on the season, the position of the sun, and the shady spots available during the day. The classes, which are conducted outdoors, simply move to a more comfortable spot when it becomes too hot or too sunny. All the classes move into the two rooms or are dismissed when it rains heavily. Light drizzle is simply ignored if the trees fail to provide adequate shelter.

The school is bounded on two sides by the village homes and by a string of shops on the road side. Another side opens out to the fields. A hand pump forms the central focus of the school and is a site of constant activity. Men, women, and children from the village come there continuously to fetch water, bathe, and clean themselves. The second grade classroom is conducted under a tree in the yard.

I spent a total of 30 weeks with a group of 51 children who were in the second grade for the first 20 weeks of the study and in the third grade for the latter 10 weeks of the study. The data collection ranged over three academic semesters of the school. Ethnographic methods of inquiry and observation, including handwritten fieldnotes during participant observation, audiotaping of classroom interactions, and formal and informal interviews, were used. The study had two phases, an observation phase and a participation phase. During the participation phase, I adopted the role of teacher-researcher and participated actively with the children in the construction and initiation of literacy activities in the classroom, in the attempt to construct a literacy curriculum that was responsive to the culturally embedded needs and purposes of the child-members of the community.

THE OBSERVATION PHASE: FAILING THE CHILDREN

My observations and interactions with all the participants revealed that the setting was an alienating, nonresponsive, uncaring one. It was an unfortunate story like the ones enacted in many schools all over the world as described by Giroux (1989) and Fine (1989). The pervasive theme was "no one cares," "no one listens." Parents, teachers, principal, and children all felt disrespected, unsupported, unresponded to. No one felt a sense of ownership over the school or the curriculum. Literacy was conceived mechanistically, practiced minimally and passively. The official power structure was nonparticipatory, unidirectional, and hierarchical. The teacher controlled all the activity in the classroom, and the children worked passively and obediently. She determined the sociospatial arrangements of all official interactions, the structuring of classroom events, and the sequence of instructional phases unilaterally, without the participation of the children.

No composing sessions occurred in this classroom. Each day, the children were assigned one writing task, which consisted of copying lines from their textbook, as many as they could fit on their slates. The children copied carefully, though quickly and mechanically. (Hindi was the language of instruction.) They did not talk about their writing, nor did they read it to themselves or to their friends, although they often stopped writing to chat with their friends about topics unrelated to the subject matter of their written texts (e.g., incidents about home, siblings, festivals, and each other).

Reading took the form of decoding the letters and words from the text book. The teacher read the text once or twice a week. She read one word at a time, with the children reciting after her, following the text word by word with their fingers. Often I observed them simply reciting along, without even looking at the text. The teacher conducted a brief spelling and word recognition drill every day. The official literacy curriculum thus consisted of reading the lessons from the basal reader and copying parts of them. There was no official story reading (other than that from the basal reader) or storytelling by either the teacher or the children, nor was there any singing, craftwork, or drawing. I saw very little variation on the sparsely furnished official curricular stage. Literacy was officially defined in terms of decontextualized technical skills of reading and writing, reduced to the bare elements of the alphabet. Reading was defined as decoding of print, and writing was understood as the mechanical transcription of letters.

BUILDING CIRCLES OF MUTUALITY: THE PARTICIPATION PHASE

During my participatory intervention phase, we explored the possibilities and potentialities offered by the children, in an attempt to construct a curriculum that would be responsive to their needs and purposes. Although there was little we could do to alter the larger institutional structure, several possibilities opened up as we collaboratively constructed our classroom into a bonded context, within which we could and did take action. We reconstructed the social structure of the classroom and assigned different roles to each other with a corresponding reordering of rights, responsibilities, and duties. We constructed a connective ideology and transformed the political structure of the classroom from a chain of oppression to several circles of mutuality. These were spaces of inclusion, participation, addressal, and response.

In the newly constructed social space, the children had the right to:

make choices,

offer consent,

perform,

play with language,

make requests,

offer suggestions,

display their knowledge for their peers and me,

help their peers by sharing competencies,

ask for help,

be helped by the teacher and their peers,

express their needs and wishes,

have these needs attended to, and

respect the decisions of the teacher.

As teacher, I:

provided a model,

addressed questions,

solicited suggestions,

made suggestions,

provided the text,

performed for them,

played with them,

conducted the performance,

listened to them and responded to them, and was their addressee, evaluator, and collaborator, sharing my competencies and leading them on to higher competencies.

The children began to appropriate a more central role in the construction of the events of the classroom, as we entered into several negotiations and collaborations while transacting the literacy curriculum. They played a decisive role in constructing the literacy we practiced, and it was in response to their demands that the curriculum took a performative shape. They "decided" that the curriculum should be woven around poetry, song, drama, and story. The following are some of the literacy events that occurred on the new curricular stage.

Poetry and Song

- Recitation of rhymes, poems and songs.

- Copying teacher models from the blackboard.

- Copying peer models.

- Teacher dictation of poems and songs.

- Peer dictation of poems and songs.

- Composing poems (extending and modeling an official sample).

Story

- Reading stories from the text book, and library books, and using child-produced texts.

- Recomposing stories collaboratively from text book and library books.

- Copying collaboratively composed stories from the blackboard.
- Teacher dictation of collaboratively recomposed stories.

- Semidictated composing, that is, extending partially dictated stories.

- Retelling stories heard or read.

- Rewriting stories heard or read.

- Composing their own stories:

    a.   Narrativizing events and experiences, real and imagined.
    b.   Extending story-starters and story ideas provided by teacher.
    c.   Picture compositions:
         —Teacher draws figures requested by the children and they compose the text.
         —Children draw and compose descriptive text.
         —Teacher draws on the board and teacher and children compose the descriptive text or story collaboratively.
         —Teacher brings printed pictures, and children compose oral stories collaboratively and written stories individually and collaboratively.

Drama

- Enacting stories from the text for each other as a class and for the rest of the school:

    a.   Story theatre: Teacher narrates; children act; children narrate and act.
    b.   Readers theatre: Teacher reads dramatically; children read dramatically.

- Enacting poems.

- Enacting songs.

In the following sections, I provide a brief descriptive analysis of the developmental histories of two of my focal children in order to illustrate how they appropriated literacy as they grew as writers and as persons during the intervention phase.

RAJESH: FINDING A VOICE

Rajesh is a thin, gaunt-looking boy with short cropped hair and a very wide smile. His large, black eyes leap out from his thin face; his look is as tentative as his smile. He has a high-pitched voice and a shy, retiring demeanor.

Rajesh lives with his mother, sister, and younger brother in Hamirpur, which is a mile from the school. Hamirpur is like any other village in the area, (with dirt roads and mud huts lined one next to the other. Rajesh lives in a mud hut with a raised platform in front and a courtyard inside with a couple of rooms around it; one room served as the family kitchen and store and the other as the bedroom. The family did all their living in the verandah and the courtyard. Because there was no electricity, they lit oil lamps when it got dark in the evening and went to bed early to save on fuel costs, as did most of the people in the village.

Rajesh's father, now deceased, used to hire himself out as a laborer in the fields. His mother now does the same work. She and a neighbor argue about Rajesh's age, finally agreeing on 10 years. Rajesh is the only member of the family who has any education, and his mother has her hopes pinned on him. She hopes that he will "progress in life and not be a 'mere' laborer like she and her husband." She values education greatly and intends to educate her son until high school.

During the observation phase, I noticed that Rajesh was an uncertain follower. He had beautifully formed handwriting, of which he was very proud as it earned him the esteem of his teacher and friends. He worked and played in his friendship group. He knew they all were better spellers than he, but reveled in the fact that his handwriting "is better than anyone else's." Rajesh was a copier. Having no faith in his ability to spell, he copied faithfully from the text and the blackboard, but most of all he copied from his friends. For him, writing meant copying from the text or the blackboard or from someone else's text in a beautiful hand. Owning it or "authorship," meant having it on his slate or page. His focus was on the precise and ornate formation of the letters. The letters seemed to symbolize only sounds and words, although not his own. At this point, he was "drawing" letters, which had aesthetic meaning for him and gave him the sense that he was writing, much in the sense in which an early writer scribbles, pretending to write. He had not yet reached second-order symbolism. Rajesh was afraid to take risks or follow an independent path, unable to perceive his own competencies and own them enough to use them for himself. Even though he relied so heavily on copying, he did have a fairly sound sense of the letter–sound association.

Rajesh seemed to be afflicted with a fear of autonomy, which might be rooted in his personal history. He is the first literate in his family. Landless, fatherless, the eldest son of a widow, he knows the family's hopes are all pinned on him. This is probably a tremendous pressure for a 10-year-old, unsupported by any literate member or literacy in his home. Lower caste laborer, widow in a feudal patriarchal casteist society, his mother's social place, and his too, consequently, is not one that inspires hope; it is one that is based on respect for the authority of one's "betters." It is in following rules that survival and security lay, and this is what he seemed to do. Furthermore, the literacy instruction in the classroom emphasized following, in terms of correct modeling of the rules of language (e.g., spelling and handwriting), and this is what he worked at. His guiding purpose was to learn literacy and to get it right.

As a result of the intervention, the participant structure, the pedagogical environment, and the definition of literacy and its demands changed, and shaped Rajesh's development as a writer. He began to make tentative moves toward finding his own words. He learned to copy selectively, learning that one can copy not only words, but speech, even if it is someone else's, in order to express one's own meaning. He copied the following sentences from another girl's book:

Mamiji(me) teaches us poems. She greets us with a namaskar. We greet her with a namaskar.[1]

He wanted to establish a relationship with me and this was his way of using writing to do so. He showed his first signs of independence in his drawing, an element introduced by me in the literacy curriculum. He began to draw his own figures and to appropriate drawing as a symbolic support for his writing, using his figures to contextualize his writing. He began by writing simple descriptive sentences such as the one under the figure of a parrot, drawn jointly by him and me: "The parrot speaks. The name of the parrot is Mithu. Ram Ram," and progressed to writing a short narrative a few days later with help from me. I prompted him with questions and at first composed each sentence for him, after which he wrote it out himself, coming to me after each sentence and using our talk as support for his writing. He composed some of the sentences himself; the narrative structure was his own, but he needed oral support and confirmation to organize his writing. He came for help frequently, driven by his need to become a writer in this new sense. He began to focus less on his handwriting, which was valued less now by his friends too.

Three months into the study, Rajesh wrote simple narratives by himself, relying less on supportive talk from me and more on contextual and personal supports like the topic and its relevance to him and his own purposes. He wrote about his friend Dashant and the game they played together. I started him off with the first sentence, "My friend's name is Dashant," after which he wrote:

If Dashant comes to my house, then I will play bat ball with him. And we [will have a] match and who ever has more runs he wins. I will win.

---

[1]Indian greeting meaning *I bow to you.*

He did not need drawing as a supportive context. Rajesh seemed to move to a second order symbolism: He was writing speech, not mine but his own. He seemed to have transformed our interpersonal composing into intrapersonal composing. He announced his intention to "win," which, given his tentative, shy, retiring demeanor, I interpreted as a sign of increased confidence in himself and the possibilities of his life.

Inventing imagined worlds, Rajesh began to use writing to imagine and fantasize with. In an official assignment in which the children were asked to write about all the things they liked to do, he wrote the following:

> I like the fair a lot and I like drama and I like apples and I like mangoes and I like my mother and father and I like my mamiji and my teacher and I like food and I like books and there are many mangoes in my orchard a when the mangoes ripen then I will give my mamiji mangoes from my orchard and then she will like them a lot.

Rajesh has no father and no orchard, and he knows I know this, but he has learned to invent imagined worlds with his writing. He has acquired symbolic power and is able to create symbolic worlds, hoped-for worlds and wished-for worlds, which is also evident from his next story:

My Story

> Tonight I dreamt that I went to my mamiji's (myself) house and I liked the house very much. Mamiji received me very lovingly and I sat in mamiji's car and I went all over the city. I liked that very much. Then with mamiji, I went to Bahenji's (the class teacher). There I met Bahenji's mother and she received me very lovingly. She sent for tea from the restaurant and I went with love. On the way I met Ekta (the class teacher's daughter) in the lane. I did not recognize her but she recognized me. She took me home and we sat for a while. Then Ekta showed me some flowers and I liked the pretty, pretty flowers. Now I think I'll be leaving. Namaste to all. Namaste to Raakhi too.

Rajesh had learned to take symbolic action. He "made" a cultural bridge between our vastly different worlds, one middle-class urban and the other working-class rural, and he walked over to the other side. In this world, he was treated lovingly and with respect by all the people he knew. This was the way he wished to be treated. Using his narrative imagination in this story, he traversed social power boundaries and distances, positioned himself socially, staked his claim to love and respect, and created a respectable, hospitable place for himself in a socially distant world, with his writing. He envisioned possibilities for himself (a possible self and a possible world), and reached out for them symbolically. In appropriating literacy as an expressive, inventive tool and a self-presentational medium, he acquired the power of imagination or envisagement as he became a writer.

Toward the end of the study, Rajesh became a confident composer, writing easily without any help from me, using me as his addressee and occasional helper, leaning on his friends, for social support and occasional spellings, but writing his own words and meanings, for purposes of his own. His composed texts had a distinct dialogic character. The writing was always addressed to someone, either to me or to his friends, and its addressive context provided the support he now needed. It was the dialogic import of his writing that he valued. He found his voice through the medium he used for expressing it, and it grew stronger the more he exercised it.

SHEELA: A PERSON ADDRESSED AND ADDRESSING

Sheela is an 8-year-old, tall but slightly built girl. She has large expressive eyes set in a round face and a wide disarming, charming smile. She lives in Sannasibagh with her parents, brothers and sisters. Her house, a few minutes walk from the school, looks much like Rajesh's. Youngest of four children, Sheela's older sister, 14, is enrolled in the sixth grade in the same school, and both older brothers have at least an eighth-grade education. Both Sheela's parents are illiterate and unemployed. They are all supported by the older brother, who owns a cycle repair shop. When interviewed, Sheela's mother displayed apathy toward her daughter's education and expressed her scepticism about its value for girls, saying, "I'm going to marry off my daughters as soon as they pass the eighth grade. What will they do with literacy? This is a village."

Sheela's home environment is not unusual in the village, especially in its gender stance. Girls are expected to be silent little creatures, who should try to make themselves useful around the house as soon as they can. The hours spent in school are allowed begrudgingly, because the only end in mind for daughters is marriage as soon as they attain puberty.

At school, Sheela liked to sit at the back, far away from the teacher's gaze, where she would try not to attract too much attention. A very careful child, she was afraid of making mistakes and worked cautiously and painstakingly. Sheela was very interested in writing and reading, working busily at all the official and unofficial literacy tasks in the classroom. Like the other children, she conceived of literacy as "copying" print. She used written language like an object to be transferred from page to page and handed to others, as in the form of the poems she so liked to share with her friends. It was still an external thing, a fun thing, to be played with, a valued thing, to be stored and an attribute to have, one that lent prestige. She had not yet discovered the potency of written language as a symbolic and intersubjective transactional medium.

Early in the intervention phase, Sheela wrote, "I greet mamiji with folded hands," and she brought it to show me. It was her first independently generated sentence. It was a way of making a connection with me, adopting me as addressee and forming her circle of mutuality. She had found a dialogic context in which to embed her writing.

Like Rajesh, Sheela too began to discover drawing as a symbolic support. She copied a poem about a parrot from her friend and brought it to me, asking me to draw a parrot for her. As I was drawing, she told me she had a parrot at home. Expressing interest, I told her she could write about her own parrot. She gave me a very tentative look, willing to try me out to see what she would find, surprised too, that I should be asking her to write and draw about herself. She then took the drawing, colored it, and generated these sentences: "My parrot speaks and he calls out 'Bimla' [her sister] and calls out to me, calling out, 'Sheela'."

She built on my dialogic support to compose these sentences, as I prompted with questions like, "What does your parrot like to talk about?" She had found a real, live personal context to write about. In response to her, I wrote, "What is your parrot's name, Sheela? Do you like him a lot?" hoping to firm up the circle of mutuality that she had begun to build. Responding cautiously to my interest in her, Sheela began to write and draw her worlds, using me as her addressee. The few minutes that I spent with each child, negotiating topics, providing verbal scaffolding, or drawing supportive contexts, were moments of individual address for them and were extremely important for Sheela. Her writing developed as she discovered its transactional potential, and found that with it she could build and maintain relationships with distant others. The main purpose that seemed to drive Sheela's writing was maintaining a relationship with me and, through me, with her teacher.

My interview with Sheela's mother, during which Sheela was present, revealed her apathy toward her daughter's education. Sheela used writing to reconstruct her reality according to her own needs and desires:

I am studying from class one to class three. My mother came to enroll me. My mother understood very well that is why my mother wanted to educate me that if I educate my daughter it will be very beneficial to me. Mother says I like educating my daughter. My mother liked sending me to school so she sent me to school. If I will educate my daughter then it will be good for me.

This was a wished-for representation (Stern, 1985) and presentation of her life. She had discovered the constructive possibilities of writing, its "constitutiveness" as Bruner (1990) calls it, "the capacity of language to create and stipulate realities of its own" (p. 89) and was using it to reinterpret her own lived reality, to "distort and transcend it" (Stern, 1985, p. 182). In the same composition she wrote:

Mamiji is my friend. Friend means she is Sheela's friend [using a synonym]. Why do I like to study because my teacher teaches then I like it. I like Bahenji's way of speaking. [The class teacher and I use standard Hindi and they speak the dialect]. Bahenji and Mamiji are very good friends and I am very good friends with Bahenji and Mamiji.

She brought this to show me, beaming brightly, as though she had made an important discovery. Mrs. S, the class teacher, read it over my shoulder. Not very pleased at the declaration of friendship, she frowned gently: "What's this about friends. How can you be friends?"

Sheela was undaunted. She stood her ground without saying anything and kept smiling at us. This is very significant, considering the traditional norms of distance between adult and child, teacher and student, upper and lower caste and class, specifically in the village and generally in the Indian context. Sheela seemed to transcend all these boundaries with this declaration of friendship. Friendship is a relationship of equality, and she was declaring herself an equal person staking claim to an equal relationship. Using writing as a personally expressive and exploratory tool, Sheela had found its empowerment potential; with it she could reposition herself with regard to the people in power and alter the power relationship for herself as she did so. She had appropriated literacy as a symbolic tool to define herself in relation to others in a way that was compatible with her vision of herself. After this, she continued to write narratives peopled with "friends." She referred to another visitor to our classroom, also an upper class adult, as "mataji (mother) is my friend." Then she extended her claims to friendship to Mrs. S's daughter Ekta as well, writing, "Ekta is my friend."

Like Rajesh, Sheela used literacy to take symbolic action in the world, although they each did so in different ways. Rajesh built a bridge, trying to bridge power differences and distances. Sheela dissolved these differences by redefining herself and her relationship with the distant powerful others in the school context, an important one in her life. She declared the differences dissolved with her redefinition of our relationship in terms of friendship. Retaining the third person form of address and the Indian suffix of deference *Ji*, she acknowledged the difference of age and the deference traditionally due to it in the Indian cultural context, but with her declaration of friendship she refused the power differences.

EMPOWERMENT PEDAGOGY FROM YOUNG CHILDREN'S PERSPECTIVE

Reflecting on the focal children of this study, and their development during the course of this study, I believe they were all empowered by the literacy practice, although not perhaps in the sense in which Giroux and others conceive of empowerment, as the acquisition of "critical knowledge about basic societal structures." They were empowered in the sense that they owned themselves more as they grew in autonomy and a realization of their self-hood. The children were empowered because of the various kinds of power they harnessed, as they appropriated literacy and thus found important self-constructing tools.

Empowerment has been conceived largely in macropolitical terms, by critical educators. Lankshear (personal communication, Spring 1994) defines it in relation to power structures, pointing out that a subject is empowered in relation to a power structure, in order to take action upon or within a given structure. Giroux (1989) has taken a similar stance, defining empowerment as 'the ability to think and act critically' he conceives empowerment pedagogy as teaching for social transformation. Following Freire's (1987) lead, all these educational theorists, define power and empowerment in both large social and political terms. According to them, education for empowerment involves primarily the cultivation of a "sociological imagination" defined by Mills (1959) as "a quality of mind which enables us to grasp history and biography and the relations between the two within society" (p. 6). Freire (1987) refers to this as "conscientzia" or a critical consciousness that involves naming the world and our position in it as historically, socially, politically constituted beings, in order that we may transform the world.

It is significant that the Freirian perspective just described comes from men, who because they are men in a world structured largely by men, locate both power and empowerment in political and social structures. They view the larger structures as being within their reach (and given their place in it, it is) and can conceive of the possibility of action upon them. I suggest that this conception of empowerment and critical pedagogy is more appropriate for adults than for children. Children (and most women) given their place in the sociopolitical power structure, feel too distanced, too far down on the power ladder, to consider it within their reach. Furthermore, they see themselves as inhabiting peopled worlds, personal and interpersonal worlds, rather than structured worlds. Children, particularly, do not conceive of reality in a structural sense, in terms of social, political or logical structures, except when these structures are embodied in the people with whom they live their lives. As Donaldson (1978) points out, children make child-sense of themselves and the world, which is different from an adult-sense. In my view, this is a more peopled, personal and interpersonal, intentional, narrative sense, one contextualised in human purposes, feelings and endeavors.

More than nurturing a sociological imagination in children, empowerment involves nurturing and developing children's narrative imaginations. The children in my study gave very few cues for social dialogues of the kind referred to by critical theorists (i.e., discussions about the "realities" of their lives such as poverty and caste). They preferred instead to talk about the imagined possibilities created by poetry, stories, and songs. Children inhabit a special place as children. We should respect their childhood and allow it to grow. They are not miniature adults, and the social structure, although it impinges on their lives, imposing limits and constraints, is still too distant to matter. More than helping them to acquire the ability to think and act critically about the realities of their lives, I found it more useful to help them compose creative and imaginative stories. They need the symbolic and social tools with which to construct stories where their own role is a more powerful one. It is with stories like the ones described earlier, that children construct their identities, negotiate relationships, and position themselves in the world.

Sheela and Rajesh both illustrate that when the imagination is released its power can be harnessed for self-construction and transformation. The imagination is powerful because it enables thinking in terms of possibility, rather than actuality. The first step in transcending or transforming a "real" world of despair is to be able to conceive of a possible world and a possible, wished-for, hoped-for self positioned comfortably in it. Sheela repositioned herself in the power relationships she encountered and effected a structural change as well, changing the power realities in the world she was constructing. The larger structure remains stable only if its components remain in their designated positions; otherwise it is destabilized by any shift. Sheela seemed to make such a destabilizing shift, not by acting on distant abstract social and political structures, but by creatively restructuring her relationship with me and the teacher, the powerful others in her school life. She seemed to be empowered by a self-knowledge, a growing, creative, imaginative understanding of who she was and who she could be in relation to others in her world. She was able to envision a possible self and was finding ways of actualizing this self.

As for Rajesh, what is the point of all this literacy, given the stark reality of his life? What will change in his life because of it? A skeptical friend confronted me with this, as I recounted Rajesh's progress enthusiastically. Perhaps it is naive optimism, born out of the comfort of my own world, but I consider Rajesh with a sense of possibility, rather than futility. Nothing had changed in the external conditions of his existence, but his personal world evolved. He had grown in confidence and self-respect. He had learned to become an active composer of his own thoughts and ideas, a writer of his own texts, rather than a passive copier of other people's words. He had appropriated a valuable symbolic tool and with this had gained an important self-construction and life-transformation tool. He had not moved up in the power structure, but a power space had emerged within himself, with which he could now act more powerfully as a person among other persons in the world. He could also construct possibilities for his life symbolically, which he did, building bridges to extend his life into other alien more powerful worlds.

As the children negotiated the curriculum and participated in structuring the events in the classroom, they learned to make decisions, take risks, and make choices, and thus grew in autonomy. Most importantly, they acquired a view of themselves as persons with a voice that counted. They learned that they had the right to participate in structuring their classroom life. Furthermore, they learned that their composed texts, crafted out of their own lived and imagined experiences, were as valid as the revered text book, a legitimate part of the curriculum. They also learned that they had the right to participate in the construction of knowledge, and they gained with this a special power, the power associated with knowledge, used in especially oppressive ways in school.

The children in my study thus point toward another conception of empowerment, one missed by the critical educators discussed earlier, one centered in and around relationships. It is people who empower and depower each other in their daily interactions with each other. From the children's perspective, empowerment has more to do with relationships than with structures. Redefined in children's terms, empowerment, although a relational term, is better understood in relation to the self and to people in immediate contexts, rather than to abstract, large social and political structures. Empowerment involves transformatory action as Giroux (1989) says, but instead of a direct social transformation, for children, empowerment takes the form of imaginative self-transformation and creative symbolic action in their own lives. Most importantly, it involves an achievement of their personhood. More than naming the real world, children's *conscientzia* manifests itself in an imaginative narrative and poetic invention of possible worlds and possible selves.

LEARNING FROM CHILDREN

The main change in the classroom after the intervention occurred in terms of the restructured relationships. The classroom was constructed into a circle of mutuality in which several such circles proliferated. The chief feature of this circle was a relationship of respectful response. The children learned to write because they had someone for whom to write. Relationships were very important to the children. They wrote because the relationship mattered to them and they wanted to nurture it; the relationship nurtured their growth as writers and persons. The curriculum was responsive because it emerged from and was grounded in a set of responsive relationships. The important factor was the relationship, even more so than the literacy, although both developed simultaneously or interactively. Given the power difference in any student–teacher relationship, this relationship assumes special significance in terms of its empowering or depowering potential. A teacher occupies an important power-space in a child's world and she can be empowering or depowering depending on how she uses her power-space.

Perhaps critical theorists, planners, and policymakers could learn from children because they seem to point in an important direction. Perhaps we need to reconceive society and politics in terms of relationships, circles of mutuality based on mutual respect and response which cohere well with our commitment to participatory democracy, defined well by Dewey (1985), who said "More than a form of Government, it is a mode of associated living, of conjoined communicated experience." (p. 93)

With specific reference to education, we need to reconceive the role of schooling and literacy, taking a view of children as persons with legitimate ends of their own to pursue. The critical theorists have done invaluable work in pointing out that the political ideology underlying the institutional structure and practice in schools deserves critical examination. Yet they should guard against falling into the ideological trap of taking an exclusively political view of literacy and schools. I agree with Giroux (1989) that public education should be linked with the imperatives of democracy, in that the institutional structure of education should take a participatory form in line with the ethical principles of democracy. I argue that he defines the purpose of schooling in reductionist political terms, as do policy planners who view literacy predominantly in its potential for national development and modernization. I protest on behalf of children, at thus being objectified and instrumentalized, viewed primarily as national resources or political agents, with the school perceived mainly as a political arena. Children are not merely national resources. They are persons, and the primary purpose of schooling is to nurture their growth as persons, and to help them appropriate literacy for their own purposes. My study suggests that young children would reconceive the school as a playground rather than a political arena and redefine critical literacy as creative literacy, construing it as a tool with which to construct a self related to others in the world. This tool can be used to imagine possibilities for their lives and consequently for the larger public spheres. The critical theorists speak of schools as "democratic public spheres," Giroux (1989) and so they should be, but not ones that obliterate or swallow up the personal spheres. Viewed from the perspective of young children, literacy is not for social and political revolution or national development; it is for people to use in relation to each other. Perhaps that is another form that social and political revolution might take, a deconstruction of power structures, not by attacking them frontally, but by transforming them into empowering relationships, or as the children show, *circles of mutuality.*

REFERENCES

Bakhtin, M. M. (1986). *Speech genres and other late essays.* Austin, TX: University of Texas.

Bruner, J. (1990). *Acts of meaning.* Cambridge, MA: Harvard University.

Dewey, J. (1985). *Democracy and education.* Carbondale, IL: Southern Illinois University.

Donaldson, M. (1978). *Children's minds.* New York: Norton.

Dyson, A. H. (1993). *The social work of child composing.* New York: Teachers College.

Fine, M. (1989). Silencing and nurturing voice in an improbable context: Urban adolscents in public schools. In H. A. Giroux & P. Mclaran (Eds.), *Critical pedagogy, the state and cultural struggle* (pp. 152–174). New York: State University of New York.

Freire, P., & Macedo, D. (1987). *Literacy: Reading the word and the world.* New York: Bergin & Garvey.

Giroux, H. A. (1989). Schooling as a form of cultural politics: Toward a pedagogy of and for difference. In H. A. Giroux & P. McLaren (Eds.), *Critical pedagogy, the state and cultural struggle* (pp. 125–152). New York: State University of New York.

Mehan, H. (1982). The structure of classroom events and their consequences for student performance. In P. Gilmore & A. A. Blatthorn (Eds.), *Children in and out of school* (pp. 59–87). Washington, DC: Center for Applied Linguistics.

Mills, C. W. (1959). *The sociological imagination.* London: Oxford University.

Sahni, U. (1994). *Building circles of mutuality: A socio-cultural analysis of literacy in a rural classroom in India.* Unpublished doctoral dissertation, University of California at Berkeley.

Stern, D. (1985). *The interpersonal world of the infant: A view from psychoanalysis and developmental psychology.* New York: Basic Books.

3

Children Reading Critically:
A Local History

Jennifer O'Brien
University of South Australia

In this chapter two related propositions are developed and illustrated. First, the critical position that I introduced in my classroom was dependent on my history, although certainly not in any predictable way. Second, critical literacy is always and necessarily local.

This is not a how-to chapter. There is no recipe for critical literacy; I cannot even say, "This worked for me" or "This is where I went wrong." What I can say is:

> This is how the particular critical positions which I introduced in these classrooms worked for my students and for me; these are the circumstances in which I introduced critically framed activities and talk; these are the personal and institutional histories that were associated with their introduction; and, several years later, this is how I now reread what happened.

From a distance of 4 or 5 years and no longer a classroom teacher, I reflect on benefits, conflicts, and dilemmas that arose as my young students and I negotiated our way through specific, local critical literacies created by new ways of working with texts and with each other.

CRITICAL LITERACY

To begin, I propose to put aside briefly the handy term *critical literacy* and replace it with "taking a critical position toward literacy."

I am doing this because in some circles, *critical literacy* has started to sound like a taken-for-granted classroom option. Critical literacy is in danger of acquiring a kind of inevitability. There's a suggestion that if teachers get students to do specific sets of activities or to answer certain questions then the result will be critical literacy. But critical literacy (or even a range of critical literacies) does not exist "out there," waiting to be introduced into classrooms. By interrupting the familiar *critical literacy* I want to bring to the fore the idea that teaching is a deliberately political act where one takes a stand; and to maintain an emphasis on both the possibilities and the uncertain outcomes of critical work.

What is available is a position that conceives of literacy as never neutral, invariably interested, and always invested with power relationships. Activities and relationships surrounding reading, writing, speaking, listening, and viewing thus have unequal real-life effects for those engaged in them. In a specific setting, such as a classroom reading lesson, a critical position creates relationships, material effects, and subjectivities particular to the location; but you can never be sure of their precise nature. This makes critical moves not only broad ranging but potentially risky and exhilarating.

I brought into classrooms not just a different set of talk and activities but new teaching practices that both underpinned and arose from my critical position. Instead of talking of introducing critical literacy into the classroom (as I have done previously) I talk of bringing a critical position, of introducing critical practices and critical text analysis, and of moving to produce critical readers. The focus is thus transferred from the critical talk and activities to the collection of behaviors and power relationships (on my part and my students' part) produced by my offering a critical position toward classroom texts. However, because I am talking about bringing together critical practices and literacy instruction, the term *critical literacy* becomes useful shorthand for what went on.

Critical literacy did not just appear in my classroom. It came along with, was inserted in, arose from, and was produced by complex sets of personal, professional, and institutional circumstances. I untangle just a few of these.

PERSONAL, PROFESSIONAL AND INSTITUTIONAL HISTORY

The directions I took in the early 1990s were to some extent made possible by my having room to manoeuver within the state educational system. For a start, at that time, teachers in South Australian state primary schools had considerable autonomy within classrooms and schools, marked by a discourse of teacher professionalism and school-based curriculum development. What is more, a climate of experimentation gave me a sense that pedagogy was not static. Early Literacy Inservice Course (ELIC) and Literacy and Learning in the Middle Years (LLIMY)[1], two influential teacher development programs, drew on a mix of whole language and progressivist pedagogies to promote innovative practices. Further, improvement in the access and participation of students living in poverty was on the government agenda. A series of programs in schools drew on the idea that a critical pedagogy would empower children living in poverty (Lankshear & Lawler, 1989). My plans to introduce critical classroom reading practices shared some theoretical positions and educational goals with these programs. In the mid-1980s, when inequalities in girls' educational experiences was a hot topic, many teachers made efforts to give both girls and boys equal access to playground facilities and classroom experiences.

As a teacher-librarian in a suburban primary school, I too wanted to make changes, so I moved on two fronts. First, I removed the materials that I judged to be most blatantly sexist and resolved to talk about and recommend only books that offered positive views of girls and women and to ignore the rest. As time went by, I saw no evidence that this strategy made any difference to children's reading habits. Second, I tried to buy books with women and girls as main characters and to build up the collection of books that might be of interest to girls. I discovered quickly that most books in these categories showed girls engaged in conventionally feminine activities and preserved familiar male–female power relationships. In short, most of the books available to girls and boys encouraged the sorts of identities as girls and as boys that antisexist programs at national, state, and school level were trying to change.

A few years later, with my uncertainties unresolved, I moved out of schools to curriculum development and further study. There I began to read poststructuralist explorations of girls' gendered experiences in schooling, investigations in the gendered construction of characters in

---

[1]*Early Literacy Inservice Course and Literacy* (Education Department of South Australia, 1984) and *Learning in the Middle Years* (Education Department of South Australia, 1989). These programs were the basis of a number of pedagogical reforms in other Australian states and were sold to a number of education authorities in the United States.

children's school books, and examinations of classroom reading practices that focused on the student readers they created.

LANGUAGE, TEXTS, AND READING LESSONS

The key concept for me was the poststructuralist focus on the centrality of language. Theorists in this tradition maintain that through our use of language we define and contest what the social world is like and the possibilities it holds for us. At the same time, our sense of ourselves (our identity or subjectivity) is produced as we engage in struggles over the meanings of the discourses of everyday life. Rather than considering social situations like classrooms as places where teachers and students have relatively fixed identities and power relationships, we can think of them as places where both subjectivities and power relationships are constructed and reconstructed through local discourses (Weedon, 1987). Viewing our identities as open to creation and recreation rather than as a fixed property that we were born with, shows us as constantly changing creatures engaged in dealing with the contradictions of everyday life, including those we meet as student and teacher readers.

Key places where ideas and gender identities are established and challenged are the texts with which society is saturated. Texts do not provide a sort of window into the world or a reflection of the world as it is; they are more than sources of information. Instead they create versions of what the social world is like and of the complex, shifting unequal power relationships between girls and boys and women and men. I intended therefore to view texts we used in the classroom not as fixed and complete objects but as places for discussion, argument, and challenge as well as for enjoyment, information, and pleasure. Furthermore, I proposed to expand the range of texts taken seriously in the classroom so that texts from family and community life, as well as those more familiar to schooling, were analyzed. And the main topic for discussion and challenge was to be the construction of gendered identities in and by these texts.

Linked to feminist poststructuralist work is the assumption that literacy is not simply an individual activity going on mainly in people's heads, not a natural extension of language development, but a set of activities that go on between people within and across a range of relationships and cultural contexts. Key contexts for literacy practices are classroom reading lessons in which relationships between teacher and students and between and among girls and boys inevitably entail networks of power. A crucial aspect of the part played by texts in maintaining gender and student identities turns on questions of power to interpret texts, to decide who can read them and when, who can say things about them and to whom, and who can authorize the meanings constructed by texts.

Research into reading instruction in the first years at school, for example, indicates that teachers often decide on the aspects of texts that will be discussed, and, despite appearing to ask young readers about their interpretations of classroom texts, give priority to their own interpretations over students'. In the end, however, the text has the final authority: Teachers generally defer to the text's truth about itself and about the world. I decided, therefore, to problematize the authority relationships between teacher and students that resulted in the teacher's textual reading being preferred to that of the students and in the text's authority being paramount (Baker & Freebody, 1989).

NEW DIRECTIONS

Back in the classroom, I proceeded to add to the range of activities around classroom reading materials. First, I introduced into reading lessons talk and activities designed to show students that texts are constructed objects that can be read in ways other than those that seem natural, universal, and commonsense. At times when students were reading, talking, writing, and drawing about specific texts, I directed their attention to the meanings that texts apparently ask their readers to make and helped them to investigate how language, visual and narrative conventions and techniques produce sets of meanings. In this way, I worked with students to ask questions about the view of the social world constructed in their texts, particularly about the inequities in gender relationships.

Second, having explored some of the ways in which reading practices are socially constructed, having made texts themselves the topics for discussion, I experimented with the idea that they could have been constructed differently.

These actions were taken within a broad context of questioning the authority relationships that were generally constructed between teacher and students and the complex of power relationships commonly built and played out in classrooms between and among girls and boys.

The examples discussed in this chapter illustrate how these insights were put into practice in my classrooms of 5 to 8-year-olds at Cairnmuir and Glenbrae, two suburban primary schools in South Australia. I discuss talk and activities around two different kinds of texts: *Almost Goodbye, Guzzler* (Cresswell & Browne, 1990), and a collection of junk mail catalogs produced for Mothers' Day.

The first is the sort of humorous short novel frequently chosen for reading aloud at school. The second is a group of texts rarely used as classroom reading material. I turn into objects of analysis a humorous, easy story and set of throwaways designed to promote consumption. But I don't neglect the broad-brush fun, or the appeal of the familiar, or the need to guide young readers through the relation between print and visuals.

THEY ALWAYS SHOW TEACHERS AS STUPID

Reading aloud time was a regular practice in my classroom that allowed students of all ages to share a previously rehearsed text with the class. Seven-year-old Jack, an accomplished reader, selected *Almost Goodbye, Guzzler.* Its appeal lay in its rather daring humor, its innovative, lively format, the familiar stereotypical representation of a ridiculous teacher (Miss Toasty) and naughty children (particularly Susie and Guzzler), and its fast-paced narrative built around a genie, a lamp, and three wishes.

Jack knew this novel would appeal to the others; he read it aloud fluently; everyone was having a lot of fun. However, from a feminist position things looked a little different, a little more complex. My students were not just getting useful reading practice and enjoyment. They were engaged with a text that achieved much of its impact through manipulation of gender-based stereotypes. So I decided to read the novel aloud myself, drawing on the poststructuralist technique of questioning the familiar, in this case the use of a well-known narrative pattern and familiar humorous gender identities. My purpose was to show how these aspects of the text produced a restricted range of possibilities for being male and female in the social world.

I show only one element of the critical literacy produced around this text. From the records[2] of classroom talk around *Almost Goodbye, Guzzler* I choose a small number of episodes that show how a few girls took up the textual investigation I proposed and my difficulty in finding appropriate ways to respond to their readings of the text and of my questions.

I aimed to make quite clear the standpoint from which I was reading this book and at the same time show how I could also read this text from more than one position with comments like these:

> Do you notice how as a teacher and a woman I reject readings of the teacher as a woman who deserves to have kids play up on her?

> I used to be a school student so I can read this as some kids getting fun out of a boring classroom.

---

[2]The materials were collected in 1992 for use in a research project at the University of South Australia. They are reproduced in full in *It's written in our head: The possibilities and contradictions of a feminist poststructuralist discourse in a junior primary classroom* (O'Brien, 1994).

I wanted to make it clear that my reading of the text challenged the obvious reading: "Do we have to agree with this writer that it's OK to be rude to make jokes about a 'boring' teacher?"

As I read aloud from *Almost Goodbye, Guzzler* I interrupted to ask a series of questions. As the responses (recorded in the first place on a wall chart) show, students found it easy to identify the novel's appeal to a particular group of readers:

Who laughs at this book?

Students

What things in this book make these readers laugh?

Consequences game ... Ridiculous things about Miss Toasty

Sending Miss Toasty to Mars

The barbecue Miss Toasty gave

It was no surprise that the questions failed to shift them from joining with the text in taking up the discourse that placed them in opposition to teachers:

Is it OK to laugh at her because she's boring?

Yes

Students were ambivalent when asked to consider how teachers stood in relation to the text:

Is this story for teachers? Why?

They might think it's funny enough to read to their class.

Is this story for teachers? Why not?

Teachers and adults wouldn't laugh at it. It makes fun of adults.

Students' use of the word *might* in this short exchange signals a number of uncertainties. Firstly, it can be read as a sign that students, recently introduced to critically framed discussion of their texts, are not sure about how to engage in this new discourse (Fairclough, 1989). Secondly, their hesitancy shows that they are aware of my contradictory position in relation to this text. Earlier, I explained that on the one hand I recognized and responded to the humor produced by the interplay between the ridiculous Miss Toasty and the naughty pupils. On the other, however, I questioned the ridicule routinely handed out to adults and to female authority figures in particular across children's books, films, and television shows.

This brief discussion highlights some of the struggles I was engaged in. Funny books written for children are not just fun; but at the same time they are fun. I had taken a contradictory set of positions toward this text and had made it possible for some of my students to get a glimpse of the complexities involved in exploring reading positions.

The transcript, recorded when I read aloud the text of *Almost Goodbye, Guzzler*, shows how I made this text a topic of study rather than adopting the standard practice of sharing stories for enjoyment and comprehension only (Baker, 1991). I explained to the class how I intended to interrupt when I was reading aloud

> O'Brien: What I'm going to do with *Almost Goodbye, Guzzler* is stop
> every so often and ask you what you think is going to be happening next.

In common with junior primary practice in South Australian schools, I used predictive questions during the course of reading aloud sessions, often as a way of checking that students were making use of the narrative devices to follow the story. This time, as I tried to explain to my students, my use of these questions was different; I grappled with the challenge of drawing attention to intertextual knowledge and to its use by writers:

> O'Brien: Because one of the things I've [pause] discovered, that I've
> realized, is that very often with books the things that happen aren't that unusual. They're things that you are quite
> used to happening. They happen over and over in stories.
> You might have already discovered that. You think [pause]
> oh yes I know what's going to happen next because you've
> already read that sort of thing in a story before. So we're going to see ...

My struggle to introduce this new discourse in terms my students could engage with is evident in this hesitant, repetitive explanation, but it had an immediate impact. Louise interrupted; the first of a number of girls to take up the text as the topic of the talk:

> Louise: What if it's different?

O'Brien: It's great, I think. Don't you think it's great if it's different? If there's something unexpected.

Christy also knew what I was talking about. She picked up on a different piece of knowledge about how texts work, one that had been the focus of many classroom textual investigations during that year: the routine representation of female characters, such as teachers, as objects of ridicule:

Christy: (aged 7, an independent reader and writer) They always show teachers as stupid

O'Brien: Yes that's true. They often do. Now we had got up to where people were collecting for the white elephant stall, isn't that right?

Some of the tensions are clear here. I was positioned by the girls' questions and comments as a fellow critical reader. At the same time, being constrained by the specific plans I had made to enact my agenda and by the exigencies of the whole group classroom setting, I did not take up their contributions more than minimally. Lainie also talked about the text. In the following example she worked with me in placing this narrative within a familiar tradition of storytelling:

Lainie: (aged 7, an independent reader and writer) In some stories they've got dark walls and things and they've got spare parts and they've got old ladies living by themselves.

O'Brien: So that's something you recognize as having old people living by themselves and the darkness.

And later, she moved to the particularities of *Almost Goodbye, Guzzler*, demonstrating her awareness that this narrative draws on common sets of understandings about what constitutes a genie and bottle story:

Lainie: I reckon like Anthea's and Steven's. The genie's going to come out and he's going to say "Thank goodness I've got out" and he starts stretching himself.... And he asks "You've got three wishes." And then the one who likes eating all the time says "I'll have bickies please."

Later, I summarized rather tentatively the position I was presenting for their consideration:

O'Brien: Do you know what? It's almost as if the story has been writ-
           ten already, you people know so much about what's going
           to happen.

This hesitancy carried traces of the contradictions inherent in my multiple positioning as teacher and critical reader. I struggled to invent in the
classroom context a critical discourse through which I could share my
own explorations of textuality and also make space for children's readings. At the same time the reading aloud session, a familiar classroom experience, carried its own complex sets of expectations for my students.

Christy had demonstrated earlier her willingness to work with me in
making a critical reading of this text; at this point she again joined in. By pick-
ing up my statement and reformulating it, she showed her capacity to apply
an idea which I had raised several times during the year: that writing for specific audiences entails drawing on culturally familiar textual practices:

Christy: It's written in our head.

Not knowing how to take up and extend her contribution, I relinquished
my position as critical reader and made several very teacherly moves: I acknowledged her contribution and participation yet at the same time appropriated her contribution by explaining what she meant:

O'Brien: It's written in your head because you've heard it and read it
           already.
Students: (hubbub of talk)

O'Brien: Listen. Can I ask you something different?

My perfunctory responses to Christy are examples of the difficulty I
found with finding a way to extend student contributions into an exchange
beyond acknowledgment or reformulation. In addition, the earlier exchange demonstrates the competing needs to get on with the story and at
the same time to engage in critical talk with the girls.

This analysis puts on clear view other contradictions in my position: I
proposed to introduce a critical position on classroom reading practices to
my students, but when faced with critical responses to my critically
framed talk, questions, and activities, I found it hard to know what to say.

This has been a partial view of the critical literacy produced around *Almost Goodbye, Guzzler*. I could have drawn on other chunks of talk to
show Jack contesting my attempts to pose analytical questions, or the
ease with which I deal with talk that positioned us more in more familiar
ways, for example, in a struggle over the meaning of the text or the lesson.

And to counter the charge that I was excessively serious about what was only a piece of fun helping children to become good readers, I could have chosen others showing the riotous fun we all had with this funny book and discussions we had about the nuts and bolts of reading a book that moved the action along by means of conventional narrative prose combined with speech balloons in comic book-style illustrations.

SHOW MUM YOU LOVE HER

In this second example of critical literacy, I am again concerned with helping children to probe the representation of women. I use as the jumping off points firstly the cultural institution, Mothers' Day, and secondly, a set of junk mail brochures produced for that occasion. This account shows how I drew extensively on the cultural resources available to children to move them toward rereading the limited life options for women suggested in Mothers' Day cataloges.

My personal and professional histories came together in the critical activities I designed around Mothers' Day catalogs. In common with many other primary schools, Mothers' Day was a big event at Cairnmuir, a school situated in a socially and economically mixed suburb with growing numbers of single parents, mostly women, and of households affected by unemployment. Much formal and informal classroom talk covered the themes of gift giving and the central roles of mothers and other female caregivers in maintaining the material and emotional fabric of the family unit. As in many other schools, it was the practice for teachers to organize children into making gifts for their mothers.

As a feminist woman I rejected a range of messages carried by Mothers' Day as practiced in contemporary Australia: women's special responsibility for maintaining family relationships, motherhood as sacrifice and self-denial, family responsibilities as women's central duty, the idea that a gift presented on one day can repay all debts incurred across a year.

I must add that I am by no means suggesting that Mothers' Day is not a significant cultural event, one full of meaning for many people, I certainly was not suggesting that children should not join in. Rather, I wanted to make room for some different ideas about what goes on around Mothers' Day. One of the most visible manifestations of Mothers' Day is the proliferation of junk mail catalogs that pour into letter boxes. These are a sign of Mothers' Day as a commercial, consumerist festival.

Although mass advertisements like junk mail are commonly read and used in community life, school reading practices, which involve literature and books written for use in the classroom, rarely take account of texts like these (Baker & Freebody, 1989). At school, for example, they are often used not for literacy activities but as a source of mathematics activities (e.g., What can you buy for your mother if you have $20 to spend?).

On this occasion, I wanted the girls and boys in my class at Cairnmuir Primary to use junk mail catalogs as reading material and to consider junk mail as texts that create specific versions of the social world in order to persuade people to spend money.

I wanted students to think about who benefited from texts like these, to think about how junk mail created a limited range of truths about women's lives, and to challenge these versions of women's lives by coming up with other possibilities.

With these purposes in mind, I gave students the following tasks to guide reading, writing, drawing and discussion:

- Draw and label six presents you expect to see in the catalogs and draw and label some presents you wouldn't expect to find.

- Draw and label six kinds of presents you can find in Mothers' Day catalogs.

- What groups of people get the most out of Mothers' Day?
- Make two lists: How the mothers in the catalogs are like real mothers and how the mothers in the catalogs aren't like real mothers.

- Draw and label any presents you were surprised to find in the Mothers' Day catalogs.

- Draw and label the people who are shown giving the presents to the mothers.

- Make a new Mothers' Day catalog full of fun things instead of clothes and things for the house.

Students worked in small mixed age groups drawing on what they knew about how mothers are usually constructed in the mass media in order to make lists of expected and unexpected presents. They were fascinated by how much they knew and about how accurate their predictions had been. For instance, their lists included watches, underwear, clothes, household appliances, and flowers.

Some students had difficulty with the question Who gets the most out of Mothers' Day, so I asked: Who produces these catalogs? Why are they in your letter box? Why do they go to all that trouble just to let you know that these things are available? With questions like these as cues, advertisers, publishers, shopkeepers, manufacturers, and other players in commercial life seemed obvious answers.

Students discovered that the "catalog mothers" were young, pretty, slim, and rarely engaged in the kinds of activities and contexts that they associated with their own mothers and caregivers. As Angie and Ahmed said: "They never show mothers smoking and they never show fat mothers."

Students produced new catalogs portraying their mothers and caregivers in a whole range of new contexts and activities: on holidays, enjoying rides in planes, going out to dinner, relaxing, watching movies, and jumping on trampolines.

I considered this a successful series of activities. While clearly having a good time, students had a chance to consider the circumstances in which mass-advertising texts were produced, to speculate on who produced the text, and with what ends in mind. I encouraged them to recognize techniques used in the narrow and exclusive portrayals of women and mothers. They were also required to think differently to create other kinds of possibilities for mothers.

The following year I was moved to another school. Here at Glenbrae Primary, children lived in communities marked by poverty and unemployment to a greater extent than was the case at Cairnmuir. The girls and boys in the class I taught came from a wider range of ethnic, racial, and cultural backgrounds; several children had recently arrived in Australia. Informal discussion revealed that for many children in the class Mothers' Day was not a familiar institution; others simply could not afford to buy presents. With this group of children, I wanted to add to the usual Mothers' Day questions like What are you giving your mother for a present? or Are you making your mother something? with a view to beginning a wide ranging discussion of Mothers' Day as a cultural practice and to raising questions of how race and culture are represented in everyday mass-advertising texts. So I decided that we should look for the groups of mothers who were not included in the catalogs, and to explore what that exclusion meant for the construction of the ideal woman in capitalist consumer society.

I opened class discussion with a series of questions intended to put the taken-for-granted cultural practice of Mothers' Day on the agenda:

- What happens on Mothers' Day?

- Why do we have Mothers' Day?

- What is Mothers' Day for?

- What part do these groups of people play in Mothers' Day (mothers, children, fathers, grandmothers, teachers, restaurant owners, shopkeepers)?

- Whose family celebrates Mothers' Day?

- Why do we have a special day for mothers?

- What do fathers have to do with Mothers' Day?

- Where do children get the money to buy presents?

- Where do presents come from?

Some children told of familiar practices such as their fathers providing money for them to spend on their mother's present; others told of how they and their families were in the process of negotiating new sets of social and cultural practices around Mothers' Day, such as dining out as a family. Jessie lived with her father. She explained that her grandmother was the focus of their celebrations.

Next, students turned to the catalogs to investigate how mothers' desires are constructed through the gifts included in them. As they cut out pictures of gifts, together we formulated tentative categories.

Students analyzed the catalogs to investigate the sorts of women portrayed as receiving presents, cutting out pictures of presents recommended for mothers and categorizing them. Using the information displayed as a result of the categorization, students wrote and drew in response to the following questions: According to these catalogs, what do mothers like doing? According to these catalogs, what sorts of things do mothers like? At this point we began to explore the ways in which pictures and language work together to construct identities as women and mothers. We talked about the idea that these texts produce a limited but very purposeful version of what mothers are like and what they do.

I then turned the discussion to aspects of the social world on which junk mail catalogs were silent, and to groups of women whose absence was notable, asking Whose mother isn't here? Students cut up catalogs and pasted photographs of mothers under heading that included cultural groups in the class. They found that most of the women in the catalogs were young, Anglo-Australian, and pretty: They identified Greek, Lebanese, Cambodian, Vietnamese, and Aboriginal mothers as missing. This activity led to a lively and extended discussion about the fact that so many groups of women (including heavily built and older women) were missing from the catalogs.

All the classroom talk so far had been about mothers; it was now time to include mothers' voices. Always on the look out for purposeful reading, writing, and talking tasks, I helped students to develop a questionnaire so that they could collect data on their own mothers' and caregivers' attitudes and preferences. This survey asked mothers, aunts, and grandmothers to list gifts they enjoyed receiving as well as activities they liked and disliked.

Students shared completed surveys in small groups, reporting many trends. They discovered that their mothers and caregivers enjoyed, appreciated, and desired much that was not in the catalogs, especially intangibles like rest, leisure, happy family relationships, being appreciated, and "peace and quiet." The survey also showed that mothers preferred many gifts that did not turn up in any of the catalogs: horror novels, cats, roller blades, tickets to the movies, Greek food, and photographs.

As the investigation proceeded, I collected the reading, writing, and drawings produced by the children and used these to make a big book. Children later used this book to reread their discussions and their investigations into the commercial and cultural institution that is Mothers' Day.

This set of activities was quite successful in drawing attention to the gaps between the social worlds constructed in the catalogs and the students' worlds. Students found that the women's world constructed in Mothers' Day advertising was one of very limited possibilities and also that the catalog represented only those aspects of women's lives that resulted in consumer spending.

In this account I have emphasised students' roles as critical analysts of Mothers' Day catalogs. However, during the course of the activities I described, students functioned on a number of other levels in addition to the critical[3]. Although it is hard to untangle these, I briefly survey other reading practices in which students participated. For a start, they were required to practice cracking the code of the English writing system when writing labels in their new Mothers' Day catalogs, when administering the survey of mothers' preferences, compiling data drawn from the surveys, drawing conclusions, and writing reports. Further decoding work, in the shape of learning about how specific kinds of texts function, occurred when students handled junk mail catalogs, data collection tables, and survey questionnaires.

---

[3]This review of Mothers' Day catalog activities uses the four-tiered model of the reading practices proposed for a complex, multivoiced society proposed by Freebody and Luke (1990) and revised by Luke (1995). This model suggests that students need to learn to bring required cultural resources to bear on texts in four (nonhierarchical) ways. They operate as code breakers able to bring the requisite knowledge about how writing systems work in order to read and write the text in question. They operate as text participants able to determine the range of cultural meanings produced by the text. They operate as text users able to assess and choose from the possible uses to which the text can be put. They operate as text analysts and critics prepared to ask in whose interest the text functions and as a consequence to challenge available meanings and to develop alternate reading positions (Luke, 1995).

The classroom activities required students as text users to interact in both conventional and unexpected ways with the texts they handled. For example, while students mined the junk mail for representations of mothers, they used questionnaires quite conventionally to gather data, charts to record findings, and reports to present conclusions.

When making meaning from the catalogs, students drew on cultural knowledge of Mothers' Day acquired in their family and community lives. They were able to use these same resources to question the representations of mothers, to identify gaps, and to suggest possible changes.

LOOKING BACK

There are no formulas for producing critical literacy in classrooms and no guaranteed results. A critical stance provides a space for questioning the usual ways of doing literacy, without providing easy answers. Although my history could be construed as giving me a more-or-less straightforward passage into critical classroom practices—no one ever challenged my agenda—it became apparent to me that what I was up to was risky if not dangerous in a number of ways. It was at times disruptive to the usual classroom order, interrupting parent, child, and teacher expectations about what school reading, writing, and talk were for; it encouraged discordant points of view to be expressed; from time to time it involved children in questioning the rules by which they and their families and communities lived out their lives.

The critical turn in textual study raises important issues for teachers and their relationships with their students and with classroom texts. For example, there are dangers in setting teachers up as experts providing enlightenment to students as passive dupes (Buckingham & Sefton-Green, 1994). Indeed, much of the work on which I based my critical position assumed that children were essentially passive readers or listeners (Baker & Freebody, 1989). For much of the time I too assumed that without my mediation students would not find ways of contesting, subverting, or resisting texts. Although I made room for children's readings, I think it fair to say that I regarded my agenda as pre-eminent, even though discussions continuously showed that students were very active constructors of readings, surprising to an adult who could pick a dominant meaning at 100 paces. The classroom encounters I discuss in this chapter, show that children are not passive readers, they are inventive and skeptical. Often they do not have the language to talk about these things, but they do challenge the text, sometimes in unexpected ways.

My working assumption at that time was that without my intervention these readings would not have emerged. Now, I would be interested in finding out the readings children made, and then weaving, shuttling between their readings and mine, considering how they were different and how these differences were constructed by our social, economic, and cultural positioning. Working with Mothers' Day catalogs, for example, I would investigate how Mothers' Day catalogs and other junk mail are used at home. I would expect to find an extensive range of reading practices, including positions of scepticism and uses that subverted, bypassed, or extended retailers' consumerist agendas.

Exploring texts in new ways is hard work for teacher and students; the script for classroom exchanges has not been already spoken by many practitioners. Conventional readings of texts and of teacher–student relationships offer ready-made responses to all parties, much as writers of children's novels make use of a range of already available characterizations, storylines, and locations. Reading lessons are already made. Their words are already said. Student–teacher relationships are expressed in recognizable forms. However, new ideas about working with texts require new practices. The challenge is to adopt practices that will not only open up new possibilities but will begin to deal with taking action. Discursive practices in classrooms, however, form only part of the complex discursive and material practices in the communities outside schools, where children live out the rest of their lives. All these sites are implicated in the challenges to inequities I propose.

The classroom practices I have described raise many questions. Many teachers worry that I am putting words in students mouths' or that students say what the teacher wants to hear. I am; and they do, of course. But these objections are based on a misleading theory that a teacher who does not challenge the authority relationship constructed between texts and their readers is in some way remaining neutral or that texts themselves are neutral unless a teacher intervenes. All texts (and all teachers) have political positions, acknowledged or unacknowledged. My position is that teachers need to adopt a pedagogy that makes it possible for them and their students to investigate the positions taken up by texts and the sorts of readers they produce in the process.

ACKNOWLEDGMENTS

I would like to acknowledge Barbara Comber and Allan Luke's contribution to my thinking and writing about the work around Mothers' Day and the junk mail catalogs.

REFERENCES

Baker, C. (1991). Literacy practices and social relations in classroom reading events. In C. Baker & A. Luke (Eds.), *Towards a critical sociology of reading pedagogy* (pp. 161–188). Philadelphia: John Benjamins.

Baker, C., & Freebody, P. (1989). *Children's first school books: Introductions to the culture of literacy.* Oxford: Basil Blackwell.

Buckingham, D., & Sefton-Green, J. (1994). *Cultural studies goes to school: Reading and teaching popular media.* London: Taylor & Francis.

Cresswell, H., & Browne, J. (1990). *Almost Goodbye, Guzzler.* London: Young Lions.

Education Department of South Australia. (1984). *Early literacy inservice course.* Adelaide, Australia: Education Department of South Australia.

Education Department of South Australia. (1989). *Literacy and learning in the middle years.* Adelaide, Australia: Education Department of South Australia.

Fairclough, N. (1989). *Language and power.* London: Longman.

Freebody, P., & Luke, A. (1990). Literacies programs: Debates and demands in cultural context. *Prospect: Journal of Adult Migrant Education Programs, 5*(3), 7–16.

Lankshear, C., & Lawler, M. (1989). *Literacy, schooling and revolution.* New York: Falmer.

Luke, A. (1995). The social practice of reading. Paper presented at the Australian Reading Association 21st National Conference, Darling Harbour, Australia.

O'Brien, J. (1994). *It's written in our head: The possibilities and contradictions of a feminist poststructuralist discourse in a junior primary classroom.* Unpublished Master of Education thesis, University of South Australia, Adelaide, Australia.

Weedon, C. (1987). *Feminist practice and poststructuralist theory.* Oxford: Basil Blackwell.

4

Constructing a Critical Curriculum
With Young Children

Vivian Vasquez
American University

As a Canadian teacher, I was introduced to critical literacy in the mid-1990s while taking a course through Mount Saint Vincent University at the University of South Australia. Until that time, the whole language movement (e.g., Goodman, Watson, & Burke, 1987; Harste, Short, & Burke, 1996; Harste, Woodward, & Burke, 1984; Newman, 1985) seemed to me the most generative theoretical position from which to support the needs of learners. Whole language gave me a way of envisioning and supporting learning as a social experience, of creating spaces in classrooms for placing children at the center of pedagogy, and, through inquiry into literacy teaching and learning, for ensuring that student voices be heard.

Whole language, however, is not a static position. As my understanding grew, and I encountered new experiences, I moved toward a critical position within whole language. The journey toward critical literacy was rooted in my early experience as literacy learner. As a young child, female, and a member of a visible minority I frequently found my identity was constructed and maintained as voiceless, as incapable of action, or of making a difference in the lives of others or, indeed, in my own life.

This is not only personal experience; much of what takes place in schools and in the world is inaccessible to certain marginalized groups, including visible minorities and females. A critical perspective suggests that deliberate attempts to expose inequity in the classroom and society need to become part of the discourse of whole language (Edelsky, 1994). I see a need, therefore, for teachers committed to a whole language perspective to construct a critical curriculum that is socially just and equitable, where issues including race, class, gender, and fairness are constantly on the agenda.

The kind of curriculum I have in mind is one which cannot be prepackaged or preplanned because it is built on children's cultural questions about everyday life. Rather, it arises as teachers and children tune in to issues of social justice and equity unfolding through classroom conversation and begin to pose critical questions. Conversations like these lead us to ask in what ways we are already readers and writers of the world and in what ways can we equitably and democratically reread and rewrite the world in order to move toward becoming the literate people we want to be in the new millenium.

Furthermore, because a critical curriculum arises from a critical sociological analysis of the contemporary economic and political conditions of teachers' communities and times (Luke, cited in Comber & Kamler, 1997), it cannot be traditionally taught; it needs to be lived. In other words, as teachers we need to incorporate a critical perspective into our everyday lives in order to find ways to help children understand the social issues around them (Vasquez, cited in Church, 1996).

Working from within a critical perspective, my desire is to construct spaces where social justice issues can be raised and a critical curriculum can be negotiated with children. Critical literacy makes it possible for me to revision my thinking as a whole language teacher by providing a framework from which to address issues of social justice and equity.

Following the postmodern view that the world is not full of knowable moments but is always in a state of flux, full of contradictions, tensions and overlapping categories, I imagine negotiation and contestation at the centre of these critical conversations, rather than a more familiar process of discovering the best way. I envision learning as a process of adjusting and reconstructing what we know rather than of accumulating information.

Shortly I propose to tell what happened when the children in my classroom and I seized on one particular school event—the annual 'French Café'—to construct a critical curriculum. First, however, I want to provide some context for this incident by outlining briefly some earlier experiences with putting a critical literacy curriculum in place, and explaining my use of an audit trail to document and analyze this curriculum and to initiate critical conversation with young children.

INQUIRIES INTO CRITICAL LITERACY

Between 1993 and 1996 as a member of a teacher-research group I carried out two interrelated inquiries into critical literacy in practice. I worked first with children between the ages of six and eight in a grade one/two classroom and later with 3- to 5-year-olds. Both groups were representative of the very diverse, multiethnic middle-class community in suburban Toronto in which the school was situated. With the aim of understanding how to construct a critical literacy curriculum, I collected observational narratives and artifacts such as children's drawings that I felt dealt with social justice and equity issues around the political and social questions asked by my students.

Analysis of the data I gathered brought both excitement and concern. On the one hand, I found that issues raised by the children led to conversations that moved well beyond the traditional topics of study often associated with primary school curriculum. Our critical literacy curriculum brought about richer experiences and deeper understandings of social justice and equity issues, along with ways of creating curriculum focusing on these issues. On the other hand, it concerned me that I had not always been able to generate further inquiry into social issues nor make connections between issues.

A third inquiry into critical literacy took place in a half-day junior kindergarten classroom where I worked with sixteen 3- to 5-year-old children, again representative of the diverse multiethnic community in a middle-class neighborhood. Building on the previous two inquiries, I focused on using issues from the social lives of children to construct a critical curriculum. This time, the investigation stretched over the course of a school year. Once again I gathered data during the course of the inquiry. On this occasion, data collection took the form of an *audit trail*, a public display of a researcher's gathered notes and artefacts that allows outsiders to retrace the researcher's thinking as she moves toward her conclusions (Harste, 1998). The audit trail was displayed on a bulletin board covered with artifacts of learning such as photographs, letters, book covers, and transcripts of conversations.

AUDIT TRAIL AS A TOOL FOR GENERATING AND CIRCULATING MEANING

Retracing thinking invites theorizing. As I constructed the audit trail, I began to think about using it as a tool for critical conversation with young children. It seemed to me that making theoretical connections through the use of artifacts might enable the children to revisit, reread, and reimagine possibilities for living a critically literate life in a way that would be generative for curriculum construction. By the end of the school year, the audit trail had become a joint construction between teacher and children and a means of generating and reflecting on the classroom curriculum. The audit trail, or learning wall, spanned a 40 foot × 6 foot length of wall space in our classroom and consisted of more than 130 artifacts, accessible to anyone who entered our class space. Artifacts included photographs, book covers, posters, drawings, transcripts of conversations, quotes from children, newspaper clippings, and internet printouts representing our theories of the world about things that mattered to us. Each of the artifacts became a way for us to make visible the incidents that caused us to want to learn, the issues we had critical conversations about and the action we took to resist bing dominated and to reposition ourselves within our community. They became our demonstration of and our site for constructing critical curriculum for ourselves.

Over the course of the school year, children regularly referred to various artifacts in the audit trail, often pointing at or touching artifacts on the learning wall as a way of connecting issues and events during our class meetings or when engaged in small group conversations. Issues recorded on the audit trail arose from and generated curriculum topics including rain forests, the environment, gender, fairness, the media, and a range of questions concerned with power and control. Over a period of 10 months, various issues were sustained and continuously revisited. The underlying questions or conversations included:

- How we are written into the world.

- How we can re-read and re-write ourselves in the world.

- How inequitable situations arise and are maintained.

- How language acts on us.

- How to compose a place for oneself.

- What is it we value beyond school?

- What does it mean to have social consciousness?

- What theories about the world do we have and how do we change our theories of the world?

As a classroom community, we used and constructed our audit trail to make visible demonstrations of how we generated and circulated a different set of meanings from the traditional social systems in place at our school. Our trail became a mediating site through which we began to destabilize traditional social systems in place at our school or at least make these systems more amenable to change, and become a site for:

- representing the stories we wished to tell about learning,

- writing curriculum,

- exposing issues from the unofficial world of school,

- demonstrating critical literacy as a frame of mind rather than as an isolated incident,

- generating issues for critical inquiry,

- ongoing and generative theorizing,

- making visible the intertextuality of different contexts,

- expanding the culture's conversation through providing space for learning the language of power and decentering truth,

- changing what counts as knowing, and

- demonstrating the construction of a more socially equitable classroom.

Because our audit trail was publicly visible, parents and guardians witnessed its growth and were privy to the issues that unfolded through our critical conversations. I also sent home newsletters regularly sharing what we were up to in the classroom. Parents and guardians, as well as other teachers who showed interest, were very supportive. However, we did encounter resistance from other classroom teachers who worried that a curriculum addressing social issues and leading to social action could create students who are radical, rude, and disrespectful. At issue seemed to be ideas of control, of who should and should not have access as well as the fear of the unknown, the untried.

Close to the end of the school year, Alyssa, one of my 4-year-old students, excitedly announced to the class that her mom and dad had just gotten back from attending a conference. Her excitement led to wide-ranging discussions about conferences and a decision to have one of our own. Thus, in June of 1997, we organized *Celebrating Our Questions: A Junior Kindergarten Conference.* Speakers included a vegetarian and an animal rights activist. Parents and guardians were invited to attend as were some of the other junior kindergarten. and senior kindergarten classes. At the close of our conference, Lily, a parent of one of the children in my class approached me. With tears in her eyes she said, "Vivian, the difference between what happened here this year and what happens in other places is that these children ask questions that matter."

I offer this parent's words as food for thought and pose the following question: In their own settings how might teachers get at questions that matter in order for their students to be able to reread and rewrite the world toward becoming the literate people they want and need to be in the new millenium.

I now reconstruct one critical incident—which I call the French Café protest—recorded during that year on the audit trail. This event illustrates the critical literacy curriculum that emerged from one child's questions about inequity as experienced by the youngest children in our school.

THE FRENCH CAFÉ

It was 9 a.m., time for morning announcements. Our principal welcomed guests to the day's special event, the Annual French Café. (In Ontario Elementary Schools, French is taught as a mandatory second language subject due to what is known as the Official Languages Act which, outlines French and English as Canada's two official languages).

"What's a French Café?," some of the children asked.

"Well, it's like a restaurant set up for the day by some of the older children in our school," I answered.

"Why did he say 'welcome guests?," the children asked.

From the doorway of our classroom Curtis watched the trickle of parents and guardians who had come to our school to have croissants and coffee or juice at the Café. "Look! Where are they all going? To the Café? Those are the guests that he's saying welcome to! Who else is going to this?" Curtis kept track of the visitors making their way to the gymnasium where the Café was being staged, then came to our class meeting with the hypothesis that everyone except some younger kids would visit the Café at some point during the day. "I think that because I already saw older kids and younger kids, and mommies and daddies and babysitters going to the Café," he concluded.

"You think all the kids are going, Curtis?" one of the other children asked. Curtis returned to his observation post for the day to wait for evidence of the Grade 1 classes attending the Café. "The Grade 1s are coming, the Grade 1s are coming!" he announced. "So that means the Grade 1 are going, the Grade 2s are going, the Grade 3s are going … everyone. Why can't we go? Who else can't go?," he asked.

"You have some observations …," I began, but Curtis took a piece of paper, wrote 1, 2, 3, 4, 5, 6, 7, 8, ticked off the groups of children he had observed entering the Café (Fig. 4.1), and then said, "If we had Grade 13s they would probably go too! Can I ask if the other kindergartens and the other junior kindergarten class is going?" Three children went to find out.

When they returned, they called an emergency class meeting to share the information they had gathered. Here the following conversation took place:

Curtis: OK, the two kindergarten classes are NOT going and the other junior kindergarten class is NOT going and we are NOT going!

Melanie: This is impossible.

Vivian: Then what is possible? How can we change what's possible?

Curtis: Maybe we can make a survey to see how much of each kids want to go.

Stefanie: Yes, let's find out from the other kindergartens.

Leigh: If more people want to go then next year maybe they'll let us go.

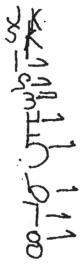

FIG. 4.1.   Curtis' observation sheet.

Curtis: Can we tape that it's not fair?

Vivian: At our Speakers' Corner? (In Speakers' Corner children can
            tape record conversations or ideas about various issues.
            These can then be played by others in the classroom or
            outside).

Melanie: That's a good idea. Then, we can send the tape of us talking
            so they'll know that we want to go.

Tiffany: Yeah, we think it's not fair.

Curtis: Who wants to do a survey?

Vivian: Tell me about your survey.

Curtis: We'll ask all the kindergartens and junior kindergartens
            yes or no, do you want to go to the French Café?

Melanie: You did that already.

PJ: We didn't answer yes or no.

Curtis: We just didn't do a writing one.

Tiffany: We just said SAY, SAY if you want to.

Melanie: Right. Not sign yes or no just SAY, but we could still do a
            writed out one.

Vivian: What reason could you give for doing that?

Melanie   So we'll know.
& Curtis:

Vivian: What information do you think the written information will
            given you that you don't already have?

Tiffany: Like a different answer?

PJ: Everyone will still say yes. I will.

Curtis: So we won't find out new stuff. We already know what
             we'll find out?

Melanie: Yup, we know what we want to find out about already.

Vivian: Who were you planning giving the survey to?

Curtis: Just for us to find out how many people want to and so we
             can tell the people who is the chair of the French Café.

Vivian: I have a suggestion for another way to pass on information
             to the French Café organizers. I think that maybe a petition
             might be a way to show that many of us, maybe most of the
             J.K.s and S.K.s might feel the same way. (J.K. students are
             4-years-old, whereas S.K. students are 5-years-old)

Curtis: Do we get everyone to write letters to them?

Vivian: Sort of but that would take a long time. What I'm thinking
             about is called a petition. Instead of asking a question for
             people to answer, you write out what you are thinking and
             then have people sign their name after it.

Melanie: Then what happens?

Tiffany: Then we bring it to the chair?

PJ: Why lots of names and one letter?

Vivian: Well you don't really need a lot of letters in this case, espe-
             cially because they would all be saying pretty well the
             same thing. What you would do is to ask people who agree
             with you to sign it. The more names you have, the stronger
             your petition is!

Curtis: Oh that's like one brain is strong but lots of brains is stronger!

Soon after our class meeting, groups of children began to work on
their tasks. Curtis and a group of three, soon known as the French Café
Petition Committee, wrote a covering letter for the petition (Fig. 4.2). A
copy of the letter was attached to a blank sheet of paper and delivered to

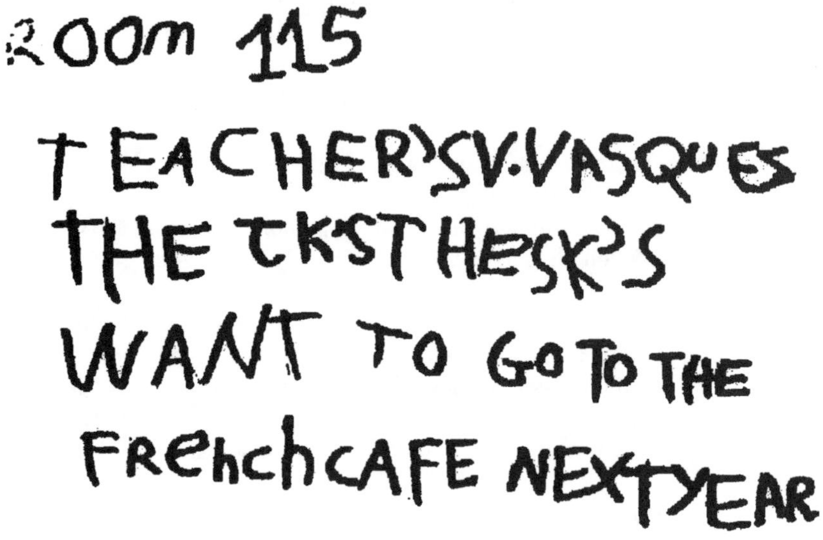

ROOM 115

TEACHER'S V. VASQUES
THE CKST HESK'S
WANT TO GO TO THE
FRehch CAFE NEXTYEAR

FIG. 4.2. French Café petition letter.

each of the other junior kindergarten and kindergarten classrooms. The children explained the reason for the petition to the other classes and arranged to collect it.

At the same time, another group of children began creating a Speakers' Corner tape to be delivered with the petitions in order to strengthen their case (Fig. 4.3). The following day, the children eagerly entered the classroom, excited about going to the other junior kindergarten and senior kindergarten classes to gather the signed petitions. During our class meeting, the committee shared the results of the petition, showing the children the names that had been collected.

In her account of the social worlds of children learning to write, Dyson (1993) talks about how children nudge the bounds of the official imaginative universe that prevails in schools. In so doing they challenge current theoretical and pedagogical thinking. She said, they do this while constructing and participating in the complicated world of school. In the same way, Curtis and his French Café Petition Committee "nudged the bounds" as they repositioned junior and senior kindergarten children as equal participants of life at our school. In doing so, they moved toward an alternate possibility: not only envisaging but actualizing a different school world.

As a result of the children's action, the junior and senior kindergarten students will be included in future Cafés. The petition and Speakers' Corner tape was met with little resistance from other teachers. I think this re-

Today there's something going on in the gym and we want to know why aren't we invited? Because only the grade ones and twos can go so that's not fair to us or to anyone.

And maybe (on the next on the , maybe on the next party, maybe) on the next party we can have it at our class.

But we figured out something. If we have dances here then they won't have dances there and if they have dances there we won't have dances here. And that's not fair to us or to the whole world because we don't get to go.

Maybe they don't understand.

Or maybe they think that we're bored or that we're not old enough but we are not going to be bored if we were even invited.

So, this is a French Café and we hope that we can go next year.

Thank you.

FIG. 4.3.   French Café speaker's corner tape.

sponse stemmed in part from surprise at the children's action and in part from seeing these young children differently. Through taking social action, the children learned not only a different way to resist and exercise their democratic abilities but also the possibilities available through collectively working through a problem. My role was not to tell the children what to think or how to act, but, based on their inquiries, to offer alternate ways of taking action and a way of naming their world within the stance they chose to take. In the words of the editors of *Rethinking Schools* (Bigelow, Christensen, Karp, Miner, & Peterson, 1994):

> We want students to come to see themselves as change makers. If we ask the children to critique the world but then fail to encourage them to act, our classrooms can degenerate into factories for cynicism. While it's not a teacher's role to direct students to particular organisations, it is a teacher's role to suggest that ideas need to be acted upon and to offer students opportunities to do just that. (p. 5)

Being able to actualize critical literacies calls for making problematic the current dominant school definition of community.

The actions taken by these 4- and 5-year-olds makes problematic the existing power structure that treats kindergarten students as innocent neutral beings to be readied not only for the real world of school, that is, for first grade and the grades that follow, but for society in general, and their position within the social hierarchy.

According to Comber and Kamler (1997) a critical perspective offers teachers a way to think about what student are learning to read and write, what they do with that reading and writing, and what that reading and writing does to them and their world. Through engagement in a critical curriculum my students and I raised various social justice and equity issues using them to interrogate, obstruct, contest, and/or change inequitable situations.

REFERENCES

Bigelow, B., Christensen, L., Karp, S., Miner, B., & Peterson, B. (1994). *Rethinking our classrooms: Teaching for social equity and justice.* Milwaukee, WI: Rethinking Schools Ltd.

Church, S. (1996). *The future of whole language.* Portsmouth, NH: Heinemann.

Comber, B., & Kamler, B. (1997). Critical literacies: Politicising the classroom. *Interpretations, 30*(1), 30–53.

Dyson, A. H. (1993). *Social worlds of children learning to write in an urban primary school.* New York: Teachers College Press.

Edelsky, C. (1994). Education for democracy. *Language Arts, 71*(4), 252–257.

Goodman, Y. M., Watson, D. J., & Burke, C. L. (1987). *Reading miscue inventory.* New York: Richard Owens.

Harste, J. C. (1998). The work we do: Journal as audit trail. *Language Arts, 75*(4), 266.

Harste, J. C., Short, K., & Burke, C. L. (1996). *Creating classrooms for authors and inquirers.* Portsmouth, NH: Heinemann.

Harste, J. C., Woodward, V. A., & Burke, C. L. (1984). *Language stories and literacy lessons.* Portsmouth, NH: Heinemann.

Newman, J. (1985). *Whole language theory in use.* Portsmouth, NH: Heinemann.

Exploring Critical Literacies
in Primary Schooling:
Unresolved Questions

5

From Prescription to Participation: Moving From Functional to Critical Literacy in Singapore

Yin Mee Cheah
Learning Ventures

In the 1993 Principals' Conference, a prestigious gathering of the top educators in Singapore, the Director of Education (Yip, 1993), in his keynote speech, reminded the audience that:

> They must not lose sight of the fact that education is not an end in itself.... education is linked to national development.... Education in Singapore provides not only quality manpower to forge our economic well-being, but is itself the glue which forms the social and cultural cohesion that is so critical to our multi-racial society. (p. 6)

This ideology that underlies the purpose of education in Singapore is central to any attempt to understand literacy issues in this island nation. Implied in Yip's speech are two main features, that is, education is as much for national development and nation building as it is for individual development, and education has a pragmatic goal of ensuring economic success. These characteristics of the education system, education for economic and social survival, reflect the broader ideology of the People's Action Party (PAP) government in Singapore. The two major expressions of this ideology have been survivalism and pragmatism, and according to Chua (1995):

> The first [survivalism] creates a state of uncertainty, providing operational room for the second concept [pragmatism], which given the context, meant "doing whatever is necessary to survive," including the acceptance of overt state intervention, even authoritarianism. (p. 37)

Although Chua (1995) went on to claim that a new ideology, communitarianism, was introduced to meet social changes that had arisen from increasing stability and economic growth in Singapore, these twin concepts remain very much a part of the ideological character of Singapore. Communitarianism, as exemplified by the establishment of a government policy on Shared Values,[1] reinforces the values of pragmatism and survivalism because, among others, the document emphasises the placing of nation before community and society above self. This again serves to diminish individualism and to sanction state intervention and authority.

This need to place the nation first and to actively forge a nation from the disparate groups of immigrants that make up Singapore, has been attributed to Singapore's history as an ex-British colony and to its short-lived merger with Malaysia as part of a larger nation. Singapore's expulsion from Malaysia in 1965, after only 3 short years, highlighted even more the vulnerability of this small island state, and this history is said to be the reason why "a sense of crisis pervades the Singaporean state's experience of itself" (Ang & Stratton, 1995, p. 72). The politics of survival also underline the constant need to stress a pragmatic approach to government and to use economic survival as a carrot to unite the nation.

On the other hand, the Singapore success story is well-known: a small island of 650 square kilometres, 3.2 million people, no natural resources, eleventh richest country in the world, and a low crime rate. Singapore's economic success is legendary, just as its government is known for its efficiency and its freedom from corruption. Much of this success has been the result of careful planning by the PAP government, and through the ideology of survivalism and pragmatism, the government has persuaded the population of the need for regulation and control. Despite some unpleasant social policies implemented under this ideology, Singaporeans have

---

[1]The White Paper on the Shared Values was passed in Parliament in January 1991. The five core values identified were: nation before community, and society above self; family as the basic unit of society; community support and respect for the individual; consensus, not conflict; racial and religious harmony.

learned to accept the need to be pragmatic and to sacrifice some aspects of personal and social freedom in return for economic and social well-being. Thus, although freedom of speech is not an issue, Singaporeans are constrained from speaking out because of the emphasis on a strong ideological consensus (Chua, 1995). It is against this sociopolitical backdrop of a nation long used to a top-down system of government, to a system of soft authoritarianism, to the belief of placing society above self, and to unquestioning authority (Jones, 1994), that we need to situate the issues of English literacy and education, for the sociopolitical beliefs and practices influence the way literacy is practised and taught in the school system.

In the rest of this chapter, I discuss issues of English literacy in Singapore. Specifically, I show how a pragmatic approach to literacy and the choice of English literacy has resulted in a functional view of literacy acquisition. At the same time, the need to keep up with global economic changes has also meant a review of the ways literacy is taught and acquired. These changes are reflected, at a microlevel, in two types of literacy practised in a Singaporean classroom. Using data from an ethnographic study of a Singapore classroom, I describe the literacy practices, and discuss the implications these have for the development of any kind of critical literacy in Singapore.

LITERACY ISSUES IN SINGAPORE

The dominance of English in Singapore is understandable because the language has a number of domains of use. Tay (1982) described them as the official language, the language of education, the working language, the lingua franca for both interethnic and intraethnic communication, the expression of national identity, and the international language. In addition, Clammer (cited in Pennycook, 1994) has shown that English is also the language of religion through its association with Christianity, a religion linked to the upper middle-class group. Although there is growing interest in Mandarin Chinese because of official language policies and an interest in economic investments in China, this has not displaced interest in English as is evident from the growth in the percentage of families using English at homes from 11.3% in 1980 to 19.2% in 1990 (Tham, 1990, p. 7).

The country's education policy includes bilingualism, and this bilingual policy specifically includes English as the first language and the three other official native languages as second languages.[2] These include Mandarin

---

[2]The terms *first* and *second languages* and *mother tongues* have different meanings in Singapore. The *first language* is the first school language and in this case is English. The *second languages* are the mother tongues, but the mother tongues are not the languages first learnt. Instead they refer to those languages which are officially designated so by the government.

for the Chinese, Malay for the Malays, and Tamil for the Indians. English has been the medium of instruction in schools since 1987 following a fall in demand for vernacular schools; the pragmatic acceptance of this policy is reflected in the lack of public dissent over this issue.

Literacy in Singapore has a functional value because Singaporeans learn English for pragmatic reasons, that is to obtain better jobs and social mobility. Bloom (1986) described English as a language learned "strictly for the purpose of getting rich" (p. 402). This plus the fact that English is not a native language, but is a literacy of contact, has encouraged a tendency among the many Singaporeans to view themselves as merely second language speakers. This has two disadvantages: It cultivates a dependence on exonormative standards and yardsticks to measure competence, and it leads to a less-than-willing attitude to develop more than functional knowledge and use of English, although for many, this will be the only language they are literate in. That English gives access to economic mobility is evident from the fact that more of the English-educated are found in the upper middle-class group and in better paying jobs (Kwan-Terry & Kwan-Terry, 1993).

In this way, English can be associated with class structure. As a non-native language, English is perceived to be neutral because it belongs to no particular ethnic group, and is regarded as the most suitable language for competition in meritocratic Singapore. However, although English is not a native language, it is by no means neutral. As the *lingua franca* for interethnic communication, it is viewed as the language most suitable to help forge a new Singaporean identity and consciousness among the younger generation (Benjamin, 1976; Koh, 1989; Pakir, 1991). This suggests that English can be made to carry certain values, especially those for nation building. In this way, English is fundamentally practiced as a form of group literacy rather than one with a personal dimension for the individual. Together with the official educational policy of learning English for pragmatic reasons, that is to access the science and technological know-how of the west, a technical literacy emphasising a skills approach and functional knowledge of the language has evolved.

This approach is reflected in the 1982 English language syllabus in which the objective for learning English was functional literacy, and where reading and writing were taught with an academic slant: in short, for examination purposes. However, these narrow objectives for literacy have been revised in the 1991 syllabus. One reason is the changing sociocultural context of Singapore. As a society that is rapidly moving to the status of a developed country, Singapore's former insecurity as an independent nation has given way to a new found confidence that has arisen from its economic success. As bread-and-butter issues become less urgent, the government has moved from issues of survival to improving the quality of life for Singaporeans. This shift is also paralleled by an equally urgent necessity to meet new demands in the global market in order to maintain an economic edge. The changes in the syllabus reflect this concern although long before the syllabus appeared, the adoption of holistic language teaching approaches in the late 1980s (Cheah, 1996) had already paved the way for the new curriculum. The Minister of Education confirmed this in his declaration that "We will ... have to shift the emphasis of the education system ... away from the mastery of content towards the acquisition of thinking and learning skills that could last students through life" (cited in Ho, 1996).

This shift, as reflected in the 1991, syllabus acknowledges English as playing a significant part in a child's "present and future needs in the personal, educational, vocational, social and cultural spheres" (p. 1). This move away from functional literacy to what Ho (1994) described as a constructivist perspective, recognizes the importance of a personal dimension in language learning. However, although this seems to be the direction of change proposed, it is also important to weigh this against the background of a society that emphasizes group values above the individual's.

On the other hand, literacy and language education in Singapore has always been associated with learning only the linguistic code (Cheah, 1994; Pennycook, 1994), and attempts to link language learning with social, political, cultural, or economic issues have been rare. Indeed the term *literacy* is only used in conjunction with literacy rates in census reports, and in the Singapore context, literacy refers to the ability to read with understanding a newspaper in a specified language (Tay, 1985). It is, therefore, not unusual to find that discussions about literacy have always been centered on the assumption that it is neutral and only concerned with skills acquisition. This, coupled with a national obsession with examinations and a rigid examination system, has resulted in a literacy that is skills based and examination oriented. The term *critical literacy* used in the popular sense of a literacy that encourages critical reflection of the established mode of events, remains elusive in this context. Although there is a concern with children's ability to think creatively and critically, it is still unclear how this should be done, especially when the end goal is described as the ability to: "adopt a *critical, but not negative*, attitude towards ideas, thoughts and values reflected in spoken and written texts (in English) of local and foreign origin" (Curriculum Planning Division, 1991, p. 8, italics added).

But despite this ambiguity, the impetus for change has been set in motion by the 1991 syllabus. In this next section, I describe two types of literacy practices in a primary classroom, one for examination purposes and the second that reflects the objectives of the new curriculum.

LITERACY LESSONS IN A SINGAPORE CLASSROOM

As part of my doctoral research, I spent 4 months in a Grade 5 classroom observing English language lessons three times a week. I identified two types of literacy practices in the class (see Cheah, 1994, for details). The first is an examination-oriented literacy that is closely linked to the demands of formal examinations, whereas the second is what I describe as a participatory model of literacy that embodies the objectives of the new syllabus. Most of the time, the teacher focused on examination-type assignments designed to prepare students for the examinations, but occasionally she chose to do group discussions based on the theme for the week. I describe characteristics of these two types of literacy next to draw out their differences in order to show how the participatory model allows students more scope to move away from the more prescriptive type of language work.

THE EXAMINATION TYPE LITERACY: LEARNING THROUGH PRESCRIPTION

In this Singaporean classroom of twenty-two 11-year-olds,[3] I found that language classes consisted primarily of completing worksheets of discrete grammar and vocabulary exercises and answering comprehension questions. This work was always done on an individual basis, reinforcing the test-like conditions during these lessons. The teacher also spent 1 or 2 hours a week, outside normal school hours, reviewing mock examination papers with the children. These were taken from commercially prepared assessment books that are widely available in Singapore. And as if these were not adequate, the students were also required to complete 35 different comprehension and vocabulary exercises each during the 10-week school term. These drill and practice exercises constituted the main language curriculum for the children.

To illustrate the kind of instruction given during such lessons, I present an excerpt taken from a lesson on picture compositions. Such a genre is common in the English language test at the primary school level, and children are expected to write a story or a description based on the picture given. This particular picture was entitled *In an electronics shop*. The objective of the lesson was to prepare students for an upcoming essay writing test:

---

[3]Most Singaporean classrooms have an average of 40 students. This class was atypical, and this was because the teacher was also concurrently the Head of English. The smaller class allowed her time to also perform the necessary administrative duties.

1. Teacher: … Now look at this picture. How are we gonna start? How
2. would you start? Give me some of your openers. How would you
   start?
3. Yes?
4. Harry: I start with, one Sunday, Sunday afternoon, I say that, there's
   a
5. lot of customers at the electronics shop, and some of the customers
   were
6. buying some products, and entertainment and buying television and
7. one of the customers …
8. Teacher: Ah Harry, just give me the introduction, don't start
9. developing the story. I'm just interested in the introduction now, you
10. have started developing the story. So you are off with—
11. Harry: It was …
12. Teacher: If I read you wrong
13. Harry: warm sunny day.
14. Teacher: He says it was a warm sunny day and they decided to go
15. shopping for electrical goods and ended up in the shop. OK that's one
16. way of starting off, will you just start right away with the shop here?
17. Class: No.
18. Teacher: No, how the customer ended up in the shop. That should
    be
19. your introduction, OK, so maybe in this case we went shopping for
20. electrical goods. Any other way to start?

In this discussion, the teacher attempted to organize the discussion
around the three-part structure of the essay, that is introduction, middle,
and conclusion. This approach was used to make the discussion more sys-
tematic, and the teacher made suggestions to help the writer along. However, the net effect of these "helpful" approaches was a highly prescriptive
lesson in thinking and writing. The summary at the end lines (18–20), especially the reminder, "That should be your introduction" served to remind students that the teacher wanted them to follow the same structure
and use the same ideas. Generally, the students complied as can be seen
from these three different introductory sentences taken from samples of
the students' writing:

One fine day, my neighbor, Mr. Naza's radio had spoiled.
One sunny Saturday afternoon, Andy and I were bored at home, so we
decided to go to the Takashimaya to shop as my father's birthday is very
close.
One hot afternoon, Mr. Lin decided to do some shopping as he felt very
bored.

There was little negotiation throughout, and participation was through answering questions posed by the teacher. Discussion of the children's personal experiences or the meaning of the task in relation to their learning or their lives in general was minimal. At one point in the lesson, one student suggested that the man in the picture dropped his spectacles when he fell, but the teacher immediately disallowed this piece of information in the story because no spectacles were seen in the picture. The students did not argue, and wrote their versions of the essay as prescribed by the teacher. This pragmatic approach to learning and the ready compliance echo the politics of survival again, but this time, in the examination battlefield.

LITERACY FOR PERSONAL GROWTH: LEARNING THROUGH PARTICIPATION

The model of literacy for personal growth is inherent in the new 1991 syllabus where a learner-centred, interactive, and process-based approach has been adopted to facilitate literacy acquisition. In the classroom, this approach is best represented through the use of group work and activities instead of the usual practice of individual work. Group work allows for collaboration, fosters cooperation instead of competition, and introduces a social dimension to the learning process. The class teacher described these lessons as exemplifying real teaching for her because it was during these lessons that children were allowed to interact freely and to introduce their own ideas into their work without fear of failing. Although the teacher believed that interaction and communication were important aspects of language learning, she could not always allow this in her classes because she needed to teach for the examinations first.

To illustrate the difference between the types of lessons, I describe a group writing lesson. The teacher had read and discussed an article on Chinese New Year foods, and she wanted the children to work in groups and write their own version describing the delicacies eaten during Chinese New Year. The group that I observed was made up of four girls, Ani (Malay), Meiling (Chinese), Manjit (Sikh) and Shanti who is Indian:

1. Manjit: (repeating as she writes) In Chinese New Year, we ...
2. Shanti: (to Meiling) What you eat ah, you all?
3. Manjit: What you all eat? Dumplings ah?
4. Meiling: Don't know.
5. Manjit: Don't know!
6. Shanti: Aiyah!
7. Manjit: Then how? I don't know ...

8. Meiling: *Niang kow* [Mandarin name of a Chinese New Year cake].
9. Manjit: In English, in English [She needs to be able to write this down].
10. Shanti: Don't want all this, something other than this (pointing to the foods on the list, among which was *niang kow*).
12. Manjit: Dumplings lah, dumplings lah, got eat or not, dumplings?
13. Meiling: Cookies lah, cookies lah. We make cookies lah!

Meiling, the only Chinese in the group, was asked to provide the input for the piece (line 2), but when she said that she did not have any to contribute (line 4), the rest were upset with her (lines 5–7). She then came up with *niang kow*, which is an authentic new year delicacy, but Shanti, the self-professed leader, rejected it because it was already mentioned in the article and was, therefore, not new information. Manjit suggested dumplings (lines 3, 12), but without much success, and finally Meiling offered cookies as the answer (line 13).

The children did not seem to know much about this topic and could have resorted to the usual strategy of copying the information from the article given or from their discussion with the teacher. Indeed, a number of groups in the class did exactly that, suggesting that although group work provided opportunities to explore alternative ways of composing, many students were too accustomed to the examination-type literacy practices of reproducing information to do anything different.

However, Shanti's group showed how students could venture out of the prescriptive practices. Refusing to reproduce the information, they went back to their personal knowledge about Chinese New Year practices, and came up with their version of Chinese New Year foods. Their example of pineapple tarts is not a true traditional delicacy, but on the other hand, pineapple tarts have, in recent years, become a popular new year food so their claim was legitimate. However, they also knew that they had to justify their choice, and knowing how the Chinese often associate food with luck and wealth, they came up with a corresponding belief (gold-colored jam representing gold and wealth), which stretched the truth, but was ideal for their purpose. Here is an excerpt of their text related to the tarts:

On Lunar New Year, Chinese people eat pineapple tarts. The gold coloured jam represents gold and wealth so people give friends and relatives a bottle or two of these pineapple tarts. This is one of the famous goodies.

Linguistic and grammatical accuracy would be important criteria for judging this piece under the examination-type literacy, but these criteria marginalize second language learners because they focus on accuracy and not on composing ability. Dyson (1993) described composing as "a distinctly socio-cultural process that involves making decisions, conscious or otherwise, about how one figures into the social world at any one point in time" (p. 435). This exercise in group work is an example of the way the children were able to situate themselves as writers and to compose for themselves a place in the social and academic worlds of the classroom.

Instead of reproducing the content from the original text, Shanti's group generated a new text from their personal and cultural knowledge. Their text suggests that the traditional delicacies of Chinese New Year have, in fact, been replaced by newer varieties like pineapple tarts and cookies, which perhaps have no real cultural significance beyond a change in taste. But more than drawing on their own knowledge, they were also actively engaged in negotiating and interrogating each other's ideas, and this is one of the few times in class when the children's voices were literally heard. In fact, Meiling's knowledge about Chinese food was constantly challenged throughout the discussion, and Meiling was forced to deal with her own lack of knowledge about the topic. In the meanwhile, the non-Chinese students constructed their own version of new year foods from their own experiences of Chinese New Year.

Shanti's group showed what the children knew about literacy and about composing. Through this activity, they also successfully found a voice for themselves. But this literacy is not free, but is instead nested in the larger, more dominant model of examination literacy prevalent in the class and in the Singaporean society. Indeed, within these limits, the children could not compose the piece as they pleased. They had to work within the demands of their class, and these included writing about a given topic that they clearly knew little about and in the style and variety of language that is officially sanctioned in class, that is standard Singapore English.

Although this episode illustrates quite clearly that students were able to break out of the prescriptive model, their text was not a result of a critical evaluation of the task or the information given. In fact, they were more concerned with just completing the task. The teacher described these lessons as *practice writing* sessions, confirming that they were less important than the examination-driven texts that were always individually produced. She thought nothing of having a class of children from different ethnic backgrounds write specifically about traditional Chinese New Year delicacies. Her written comments on the piece, "You have taken pains to give detailed descriptions. However, are you sure that some of the delicacies are related to the Lunar New Year?" suggested that she wanted to see a reproduction of the type of information that she had discussed with them instead of what the students have suggested. In fact, there was never any discussion of why such foods were eaten, and whether these foods still have significance in this modern society. In short, the teacher and the class never questioned the prescribed scheme of work for English; they merely found different ways to complete the tasks. Further, the group work was more valued as opportunities for practicing English rather than for the negotiation of any kind of social or cultural meanings.

TOWARD CRITICAL LITERACY?

Critical literacy is, as Comber (1994) explained, open to "multiple interpretations" (p. 666). If critical literacy is only interpreted as the kind of literacy that contests and challenges the status quo and seeks to redefine existing the social conditions, then most educators would argue that critical literacy is nonexistent in Singapore. This is because such a tradition of critiquing and challenging the establishment is not well-established, although there are signs that more Singaporeans are beginning to articulate their views, for example, in the forum page of the local newspapers and on the Internet news groups.

But because literacy practices reflect social relations of authority and control (Lankshear & Lawler, 1987), it is not difficult to understand why the prescriptive, examination-based literacy dominates. This literacy, in turn, nurtures a dependency on teachers on the part of the students because teachers are the gatekeepers to success. The result is that students, like most other Singaporeans, rarely want to take risks, preferring instead to follow the official directives. This examination-type literacy leads to a reproduction of a particular type of school discourse and a certain set of ideas that in turn locate the students in the larger society. It is through this literacy too that the ideologies of survivalism and pragmatism are nurtured in school.

Any initiative toward any form of critical literacy may well begin with the students, and not the teachers. If the participatory-type literacy is allowed to develop, the children may take the lead in introducing a "pedagogy that starts with the concerns of the students ... through an exploration of students' histories and cultural locations" (Pennycook, 1994, p. 311). This bottom-up model is more likely especially when teachers and principals are not inclined to make changes that are not mandated from the Ministry of Education, and that will not have any direct relation with examinations. But for any kind of critical literacy to develop, students need the guidance and support of their teachers who in turn must be able to provide the right environment to nurture their thinking. However, this issue is not a priority now, but the task for teacher education is clear. Its most immediate goal is to raise teachers' consciousness in relation to the social aspects of language particularly the relationship between language and power. But it will be a while before any sort of critical education is included in the formal curriculum both for teachers and students.

That English will continue to be the language through which this literacy is explored is unavoidable because English literacy is what most young Singaporeans will acquire to some level of competency. But a critical literacy should first start with the appropriation of the language to express personal meanings and experiences, and the participatory-type literacy does help foster a personal dimension in literacy learning. Singaporeans are aware of the problems associated with this model of examination-oriented literacy (Yip, 1993), and although change is desired, the examination system is likely to remain in meritocratic Singapore. The participatory-type literacy is not critical literacy by a long shot, but it is a positive move away from the dominant model of duplicating existing knowledge and texts and echoing dominant voices. This move in the context of a society where "for the individual, being politically oppositional can be a perilous activity" (Chua, 1995, p. 207), should be seen as a significant and positive step because of the accompanying possibilities. There is the possibility that student voices and student social and cultural experiences will become a legitimate part of the classroom curriculum; the possibility that students will learn to take risks, start questioning established texts and forms of knowledge; the possibility that teachers will in time come to recognize that these new and different texts and voices are valid and necessary to enable learning; and the possibility of a new classroom culture with liberating literacy practices that can lead to cultural changes in the society at large.

REFERENCES

Ang, I., & Stratton, J. (1995). The Singaporean way to multiculturalism: Western concepts/Asian cultures. *Sojourn, 10*(1), 65–89.

Benjamin, G. (1976). The cultural logic of Singapore's 'multi-culturalism'. In R. Hassan (Ed.), *Singapore: Society in transition* (pp. 115–133). Kuala Lumpur: Oxford University Press.

Bloom, D. (1986). The English language and Singapore: A critical survey. In B. K. Kapur (Ed.), *Singapore studies: Critical survey of the humanities and the sciences* (pp. 337–458). Singapore: Singapore University Press.

Cheah, Y. M. (1994). *Literacy and cultural identity: An ethnographic study of English language education in Singapore.* University of California, Berkeley, CA.

Cheah, Y. M. (1996, April). *Shaping the classrooms of tomorrow: Lessons from the past.* Paper presented at the RELC Seminar, Singapore.

Chua, B. H. (1995). *Communitarian ideology and democracy in Singapore.* London: Routledge & Kegan Paul.

Comber, B. (1994). Critical literacy: An introduction to Australian debates and perspectives. *Journal of Curriculum Studies, 26*(6), 655–668.

Curriculum Planning Division. (1991). *English language syllabus (primary and secondary).* Singapore: Ministry of Education.

Dyson, A. H. (1993). *Social worlds of children learning to write in an urban primary school.* New York: Teachers College Press.

Ho, W. K. (1994). The English language curriculum in perspective: Exogenous influences and indigenization. In S. Gopinathan, A. Pakir, W. K. Ho, & V. Saravanan (Eds.), *Language, society and education in Singapore: Issues and trends* (pp. 235–266). Singapore: Times Academic Press.

Ho, W. K. (1996). Singapore: Review of educational events in 1994 and 1995. *Asia Pacific Journal of Education, 16*(2), 79–87.

Jones, E. (1994). Asia's fate: A response to the Singapore school. *The National Interest,* 18–28.

Koh, T. A. (1989). Culture and the arts. In K. S. Sandhu & P. Wheatly (Eds.), *The management of success: The moulding of modern Singapore* (pp. 710–748). Singapore: Institute of South-East Asian Studies.

Kwan-Terry, A., & Kwan-Terry, J. (1993). Literacy and the dynamics of language planning: The case of Singapore. In P. Freebody & A. R. Welch (Eds.), *Knowledge, culture and power: International perspectives on literacy as policy and practice* (pp. 142–161). London: Falmer.

Lankshear, C., & Lawler, M. (1987). *Literacy, schooling and revolution.* New York: Falmer.

Pakir, A. (1991). The range and depth of English-knowing bilinguals in Singapore. *World Englishes, 10*(2), 167–179.

Pennycook, A. (1994). *The cultural politics of English as a international language.* London: Longman.

Tay, M. W. J. (1982). The uses, users, and features of English in Singapore. In J. B. Pride (Ed.), *New Englishes* (pp. 51–70). Rowley, MA: Newbury House.

Tay, M. W. J. (1985). *Trends in language, literacy and education in Singapore (Census monograph no. 2).* Singapore: Department of Statistics.

Tham, S. C. (1990). Multi-lingualism in Singapore: Two decades of development. Singapore: Department of Statistics, Ministry of Trade and Industry.

Yip, J. S. K. (1993, September). *The teaching profession: Responding to change.* Paper presented at the Second Principals' Conference, Singapore.

Resistance and Creativity in English Reading Lessons in Hong Kong[*]

Angel Mei Yi Lin
City University of Hong Kong

In this chapter, I present a fine-grained analysis of a videotaped lesson segment of a Form 2 (Grade 8) English reading lesson in a school located in a working-class residential area in Hong Kong. The excerpt was taken from a larger corpus of similar lesson data videotaped in the class over 3 consecutive weeks. The analysis shows how these limited English-speaking Cantonese school children subverted an English reading lesson that had a focus on practicing skills of factual information extraction from texts, and negotiated their own preferred comic-style narratives by artfully making use of the response slots of the Initiation–Response–Feedback (IRF) discourse format used in the lesson. The analysis shows the students' playful and artful verbal practices despite the alienating school reading curriculum that seems to serve to produce an uncritical labor. The implications for teaching are discussed.

[*] This article first appeared in *Language, Culture and Curriculum*, Vol. 12, No. 3, 1999, pp. 285–296. Reprinted here with permission of the journal.

SOCIOPOLITICAL BACKGROUND: LANGUAGE AND POWER IN HONG KONG

Hong Kong was a British colony situated on the southern coast of China. Since its cession from China to Great Britain in 1842 as a result of China's defeat in the Opium War, it had changed from an agrarian fishing port to a labor-intensive industrial city in the 1960s and 1970s. In the 1980s and 1990s, with the boom of China trade following "the open door" policy of China, Hong Kong had gradually changed from a light industry-based, manufacturing economy to an economy primarily based on the re-export of products processed in China, and business and financial servicing for China (Ho, 1994). It also has an increasing demand for a low-level, white-collar workforce with some functional skills in English (e.g., shipping, export–import, accounts clerks; receptionists; telephone operators; typists; secretaries). Whereas the universities are producing the bilingual middle-management workforce, the majority of secondary schools are producing the nonmanagement, white-collar labor for the day-to-day routine work that requires some English.

Despite its international cosmopolitan appearance Hong Kong is ethnically rather homogeneous. About 98% of its population is ethnic Chinese, and Cantonese[1] is the mother tongue of the majority. English native speakers account for not more than 2% of the entire population. They had constituted the dominant class, at least until July 1997 when the sovereignty of the colony was returned to China, and Hong Kong became a Special Administrative Region (SAR) of China.

Notwithstanding its being the mother tongue of only a minority, English has been both the language of power and the language of educational and

---

[1]Cantonese is a regional Chinese language widely spoken in the southern Chinese province of Guangdong. Phonologically it is quite distinct from Modern Standard Chinese (the national standard language of China, known as Mandarin or Putonghua); however, there are both overlaps and differences in the grammar and lexis of the two codes. Although linguists and educationists differentiate between Cantonese and Modern Standard Chinese as two distinct codes, Hong Kong Chinese people in their daily life often refer to their own language as *jung-man*, meaning "Chinese language." It is usually the linguist who sees Hong Kong Chinese as in fact speaking Cantonese as their mother tongue and reading and writing a form of Modern Standard Chinese that has been influenced by Cantonese lexis and syntax. Hong Kong Chinese themselves however usually do not pay attention to these distinctions in their daily language practices. They know that the written style is and should be different from the spoken style of their language, but they consider themselves using *jung-man* all the same. They can distinguish spoken Mandarin or Putonghua from Cantonese but they see them as different regional ways of speaking *jung-man* and generally do not see them as constituting totally different languages. Ethnically and culturally they regard themselves as Chinese and *jung-man* as their familiar native language in contrast to English, which they do not ordinarily speak among themselves and which they largely see as a language of the *gwai-lou* (a Cantonese slang word referring to Westerners) or the middle-class yuppies, who tend to code-mix or code-switch between Cantonese and English.

socioeconomic advancement, that is, the dominant symbolic resource in the symbolic market (Bourdieu, 1991) in Hong Kong. Even after Hong Kong became an SAR of China, English has maintained its status as the primary language of higher education and business, partly due to its global domination as a major language of science, technology and business. For instance, it is still the medium of instruction of most universities and an important language requirement for most white-collar, professional, executive, and civil service jobs. Although Putonghua (Mandarin Chinese, the standard national language of China) is rising in its political importance, it seems unlikely that it will take over the socioeconomic and higher education functions of English in the near future.

The symbolic market is embodied and enacted in the many key situations (e.g., educational settings, job settings) in which symbolic resources (e.g., certain types of linguistic skills, cultural knowledge, specialized knowledge and skills, etc.) are demanded of social actors if they want to gain access to valuable social, educational and eventually material resources (Bourdieu, 1991). For instance, a Hong Kong student must have adequate English resources, in addition to subject matter knowledge and skills, to enter and succeed in the English-medium professional training programs of medicine, architecture, legal studies, and so on, in order to earn the English-accredited credentials to enter these high-income professions. The symbolic market is therefore not a metaphor, but one with transactions that have material, socioeconomic consequences for people.

THE SCHOOLING AND EXAMINATION SYSTEMS: INSTITUTIONS OF SOCIAL SELECTION

The schooling system can be said to be largely subsumed under the public examination system, a major institution of social selection (Bourdieu & Passeron, 1977) in Hong Kong. The secondary school curriculum is, for instance, in reality, if not in name, heavily influenced by the public examination syllabuses. Public examinations are important because the job market uses public exam results as an important screening criterion on job applicants. A student's higher and professional education opportunities are also dependent on her or his public examination results. Schools in turn depend on its graduates' public examination results to acquire prestige and status among parents and in the community. Teachers are therefore under school administrators' constant pressure and monitoring to produce good public examination results by the students. It is not difficult for a success-oriented student to discover that public exam-taking skills constitute the most important factor for success in school and in society (at least initially) and that the rules of the game do not hinge on gaining education or learning but exam-taking skills.[2]

THE LARGER STUDY: UNCOVERING INSTITUTIONS OF SOCIAL REPRODUCTION

The data and analysis reported in this chapter have been taken from a larger study (Lin, 1996a) that examines how English lessons were organized in junior forms (Form 1–3; comparable to Grades 7–9 in North America) in secondary schools in Hong Kong. The purpose of the study was to find out whether schools situated in different socioeconomic contexts provide their Cantonese-speaking students with differential access to the socioeconomically dominant English linguistic and cultural resources in Hong Kong, and thus serve as institutions of social reproduction (e.g., perpetuating or reproducing the lack of linguistic and cultural capital for success among socioeconomically disadvantaged children).

In the study, I visited and videotaped all the English lessons on at least 5 consecutive school days in each of the eight English classes of the eight teachers participating in this study. The eight teachers were in seven schools from a range of socioeconomic and academic backgrounds. I informally interviewed small groups of the students, and collected other curricular, assessment, and background information on the classes and the schools. The data excerpt included in this chapter has been taken from a corpus of lesson data videotaped in the class of one teacher (Mr. Chan)[3] over 3 consecutive weeks.

Mr. Chan's class consisted of 39 students (19 male and 20 female), ages 13 to 14. The school is located in a town close to an industrial area. The students in the class largely came from families who live in the nearby public housing estates. Their parents were largely manual workers and their education level ranged from primary school to junior secondary school. They spoke only Cantonese at home and most of the boys loved to read comic strips (translated from Japanese to colloquial Chinese, which is close to Cantonese in style; Usui, 1992). They did not read any English apart from school textbooks. Their English fluency, as can be seen from how and what they spoke in the classroom, seemed to be rather limited for their grade level. There were many words in the text that they did not understand or did not know how to pronounce.

Mr. Chan appeared in every way to be a caring and responsible teacher. He was however at a disadvantage in his teaching of this class due to his level of English fluency. I must point out that this is by no means an individ-

---

[2]For instance, many students are willing to pay expensive tuition fees to private exam-oriented tutorial centres to get tips and training on exam-taking skills.

[3]All personal names are pseudonyms.

ual fault of the teacher: The English language teaching courses he took in the 2 year part-time Postgraduate Certificate of Education Program at the university do not seem to be designed to provide non-English majors with the necessary access to English linguistic resources, for example, no fluency development component in the program. It also appeared to be a language he used primarily in the school context, with little overlap with his life outside of school. For example, his own leisure activities, like those of many people in Hong Kong, did not require much use of English.

The overall organization of Mr. Chan's reading lessons can be outlined in terms of the following sequence of phases:

- The Prereading Phase: This phase can be further divided into the warm-up questioning phase and the reading-questions introduction phase:

  (a) *The Warm-Up Questioning Phase:*   The teacher starts the reading lesson by asking students some prereading questions that are generally related to the topic of the text and elicit students' personal experience and knowledge about the topic. This is a standard procedure recommended by most second language (L2) reading teaching methodologies (e.g., Barnett, 1989). According to these teaching methods, the aim of this pre-reading, warm-up procedure is to arouse students' interest and motivation to read the text, and to activate the relevant background knowledge schemata that will facilitate the students' comprehension of the text.

  (b) *The Reading-Questions Introduction Phase:*   After asking some prereading questions, the teacher typically begins to introduce comprehension questions that are specifically related to the content of the text. However, no answers are expected at this stage, the students are asked to find answers to these questions from the text. Again, this is a typical procedure recommended by L2 reading methodologies, which advise teachers to help students to become focused readers by providing them with a purpose to read and an advance organizer to guide their reading comprehension.

- The Reading Phase: After students are introduced to the comprehension questions, they are instructed to read the text to find out the answers to the set of questions just introduced. The teacher assigns a period of time in which students are to do their silent reading and to 'mark' the answers to the questions on the text.

- The Question-and-Answer Phase: Typically, the teacher begins to ask the comprehension questions and elicit answers from students only after the silent reading period, that is, after students are supposed to have finished reading the whole text and have marked the answers to the set of comprehension questions with a pencil. The lesson segment examined in this chapter is taken from the question-and-answer phase, in which the dominant discourse format used is the IRF format (Heap, 1985, 1988; Mehan, 1979; Sinclair & Coulthard, 1975).

The organization of Mr. Chan's reading lessons shows that the purpose of reading, as formulated by the teacher, seems to be one of marking the answers to the given questions in the storybook, and then to give these answers to the teacher, who is going to elicit them from the students after the students have spent some time working on their own. The teacher seems to formulate reading as merely extracting from a text answers (or information) to a pregiven set of factual questions (see the following). More creative, nonfactual (or noninformation type) questions such as: "Do you like the story? Which character do you like the best? If you were Tin Hau, what would you …" have not found their way into the reading lessons, and "reading" in the classroom (even when one is not reading informational, expository types of materials) bears a striking resemblance to reading in the examination hall. In the following section, we look in more detail how the teacher's organization of the reading phase and question-and-answer phase seems to be geared toward doing information-extraction from texts, and how some students negotiate their own story by taking advantage of the response slot of the IRF discourse format.

The list of comprehension questions the teacher wrote on the blackboard at the beginning of the reading lesson:

1. What was the name of Tin Hau before she became the Queen of Heaven?

2. What kind of work did her father and brothers do?

3. What did she do if they were in danger?

4. What did her mother always worry about her menfolk?[4]

---

[4]There is a grammatical mistake in this sentence. This sentence seems to have been influenced by the teacher's Cantonese. In Cantonese, it is grammatical to say 'Her mother worries about them what?'

5. Why did Lin suddenly stop speaking?

6. What did Lin see in her vision?

7. How did she save them?

8. Why did her mother cry?

9. What happened when Lin answered her mother?

10. What did Lin become at the end of the story?

TEACHER'S TEXT INFORMATION EXTRACTION PRACTICES VERSUS STUDENTS' NEGOTIATION OF AN ALTERNATIVE STORY

In Mr. Chan's lesson, there is a clear division between the reading phase and the question-and-answer phase. We discuss each of them in the following.

The Reading Phase

As previously discussed, the students are expected to do their reading silently and individually and as they read they are expected to mark answers in the text to a pregiven set of questions. They are not encouraged to discuss or check with each other their answers. In fact, they are supposed to do this on their own quietly, that is, not talking with their neighbors; there is evidence in the transcript of the teacher asking the students to keep quiet and focus on their work and not to talk to their neighbors. For example, a girl appears to have finished very quickly and begins to fiddle around; the teacher asks her to keep quiet and expresses doubts about whether she has really finished her work; she responds by saying that the questions are "*Gum gaan-daan!*" (i.e., "so simple") that she has got them done already. This incident seems to reflect the student's perception of reading: One is counted as having finished reading a text as soon as one has finished answering the preset questions for the text. It seems the idea never enters their minds that written texts can be something to enjoy, to read and reread, to analyze literarily, to respond to creatively and personally, and so on. Once you have answered the preset questions, you are done with the text and done with reading. Besides, the student's own way of responding to and interacting with the text has been predefined and preconstrained by the pre-given set of factual questions.

The Question-and-Answer Phase:

After 10 minutes, Mr. Chan begins to engage the students in a "certi-
fied-lesson-knowledge-corpus coproduction process," through the use of
an I (L2–L1) – R (L1) – F (L1–L2) format (Lin, 1996b), in very much the
same way it has been used in the prereading phase. However, in this phase
the questions to be asked by the teacher in the initiation slots are already
known and given, and the answers to be provided by the students in the response slots are also supposed to be preformulated (or premarked-out in
the storybook). So, it is not so much a discussion or talking about the storybook as it is checking answers to the preset questions, which is a recurrent
practice in other lessons of this class as well (not included in this analysis;
e.g., checking answers to grammar exercises, vocabulary exercises, etc.).

Let us look at the following example, taken from the beginning of the
question-and-answer phase:

Example 1: (See Appendix for notes on transcription.)

608.8 T:	Alright (1) let's (1) look at the story, Tin Hau, Queen of Heaven. (3) Look at the first paragraph, 'Before Tin Hau became the Queen of Heaven, and Goddess of the Sea (1) she: lived (1) a mortal life as a merchant's daughter, named ... Lin Mo (1) Lin Moniang' right?=
707.1 S:	=Linmoniang= {voice soft on the tape}
707.3 T:	=so ... look at the first question, (2) what was the name of Tin Hau before she became the Queen of Heaven?=
709.5 Chan:	=Lahm-Mahk-Neuhng <Linmoniang>!=
709.8 T:	Yeh ... that answer's.. so easy, (2) (Lahm).. Lin Moniang, right?=
711.5 S:	=Linmoniang! {spoken in a joking intonation}
712 T:	Number two ... what kind of work did.. her father, and brothers do?
713.5 S1:	(Dim duhk aa <How to read it>?)
713.8 S2:	m-e-r-c-h-(? ?)
714.1 T:	Now.. who knows the answer? (2.5) r'ai? (6) let me ask question, (1.5) aah: (1) Wohng-Ji-Jung (3) number 2 (2) haa? (3) Wohng-Ji-Jung

720.5 W:	Eh... =
720.8 T:	=What do they do?
721 W:	(Fishing)=
721.2 T:	=Fishing? (1) they are fishermen? (1.5) Is it correct? (2) Haih maih yyuh-fu leih gaa heui.. deih <Are they fishermen>?
723.3 Chan:	Oh mh-haih aahk <Oh, no>!
723.8 T:	Heui-deih jouh me-yeh gaa <What do they do>?=
724 Chan:	jouh seung-syuhn ge <do merchant ships>!
724.5 T:	Right, where can you find the .. answer? (1) =
725 S:	(s-a-i-l ? ? sail)
725.5 Chan:	Line three!
725.7 =T:	(aahk) merchants- aahk..heui haih sheung-yahn leih go wo <they are merchants>! Look at second paragraph, (1) Lin ... (090)

The teacher starts off by suggesting that they will look at the story and then he reads out the title of the story (turn [608.8]). Then he draws his students' attention to a specific paragraph in the story and reads out the relevant part from which the answer to Question 1 can be found (turn [608.8]). It is only after reading out this part that he starts to ask the first question (turn [707.3]). His orientation to specific parts of the text as the basis for the answers to the set of questions is thus demonstratively clear right from the beginning.

A student shouts out an answer, "*Lahm-Mahk-Neuhng*," which is a Cantonese rendering of the name of Tin Hau before she became Heaven-Queen. It is interesting to notice how the teacher acknowledges it: he says "Yeh.. that answer's ... so easy, ... (Lahm) ... Lin Moniang, right?" (turn [709.8]). He is almost to reiterate the name in Cantonese (*Lahm*), but then he corrects himself and renders the name in English, that is, in the Anglicised form that is rendered in the English storybook. This confirms with our observation above that the feedback has to contain a reformulation of L1 answers (offered by students) in L2 as it is only the latter that is to count as part of the certified lesson-corpus coconstructed.

Then he goes on to ask, "Number two ..." (turn [712]). This is interesting: he prefaces his question with the "number" of the question like going through a list. This is a typical "question-opener" in the "checking answers" discourse format that is recurrent in other lessons of this teacher as well (not included in this analysis). Rejecting an entirely reasonable but not text-based answer, he reinitiates again in L1, and this time receiving an answer from a girl (Chan), who interestingly paraphrases and summarizes the relevant English part of the storybook ("... merchant's daughter ... father and brothers often sailed across the sea to buy and sell goods") in a concise and idiomatic Cantonese phrase, "*jouh seung-syuhn*" (turn [724]) ("do merchant ships"—this is odd in English, but the meaning and lexical structure of the Cantonese phrase is entirely acceptable and idiomatic in the Cantonese language). We see that this Cantonese construction offered by her as a response to the teacher shows remarkable sensitivity to the linguistic structure of the teacher's L1 question, "*Heuideih jouh me-yeh gaa?*" ("What do they do?") (turn [723.8]) (again, in Cantonese, this is idiomatic and is taken to mean "What they do for as a job?").

In other words, the student's L1 response seems to be a result of a great sensitivity to the teacher's question, and not necessarily reflecting the lack of English linguistic resources to answer in English on her part. This would have implications for the teacher's language use patterns, if the teacher wants to maximize the opportunities for students to use English in the language classroom.

On the other hand, the teacher highlights the need *to base one's answer on relevant parts in the text* by asking the student where she can find the answer (turn [724.5]). And this time, he asks this in English (probably this switch back to English signals an imminent need to turn to the English text), and the girl answers him in English, too (turn [725.5]).

The need to base one's answer (or to "find the answer") in the text is a recurrent concern of the teacher voiced in his recurrent prompts and follow-up questions such as "Where can you find it?", "Does the book really say so?", "Look at paragraph, line ", and so on (found in other parts of the transcript). However, there are times when a bookish answer is so boring, especially when these students feel that this story of the Chinese Heaven-Queen is so familiarly boring (some evidence of this in other parts of the transcript). And the factual nature of the set of questions has left so little room for imagination for these lively 13-year-olds. In the following example, we find the creativity of the children bursting out in a niche that they exploit and capitalize on in an otherwise probably uninteresting IRF discourse:

Example 2:

870 T: Yauh mat-yeh faat-sang aa <What happened>? ..
Leih-Lohn-Mihng (2) dong heui- daap heui maa-mih
<when she answered her mum> (1) heui maa-mih aai
heui meng ne heui daap heui go sih-houh yauh mat-yeh
faat-sang aa <her mum called her name, and when she
answered her mum, what happened>?

*872   Leih:Heui louh-dauh dik-jo lohk (deih) <Her old-man fell
off to the (ground)>. {chuckling towards the end of his
sentence} =

872.5 Ss: =Haha! haha! haha! hahahaha! {other Ss laughing hilari-
ously}

872.8 T: Me aa?! (2) daaih-seng di <louder>! {against a background of Ss' laughter}

*873.2 Chan: Heui louh-dauh dik-jo lohk gaai woh <Her old-man fell off
to the street>!{chuckling) =

873.5 S1:   =Hihihihik!!={laughing}

873.8 S2:   =(Go douh) yauh gaai gaa me <(Is there) a street>?

*874 T: Go douh yauh gaai me <Is there a street>?{T in an
amused tone; some students laugh}

*874.5 L: Dik-jo lohk // hoi <fell into the sea>=

*874.8 //T: =Dik-jo lohk bin-douh aa:: <Where did he fall into>?
{quite amusingly}

875 L: Hoi aa <Sea that is>.

875.2 T: Haahk.. dik-jo lohk hoi <Yes.. fell into the sea>.

875.5 S1:   Dik-jo lohk gaai hahaha <fell off to the street>

875.8 S2:   Heui louh-dauh dik-jo lohk gaai aa <Her old-man fell off to
the street>.

876 T: // Right? (1) Her father dropped into the SEA!==
876 //S3:   Hekhek! {laughing}

876.5 ==T: Right? (2) gum-yeung sei-jo laak <in that manner died>. ...
             SHH! (1) hou-laak <okay> .. jeui-hauh laak <finally> ..
             SHH! number ten ...

The question (turn [870]) has been asked in English earlier, but no student response has been forthcoming, and the teacher is asking it again in
Cantonese, and also specifically directs it to a student (Leih-Lohn-Mihng),
ensuring that someone is going to answer it. Now, something interesting
happens. Leih says something (turn [872]; the Cantonese word *louh-dauh*
literally means *old-bean* and is a common colloquial, not very respectful
word for *father*) which rouses other students to hilarious laughter (turn
[872.5]).

The student has exploited the Response slot to do something playful,
to slip in a contribution that will turn the whole story into a comic-strip
type of story, which they so enjoy reading outside the classroom (based
on what they told me when I chatted with them after school, and on their
responses to questions about the kinds of extracurricular reading they do
in a questionnaire I gave them). In their favorite comic strips (which have
been translated to Cantonese-style-Chinese from Japanese), the characters usually do funny, impossible things. For example, a boy changes into
a girl when he falls into cold water and changes back to a boy when he's
showered with hot water; or, the father of the boy changes into a big
black bear when coming into contact with hot water, and so on and
amusement and enjoyment come from the superimposing of impossible
and unpredictable fantasy with the familiar, predictable, and boring
mundane world. It seems that the boy who provides this funny answer
(turns [872], [873.2]) is a skillful storyteller with a ready audience, and
this is reflected in the overwhelmingly positive response from his fellow
students (i.e., their hilarious laughter, showing their great amusement
derived from this twist of the story effected by his answer: Her father fell
off into the street (from a merchant ship amidst a stormy ocean). His
change in the plot will make a very funny and imaginative comic-strip
type story.

The teacher cannot hide his amusement himself (turns [874], [874.8])
but insists on the text as the authoritative basis for answers to the question. He challenges, "*Go douh yauh gaai me?*" (Is there a street?) (turn
[874]), and goes on to demand that the student give him a text-based answer, which he can acknowledge, reformulate into English, affirm and
certify (turn [876]). Throughout the teacher has been demonstrating to
his students that reading means finding answers to pregiven questions in
the text; and there is little more you can do or play around with while
reading a text.

WHAT COUNTS AS LITERACY? AND LITERACY FOR WHAT PURPOSES?

The organization of Mr. Chan's reading lesson is not an isolated example. Similar examples can be found in other classes in my larger corpus of classroom data (Lin, 1996a). The point of English reading lessons in Hong Kong schools seems to be primarily one of practice in extracting prescribed information from texts. This seems to have followed naturally from the pragmatic emphasis of the school English curriculum and the way English reading comprehension is assessed in public examinations. English seems to be conceived as mainly for academic and job-related purposes in Hong Kong. The information-extraction approach to reading seems to dominate most English reading practices in school, even when the texts being read are stories and not a type of technical, academic or job-related manuals that might more typically require information extraction in many contexts. The schools thus seem to serve as training grounds to churn out graduates skilled in extracting specific information from English texts to accomplish prescribed tasks.

School children, however, might seize whatever opportunities they can find in the classroom to negotiate their own sense of the text, for instance, text not as an information-holder, but as a source of enjoyment. When the prescribed school text proves to be unimaginative or unengaging, they exercise their own creativity to recreate a new plot, to negotiate a comic type of story, which suits their taste. It seems that they are negotiating their own kind of literacy for their own purposes, despite the illegitimacy of their own literacy and their own purposes in the school context.

CODA: RETHINKING THE TEACHER'S ROLE

In this concluding section, an alternative model of literacy is proposed that emphasizes affirming and capitalizing on what children bring to the classroom: their indigenous linguistic, discourse, and cultural resources.

Analysis of students' classroom practices shows that the students' artful story coconstruction practices can be a potential resource in the English lesson if the teacher can harness and build on it. Although one might simply dismiss the students' discourse practice exemplified previously as an instance of student uncooperative behavior, one might also take a very different approach to it: There is the possibility of capitalizing on this kind of popular storytelling resource of the students in a writing program, for instance, by allowing students a chance to coconstruct, retell, and rewrite the story that they have read in the textbook. More research and curricular development are needed in this direction if we see L2 literacy education not just as the training of students in the uncritical, factual extraction of information from texts, as is expected of low-level, white-collar workers in the workplace.

The critical teacher thus needs to reflect on her or his role: Does he or she really want to play the role of producing uncritical students for examinations and uncritical labor for the workplace? Or, does he or she want to foster in students a critical attitude towards texts, the curriculum, and their own socioeconomic positioning in the society? Although there is no denying that the teacher needs to prepare students for examinations that emphasize literacy as uncritical information extraction, the teacher can perhaps discuss various perspectives on reading with students, and in this way, work with students toward a critical understanding of the curriculum and how they can widen their own repertoire of literacy skills beyond those prescribed by the curriculum, without negating or excluding their creative linguistic and sociocultural resources from the classroom.

Teachers in working-class schools can choose to serve as part of the society's machinery in stratifying and reproducing labor to fill low-paying jobs, or to work with students toward uncovering their creative potential and toward a critical exploration of the kinds of literacy they can achieve beyond those prescribed by the curriculum and the examination syllabus. We need more work in exploring feasible alternative classroom practices. As things stand now, we are a long way from reaching this objective. It is, however, my hope that this chapter might arouse some discussion that can lead to future efforts in this direction.

REFERENCES

Barnett, M. V. (1989). *More than meets the eye: Foreign language reading: Theory and practice.* New Jersey: Prentice Hall.

Bourdieu, P. (1991). *Language and symbolic power.* (G. Raymond & M. Adamson, Trans.). Cambridge, MA: Cambridge University Press. (Original work published 1982)

Bourdieu, P., & Passeron, J.-C. (1977). *Reproduction in education, society and culture.* (R. Nice, Trans.). London: Sage.

Heap, J. L. (1985). Discourse in the production of classroom knowledge: Reading lessons. *Curriculum Inquiry, 15*(3), 245–279.

Heap, J. L. (1988). On task in classroom discourse. *Linguistics and Education, 1,* 177–198.

Ho, H. C. Y. (1994). The state of the economy. In P. K. Choi & L. S. Ho (Eds.), *The other Hong Kong report: 1993* (pp. 75–94). Hong Kong: The Chinese University.

Lin, A. M. Y. (1996a). *Doing-English-lessons in secondary schools in Hong Kong: A sociocultural and discourse analytic study.* Unpublished PhD dissertation, University of Toronto, Canada.

Lin, A. M. Y. (1996b). Bilingualism or linguistic segregation? Symbolic domination, resistance, and code-switching in Hong Kong schools. *Linguistics and Education, 8*(1), 49–84.

Mehan, H. (1979). *Learning lessons: Social organization in the classroom.* Cambridge, MA: Harvard University.

Sinclair, J. M., & Coulthard, R. M. (1975). *Towards an analysis of discourse: The English used by teachers and pupils*. London: Oxford.

Usui, Y. (1992). *Crayon Shin-Chan comic series* (Vol. 9). Hong Kong: Tong Li Hong Kong Publishing.

APPENDIX: NOTES ON TRANSCRIPTION

1. English is transcribed orthographically and Cantonese is transcribed in the Yale system. English translations of Cantonese utterances are placed in pointed brackets < > following the Cantonese utterances. The English utterances, Cantonese utterances, and the English translations are each written in a different font type.

2. The numerals preceding each turn is the transcribing machine counter no.; a speaking turn is referred to as: turn [counter no.]

3. 'T' represents 'Teacher'; 'S': Student; 'Ss': Students; 'Boy' or 'Girl' stands for any male or female student voice picked up by the tape and whose identity not available. Words like 'Girl 1,' 'Girl 2,' 'Boy 1,' 'Boy 2,' 'S1,' 'S2,' and so on, are used to differentiate between two different boys/girls/students speaking one after the other. The same words may be used at other points in the transcript to differentiate between another two students speaking, but that does not indicate that they are the same two students who have spoken earlier.

4. Pauses and gaps: A short pause is indicated by '..' and a longer one by '...'. Pauses longer than 0.5 second are indicated by the number of seconds in brackets, for example, (2) indicates a pause of 2 seconds. Gaps between speaking turns are indicated by: ((no. of seconds)), for example, ((5)) indicates a gap of 5 seconds.

5. Simultaneous utterances: The point at which another utterance joins an ongoing one is indicated by the insertion of two slashes in the ongoing turn. The second speaker and her/his utterance(s) are placed below the ongoing turn and are preceded by two slashes, for example:

> 017.8 T: //Sheung-hok-kei <Last term> {spoken in an Anglicized tone} no, haha! {T sounds amused}

> 017.8 //Boy 3: Mat-yeh giu jouh sports day aa <What is a sports day>?
> If the first ongoing turn is very long, the second utterance is placed under the line of the ongoing

turn where the point of intersection appears, for example:

508.5 T: Mh-hm mh-hm {clearing his throat} (3) mh-hm alright {all students are quiet now} (2) today we'll talk about unit 3, (2) open your book (2) story//book (1.5) who don't have the storybook, ==

510.5 //Boy: storybook

511 ==T: raise up your hand (4.5), I want to make sure everybody can read the story, right you two share- share the book. (2.5) How about you? (3) Take out the book. (3 sec) Right you two share the book (3.5) Jeung-Yiuh-Jung.. yeh aah. (5) Right unit three, Tin Hau, Queen of Heaven.=

6. Contiguous utterances: Two equal signs == are used to connect different parts of a speaker's utterance when those parts constitute a continuous flow of speech that has been carried over to another line, by transcript design, to accommodate an intervening interruption; see example under (5) above.
The latching of a second speaking turn to a preceding one is indicated by a single equal sign, '=', for example:

517 Boy: (Bin yau ying-man ge?) < (How come there's English?) >=

517.3 =T: Shh: do you know .. Tin Hau?

7. Contextual information: Significant contextual information is given in curly brackets: for example {Ss laugh}

8. Accentuation: Accentuated syllables are marked by capitalization. Lengthening of sounds is marked by colons: for example SHOU::LD

9. Transcriptionist doubt: Unintelligible items or items in doubt are indicated by question marks in parentheses or the words in doubt in parentheses, for example:

517 Boy: (Bin yau ying-man ge?) < (How come there's English?) >

524 Girl 1:   Ngoh faan (? ?) <I returned (? ?)>

10. Underlined words in the utterances are words read out from a text.

11. All personal names are pseudonames. Names spoken in Cantonese are substituted by a Cantonese pseudoname, for example, Chahn-Ji-Mahn; names spoken in English are substituted by an English pseudonym, for example, Robert. Original names of places close to the schools are substituted by other place names.

12. Asterisks (*) are used to indicate turns of particular analytical interest.

7

On the Road to Cultural Bias: A Critique of *The Oregon Trail* CD-ROM

Bill Bigelow
Franklin High School, Portland, Oregon

I suppose I began this chapter with a bit of a chip on my shoulder—with an attitude, as my students say. I teach history in a public high school (1,600 students) in Portland, Oregon, a medium-sized U.S. city in the Pacific Northwest (student population: 58,000). Conditions of teaching and learning are eroding. Due in large part to a property tax limitation passed several years ago, there is less and less money available for the schools. Teachers have been laid off, class sizes have ballooned, library budgets have been slashed, and support for professional improvement has declined.

In the midst of this crisis, school officials sought, and voters approved, a special levy dedicated in large part to buying more technology for schools. By law, the money cannot be spent to hire more teachers, or to lower class sizes. This sad juxtaposition of scholastic atrophy and technological expansion seems an apt symbol for the state of schooling in my city. Administrators and many teachers appear to regard the new technology—computers, the Internet, CD-ROMs, and the like—as progressive and purely benign, even as the magic key to the schools of tomorrow. The sole equity or justice issue most educators raise concerns access: Who gets the goodies and how much do they get? I am not anticomputer, but this love affair between educators and technological toys worries me.

My school closed a week early last spring so that workers could get an early start rewiring classrooms for the promised infusion of new Internet-linked, CD-ROM-equipped computers. To date, however, there have been no workshops to engage teachers in a critical reflection of the values that come packaged with the hardware and software. Whose lives are highlighted and whose marginalized in the new technology? What cultural biases do students absorb when they interact with the new technology? How do we equip our students to read critically the electronic curricula? These are vital questions that need to be raised at every opportunity.

In 1978, when I got my first high school job in Portland, teachers were not allowed access to the one copy machine in the school. We had a handful of film projectors, no VCRs and, to my knowledge, there was not a single computer in the school—a public school then serving 1,800 students. Twenty years later, I hope that educators do not measure progress based on how much technology we now have access to.

THE OREGON TRAIL

The critics all agree: *The Oregon Trail* is one of the greatest educational computer games ever produced. *Prides' Guide to Educational Software* (1992) awards it five stars for being "a wholesome, absorbing historical simulation," and "multi-ethnic," (p. 419) to boot. The new version, *Oregon Trail II*, is the "best history simulation we've seen to date" according to Warren Buckleitner (MECC, 1994), editor of *Children's Software Review Newsletter* (Minnesota Educational Computer Company—MECC, 1994). Susan Schilling, a key developer of *Oregon Trail II* and recently hired by Star Wars filmmaker George Lucas to head Lucas Learning Ltd., promises new interactive CD-ROMs targeted at children 6 to 15 and concentrated in math and language arts (Armstrong, 1996).

Because interactive CD-ROMs like *The Oregon Trail* are encyclopedic in the amount of information they offer, and because they allow students a seemingly endless number of choices, the new software may appear educationally progressive. CD-ROMs seem tailor-made for the classrooms of tomorrow. They are hands-on and student-centered. They are generally interdisciplinary (e.g., *Oregon Trail II* blends reading, writing, history, geography, math, science, and health). And they are useful in multiage classrooms because they allow students of various knowledge levels to play and learn. But like the walls of a maze, the choices built into interactive

CD-ROMs also channel participants in very definite directions. The CD-ROMs are programed by people—people with particular cultural biases—and children who play the new computer games encounter the biases of the programmers (Bowers, 1988). Just as we would not invite a stranger into our classrooms and then leave the room, teachers need to become aware of the political perspectives of CD-ROMs, and to equip our students to read them critically.

At one level, this article is a critical review of the *Oregon Trail* CD-ROMs. I ask what knowledge is highlighted and what is hidden as students play the game. But I also reflect on the nature of the new electronic curricula, and suggest some questions teachers can ask before choosing to use them with our students. And I offer some classroom activities that might begin to develop students' critical computer literacy.

PLAYING THE GAME

In both *The Oregon Trail* and *Oregon Trail II*, students become members of families and wagon trains crossing the Plains in the 1840s or 1850s on the way to Oregon Territory. A player's objective, according to the game guidebook, is to safely reach Oregon Territory with one's family, thereby "increasing one's options for economic success" (*Oregon Trail II* Guidebook).

The enormous number of choices offered in any one session—what to buy for the journey; the kind of wagon to take; whether to use horses, oxen, or mules; the size of the wagon train with which to travel; whom to talk to along the way; when and where to hunt; when to rest; how fast to travel—is a kind of gentle seduction to students. It invites them to "try on this worldview; see how it fits." In an interactive CD-ROM, you do not merely identify with a particular character, you actually adopt his or her frame of reference and act as if you were that character (Provenzo, 1991). In *Oregon Trail*, a player quickly bonds to the 'pioneer' maneuvering through the 'wilderness.'

In preparation for this chapter, I played *Oregon Trail II* until my eyes became blurry. I can see its attraction to teachers. One cannot play the game without learning a lot about the geography from Missouri to Oregon. (However, I hope I never have to ford another virtual river ever again.) Reading the trail guide as one plays teaches much about the ailments confronted on the Oregon Trail, and some of the treatments. Students can learn a tremendous amount about the details of life for the trekkers to Oregon: the kinds of wagons required, supplies needed, vegetation encountered along the route, and so forth. And the game has a certain multicultural and gender-fair veneer that, however limited, contrasts favorably with the

White male dominated texts of yesteryear. But as much as the game teaches, it mis-teaches more. In fundamental respects, *Oregon Trail II* is sexist, racist, culturally insensitive, and contemptuous of the earth. It imparts bad values and wrong history.

THEY LOOK LIKE WOMEN, BUT ...

To its credit, *Oregon Trail II* includes large numbers of women. Although I did not count, women appear to make up roughly half the people students encounter as they play. But this surface equity is misleading. Women may be present, but gender is not acknowledged as an issue in *Oregon Trail*. In the opening sequences, the game requires students to select a profession, special skills they possess, the kind of wagon to take, the city they will depart from. Class is recognized as an issue (e.g., bankers begin with more money than saddlemakers)—but not gender or race—a player cannot choose these.

Without acknowledging it, *The Oregon Trail* maneuvers students into thinking and acting as if they were all males—and, as we will see, White males. The game highlights a male lifestyle and poses problems that historically fell within the male domain: whether and where to hunt, which route to take, whether and what to trade, to caulk a wagon or ford a river. However, as I began to read more feminist scholarship on the Oregon Trail, I realized that women and men experienced the Trail very differently. It is clear from reading women's diaries of the period that women played little or no role in deciding whether to embark on the trip, where to camp, which routes to take and the like. In real life, women's decisions revolved around how to maintain a semblance of community under great stress, how to preserve the home in transit (Faragher & Stansell, 1992; Kesselman, 1976; Schlissel, 1992). Women decided where to look for firewood or buffalo chips, how and what to cook using hot rocks, how to care for the children, and how to resolve conflicts between travellers, especially the men.

These were real life decisions, but, with the exception of treating illness, they are missing from *The Oregon Trail*. Students are rarely required to think about the intricacies of preserving the home in transit for 2,000 miles. An *Oregon Trail II* information box on the screen informs a player when morale is high or low, but other than making better male-oriented decisions, what is a player to do? *The Oregon Trail* offers no opportunities to encounter the choices of the Trail as women of the time would have encountered them, and to make decisions that might enhance community, and thus morale. As Lillian Schlissel (1992) concluded in her study, *Women's Diaries of the Westward Journey*, "If ever there was a time when men and women turned their psychic energies toward opposite visions, the overland journey was that time. Sitting side by side on a wagon seat, a man and a woman felt different needs as they stared at the endless road that led into the New Country" (p. 15).

Similarly, *The Oregon Trail* fails to represent the texture of community life on the Trail. Students confront a seemingly endless stream of problems posed by *The Oregon Trail* programmers, but rarely encounter the details of life, especially that of women's lives. By contrast, in an article in the book, *America's Working Women*, Amy Kesselman (1976) includes a passage from the diary of one female trekker, Catherine Haun, in 1849:

> We women folk visited from wagon to wagon or congenial friends spent an hour walking ever westward, and talking over our home life "back in the states" telling of the loved ones left behind; voicing our hopes for the future in the far west and even whispering, a little friendly gossip of pioneer life. High teas were not popular but tatting, knitting, crocheting, exchanging receipts for cooking beans or dried apples or swopping food for the sake of variety kept us in practice of feminine occupations and diversions. (p. 71)

The male orientation of *The Oregon Trail* is brought into sharp relief in the game's handling of Independence Day commemoration. As pioneers, students are asked if they wish to "Celebrate the Fourth!" Click on this option, and one hears loud "Yahoos" and guns firing. Compare this to the communal preparations described in Enoch Conyers' 1852 diary (cited in Hill, 1989, but not in *The Oregon Trail*):

> A little further on is a group of young ladies seated on the grass talking over the problem of manufacturing "Old Glory" to wave over our festivities. The question arose as to where we are to obtain the material for the flag. One lady brought forth a sheet. This gave the ladies an idea. Quick as thought another brought a skirt for the red stripes.... Another lady ran to her tent and brought forth a blue jacket, saying: "Here, take this; it will do for the field." Needles and thread were soon secured and the ladies went at their task with a will, one lady remarking that "Necessity is the mother of invention," and the answer came back, "Yes, and the ladies of our company are equal to the task." (p.58)

The contrast between the yahoos and gunfire of *The Oregon Trail* and the collective female exhilaration described in the diary excerpt is striking. This comparison alerted me to something so obvious that it took me awhile to recognize. In *The Oregon Trail*, people do not talk to each other, they all talk to you, the player. Everyone in *The Oregon Trail*-constructed world aims her or his conversation at you, underscoring the simulation's individualistic ideology that all the world exists for the controller of the mouse. An *Oregon Trail* more alert to feminist insights and women's experiences would highlight relationships between people, would focus on how the experience affects our feelings about each other, would feature how women worked with one another to survive and weave community, as women's diary entries clearly reveal.

As indicated earlier, large numbers of women appear throughout *The Oregon Trail* simulation, and they often give good advice, perhaps better advice than the men we encounter. But *The Oregon Trail's* abundance of women, and its apparent effort to be gender-fair, masks an essential problem: the choice structure of the simulation privileges men's experience and virtually erases women's experience.

AFRICAN AMERICANS AS TOKENS

From the game's beginning, when a player starts off in Independence or St. Joseph's, Missouri, African Americans dot the Oregon Trail landscape. However, by and large they are no more than black-colored White people. Although Missouri was a slave state throughout the entire Oregon Trail period, I never encountered the term *slavery* while playing the game. I found race explicitly acknowledged in only one exchange, when I "talked" to an African-American woman along the trail: "I'm Isabella. I'm travelling with the Raleigh's and their people. My job is to keep after the cows and watch the children. My husband Fred is the ox-driver—best there is." Are they free, are they enslaved? Are we to assume the Raleighs are White? I asked to know more: "I was born in Delaware. My father used to tell me stories of Africa and promised one day we'd find ourselves going home. But I don't know if I'm getting closer or farther away with all this walking." The end. Like Missouri, Delaware was a slave state in ante bellum days, but this is not shared with students. Isabella offers provocative details, but they hide more than they reveal about her identity and culture.

Oregon Trail's treatment of African Americans reflects a very superficial multiculturalism. Black people are present, but their lives are not. Attending to matters of race requires more than including lots of Black faces, or having little girls "talk Black": "I think it's time we be moving on now." (This little girl reappears from time to time to repeat these same words. A man who looks Mexican likewise shows up frequently to say, with heavy accent: "Time is a-wasting. Let's head out!").

Although one's life prospects and worldview in the 1840s and 1850s—as today—were dramatically shaped by one's race, this factor is invisible in *The Oregon Trail*. *Oregon Trail* players know their occupations but not

their racial identities, although this knowledge is vital to decisions participants would make before leaving on the journey as well as along the way.

For example, many of the constitutions of societies that sponsored
wagon trains specifically excluded Blacks from making the trip west.
Nonetheless, as Elizabeth McLagan (1980) pointed out in her history of
Blacks in Oregon, *A Peculiar Paradise*, Blacks did travel the Oregon Trail,
some as slaves, some as servants, and at least some, like George Bush, as
well-to-do pioneers. Race may not have seemed important to *The Oregon
Trail* programmers but race mattered a great deal to Bush. He confided to
another emigrant that if he experienced too much prejudice in Oregon, he
would travel south to California or New Mexico and seek protection from
the Mexican government (McLagan, 1980).

And Bush had reason to be apprehensive: African Americans arriving in
Oregon Territory during the 1840s and 1850s were greeted by laws barring
Blacks from residency. Black exclusion laws were passed twice in Oregon
Territory in the 1840s, and a clause in the Oregon State Constitution barring
Black residency was ratified in 1857 by a margin of 8 to 1—a clause,
incidently, not removed until 1926.

On completion of one of my simulated Oregon Trail journeys, I clicked
to see how I turned out: "In 1855, Bill built a home on 463 acres of land in
the Rogue River Valley of Oregon," experienced only "moderate success"
and later moved to Medford, "establishing a small business that proved
more stable and satisfying." Although *The Oregon Trail* simulation never
acknowledges it, "Bill" must have been White, because in 1850 the U.S.
Congress passed the Oregon Donation Land Act granting 640 acres to free
White males and their wives—only. It is unlikely that a Black man, much
less a Black woman, would have been granted land in 1855 or have been
allowed to start a business in Medford some years later.

Why were Whites so insistent that Blacks not live in Oregon? The pre-
amble of one Black Exclusion Bill explained that "situated as the people of
Oregon are, in the midst of an Indian population, it would be highly dangerous to allow free negroes and mulattoes to reside in the territory or to
intermix with the Indians, instilling in their minds feelings of hostility
against the white race." (McLagan, 1980, p. 26). And Samuel Thurston, a
delegate to Congress from Oregon Territory explained in 1850 why Blacks
should not be entitled to homestead in Oregon:

> The negroes associate with the Indians and intermarry, and, if their free in-
> gress is encouraged or allowed, there would a relationship spring up be-
> tween them and the different tribes, and a mixed race would ensue inimical
> to the whites; and the Indians being led on by the negro who is better ac-
> quainted with the customs, language, and manners of the whites, than the
> Indian, these savages would become much more formidable than they oth-

erwise would, and long and bloody wars would be the fruits of the comingling of the races. It is the principle of self preservation that justifies the action of the Oregon Legislature.(McLagan, 1980, pp. 30–31)

Thurston's argument carried the day. But *The Oregon Trail* programmers have framed the issues so that race seems irrelevant. Thus, once students-as-pioneers arrive in Oregon, most of them will live happily ever after—never considering the impact that race would have on life conditions.

JUST PASSING THROUGH?

The Oregon Trail programmers are careful not to portray Indians as the enemy of westward trekkers. However, the simulation's superficial sympathy for Native groups masks a profound insensitivity to Indian cultures and to the earth that sustained these cultures. The simulation guidebook lists numerous Indian nations by name—and respectfully calls them *nations*. *The Oregon Trail* guidebook explains that emigrants' fear of Indians is "greatly exaggerated":

> Some travellers have been known to cross the entire breadth of the continent from the Missouri River to the Sierra Nevadas without ever laying eye on an Indian, except perhaps for occasional brief sightings from a distance. This is all well and good, for it is probably best for all parties concerned for emigrants and Indians to avoid contact with each other. Such meetings are often the source of misunderstandings, sometimes with regrettable consequences.

Emigrants often spread disease, according to the guidebook, which made the Indians "distrust and dislike" the emigrants. The guidebook further warns *The Oregon Trail* players not to overhunt game in any one place as "few things will incur the wrath of the Indian peoples more than an overstayed welcome accompanied by the egregious waste of the natural resources upon which they depend."

What orientation is highlighted and what is hidden in the simulation programed for students to follow? The ideology embedded in *The Oregon Trail I* and *II* is selfish and goal-driven: care about indigenous people insofar as you need to avoid misunderstanding and incurring the wrath of potentially hostile natives. *The Oregon Trail* promotes an anthropocentric earth-as-natural resource outlook. Nature is a thing to be consumed or overcome as people traverse the country in search of success in a faraway land. The simulation's structure coerces children into identifying with White settlers and dismissing non-White others. It contributes to the broader curricular racialisation of identity students absorb—learning who constitutes the normalized "we" and who is excluded.

The Oregon Trail players need not take into account the lives of others unless it's necessary to do so in order to accomplish their personal objectives. Thus the cultures of Plains Indians are backgrounded. The game marginalizes their view of the earth. Contrast, for example, the Indians' term *mother earth* with *The Oregon Trail* term *natural resource*. The metaphor of earth as mother suggests humans in a reciprocal relationship with a natural world that is alive, nourishing us, sustaining us. A resource is a thing to be used. It exists for us, outside of us, and we have no obligations in return.

The consequences of the Oregon Trail for the Plains Indians, the Indians of the Northwest, and for the earth were devastating. In fairness, as they play *The Oregon Trail*, students may hear some of the details of this upheaval. For example, on one trip I encountered a Pawnee Village. Had I paid attention to the warning in the guidebook to "avoid contact" I would have ignored it and continued on my trip. But I entered and " talked" to the people I encountered there. A Pawnee woman: "Why do you bother me? I don't want to trade. The things that we get from the White travellers don't make up for all that we lose." I click to hear more. "We didn't know the whooping cough, measles, or the smallpox until your people brought them to us. Our medicine cannot cure these strange diseases, and our children are dying." I click on "Do you have any advice?" Angrily, she says, "No. I just want you to leave us alone." The implication is that if I just "leave [them] alone" and continue on the trail I can pursue my dream without hurting the Indians.

However, this interpretation hides the fact that the Oregon Trail itself, not just contact with the so-called pioneers, devastated Indian cultures and the ecology of which those cultures were an integral part. For example, pioneers—let us begin to call them their Lakota name, Wasi'chu (greedy persons)[1]—cut down all the cottonwood trees found along the rich bottomlands of plains rivers—trees that "offered crucial protection during winter blizzards as well as concealing a village's smoke from its enemies. In lean seasons, horses fed on its bark, which was surprisingly nourishing" (Davidson & Lytle, 1992, p. 114).

The Oregon Trail created serious wood shortages, which even the Wasi'chu acknowledged. "By the Mormon guide we here expected to find the last timber," wrote overlander A. W. Harlan, describing the Platte River,

---

[1]The Lakota "used a metaphor to describe the newcomers. It was Wasi'chu, which means 'takes the fat,' or 'greedy person' . Within the modern Indian movement, Wasi' chu has come to mean those corporations and individuals, with their governmental accomplices, which continue to covet Indian lives, land, and resources for private profit. Wasi'chu does not describe a race; it describes a state of mind" (Johansen & Maestas, 1979, p. 6).

"but all had been used up by others ahead of us so we must go about 200 miles without any provisions cooked up." A few weeks later, in sight of the Black Hills, Harlan wrote: "[W]e have passed many cottonwood stumps but no timber" (Davidson & Lytle, 1992, p. 115).

Wasi'chu rifles also killed tremendous numbers of buffalo that Plains Indians depended on for survival. One traveller in the 1850s wrote that "the valley of the Platte for 200 miles presents the aspect of the vicinity of a slaughter yard, dotted all over with skeletons of buffaloes" (Davidson & Lytle, 1992, p. 117). Very soon after the beginning of the Oregon Trail the buffalo learned to avoid the Trail, their herds migrating both south and north. Edward Lazarus (1991) pointed out in *Black Hills/White Justice: The Sioux Nation Versus the United States—1775 to the Present*: "But the Oregon Trail did more than move the buffalo; it destroyed the hunting pattern of the Sioux, forcing them to follow the herds to the fringes of their domain and to expose themselves to the raids of their enemies" (p. 14).

However, wrapped in their cocoons of self-interest, *The Oregon Trail* players push on, oblivious to the mayhem and misery they cause in their westward drive. This is surely an unintended, and yet intrinsic, part of the game's message: Pursue your goal as an autonomous individual, ignore the social and ecological consequences; "look out for number one."

NO VIOLENCE HERE

The Oregon Trail never suggests to its simulated pioneers that they should seek permission of Indian nations to travel through their territory; and from this key omission flow other omissions. The simulation does not inform players that because of the disruptions wrought by the daily intrusions of the westward migration, Plains Indians regularly demanded tribute from the trekkers. As John Unruh (1993) wrote in *The Plains Across*:

> The natives explicitly emphasised that the throngs of overlanders were killing and scaring away buffalo and other wild game, overgrazing prairie grasses, exhausting the small quantity of available timber, and depleting water resources. The tribute payments ... were demanded mainly by the Sac and Fox, Kickapoo, Pawnee, and Sioux Indians—the tribes closest to the Missouri River frontier and therefore those feeling most keenly the pressures of white men increasingly impinging upon their domains. (p. 169)

Wasi'chu travellers resented this Indian-imposed taxation and their resentment frequently turned to hostility and violence, especially in the later years of the Trail. The Pawnees were "hateful wretches," wrote Dr. Thomas Wolfe in 1852 (cited in Unruh, 1993), for demanding a 25 cent toll at a bridge across Shell Creek near the North Platte River. Shell Creek and other crossings became flashpoints that escalated into violent skirmishes resulting in the deaths of settlers and Indians.

Despite the increasing violence along the Oregon Trail, one choice *The Oregon Trail* programmers do not offer students-as-trekkers is the choice to harm Indians. Doubtless MECC, producer of *The Oregon Trail*, is not anxious to promote racism toward Native peoples. However, because simulation players cannot hurt or even speak ill of Indians, the game fails to alert students that White hostility was one feature of the westward migration. The omission is significant because the sanitised nonviolent *Oregon Trail* fails to equip students to reflect on the origins of conflicts between Whites and Indians. Nor does it offer students any insights into the racial antagonism that fueled this violence. In all my play of *The Oregon Trail* I cannot recall any blatant racism directed at Indians. But as Unruh (1993) pointed out, "the callous attitude of cultural and racial superiority so many overlanders exemplified was of considerable significance in producing the volatile milieu in which more and more tragedies occurred" (p. 186).

THE END OF THE TRAIL

> *"Soon there will come from the rising sun a different kind of man from any you have yet seen, who will bring with them a book and will teach you everything, after that the world will fall to pieces." Spokan Prophet, 1790. (Limerick, 1987, p. 39)*

Someone can spend 2 or 3 hours—or more—playing one game of *The Oregon Trail* before finally reaching Oregon Territory. Once we arrive, the game awards us points and tells us how our life in Oregon turned out. And yet it fails to raise vital questions about our right to be there in the first place and what happened to the people who were there first.

In its section on the *Destination*, the guidebook offers students its wisdom on how they should view life in a new land. It is a passage that underscores the messages students absorb while engaged in the simulation. These comforting words of advice and social vision are worth quoting at length:

> Once you reach the end of your journey, you should go to the nearest large town to establish your land claim. If there are no large towns in the area, simply find an unclaimed tract of land and settle down.... As they say, possession is nine-tenths of the law, and if you have settled and worked land that hasn't

yet been claimed by anyone else, you should have little or no trouble legally establishing your claim at a later time.

As more and more Americans move into the region, more cities and towns will spring up, further increasing one's options for economic success. Rest assured in the facts that men and women who are willing to work hard will find their labors richly rewarded, and that you, by going west, are helping to spread American civilization from ocean to ocean across this great continent, building a glorious future for generations to come!

The Lakota scholar and activist Vine Deloria (1977) in his book, *Indians of the Pacific Northwest* offered a less sanguine perspective than that included in the CD-ROM guidebook. People coming in on the Oregon Trail "simply arrived on the scene and started building. If there were Indians or previous settlers on the spot they were promptly run off under one pretext or another. Lawlessness and thievery dominated the area" (p. 53). From 1850 on, using provisions of the Oregon Donation Act, thousands of pioneers invaded with impunity.

As Deloria (1977) pointed out, there were some in Congress who were aware that they were encouraging settlers to steal Indian land, and so shortly after, Congress passed the Indian Treaty Act requiring the United States to get formal agreements from Indian tribes. Anson Dart, appointed to secure land concessions, pursued this objective in a despicable fashion. For example, he refused to have the treaties translated into the Indians' languages, instead favoring "Chinook jargon," a nonlanguage of fewer than 300 words good for trading, giving orders, and little else. Dart's mandate was to move all the Indians east of the Cascades, but he decided some tribes, like the Tillamooks and Chinooks, should keep small amounts of land as cheap labor reserves:

> Almost without exception, I have found [the Indians] anxious to work at employment at common labour and willing too, to work at prices much below that demanded by the whites. The Indians make all the rails used in fencing, and at this time do the boating upon the rivers: in consideration, therefore, of the usefulness as laborers in the settlements, it was believed to be far better for the Country that they should not be removed from the settled portion [sic] of Oregon if it were possible to do so. (Deloria, 1977, p. 51)

Meanwhile, in southwestern Oregon, White vigilantes did not wait for treaty niceties to be consummated. Between 1852 and 1856 self-proclaimed volunteers attacked Indians for alleged misdeeds, or simply because they were Indians. In August of 1853, Martin Angel rode into the Rogue River Valley gold-mining town of Jacksonville shouting, "Nits breed lice. We have been killing Indians in the valley all day," and "Exterminate the whole race." Minutes later a mob of about 800 White men hanged a 7-year-old Indian boy. In October 1855, a group of Whites massacred 23 Indian men, women, and children. This incident began the Rogue Indian war, which lasted until June 1856 (Beckham, 1991). Recall that this is the same region and the same year in one *Oregon Trail* session where Bill built a home and experienced "moderate success"—but thanks to *The Oregon Trail* programmers, learned nothing of the social conflicts swirling around him.

Nor did Bill learn that, even as a White person, he could protest the outrages committed against the Rogue River Valley Indians as did one anonymous volunteer in a passionate 1853 letter to the *Oregon Statesman* newspaper:

A few years since the whole valley was theirs [the Indians'] alone. No white man's foot had ever trod it. They believed it theirs forever. But the gold digger come, with his pan and his pick and shovel, and hundreds followed. And they saw in astonishment their streams muddied, towns built, their valley fenced and taken. And where their squaws dug camus, their winter food, and their children were wont to gambol, they saw dug and plowed, and their own food sown by the hand of nature, rooted out forever, and the ground it occupied appropriated to the rearing of vegetables for the white man. Perhaps no malice yet entered the Indian breast. But when he was weary of hunting in the mountains without success, and was hungry, and approached the white man's tent for bread; where instead of bread he received curses and kicks, ye treaty kicking men—ye Indian exterminators think of these things. A Soldier. (Applegate & O'Donnell, 1994, p. 34)

The Oregon Trail hides the nature of the Euro-American invasion in at least two ways. In the first place, *The Oregon Trail* CD-ROM simply fails to inform simulation participants what happened between settlers and Indians. To *The Oregon Trail* player, it does not feel like an invasion, it does not feel wrong. After one of my arrivals, in 1848, "Life in the new land turned out to be happy and successful for Bill, who always cherished bittersweet but proud memories of the months spent on the Oregon Trail." (This struck me as a rather odd account, given that I had lost all three of my children on the trip.) The only person that matters is the simulation player, in this case Bill. I was never told whether life turned out equally "happy and successful" for the Klamaths, Yakamas, Cayuses, Nez Percés, Wallawallas, and all the others, who occupied this land generations before the Wasi'chu arrived. The second way the nature of the White invasion is hidden has to do with the structure of the simulation. For a couple hours or more the player endures substantial doses of frustration, tedium, and difficulty. By the time the Willamette or Rogue Valleys come on the screen we, the simulated trekkers, feel that we deserve the land, that our labors in transit should be "richly rewarded" with the best land we can find.

DATA DECEPTION AND THOUGHTS ON WHAT TO DO ABOUT IT

In the Beatles' song, *All you need is love*; in *The Oregon Trail*, all you need is data. *The Oregon Trail* offers students gobs of information: snake bite remedies, river locations and depths, wagon specifications, ferry costs, and daily climate reports. Loaded with facts, it feels comprehensive. Loaded with people voicing contrasting opinions, it feels balanced. Loaded with choices, it feels free. But the simulation begins from no moral or ethical standpoint beyond individual material success; it contains no vision of social or ecological justice, and, hence promotes the full litany of sexism, racism, and imperialism, as well as exploitation of the earth. And simultaneously, it hides this bias. The combination is insidious, and makes interactive CD-ROMs like this one more difficult to critique than traditional textbooks or films. The forced identification of player with simulation protagonist leaves the student no option but to follow the ideological map laid out by the programmers.

Nonetheless, my critique is not a call to boycott the new "edutainment" resources. But we need to remember that these CD-ROMs are not teacher substitutes. The teacher's role in analyzing and presenting these devices in a broader ethical context is absolutely vital. Thus teachers across the country must begin a dialogue toward developing a critical computer literacy. We need to figure out ways to equip students to recognize and evaluate the deep moral and political messages imparted as they maneuvre within various computer software programs.

Before choosing to use CD-ROMs that involve people and place, like *The Oregon Trail* (or, e.g., its newer siblings *The Yukon Trail*, *The Amazon Trail*, and *Africa Trail*) teachers can consider a series of questions. These include:

- Which social groups are students not invited to identify with in the simulation? For example, Native Americans, African Americans, women, and Latinos are superficially present in *The Oregon Trail*, but the stuff of their lives is missing.

- How might these social groups frame problems differently than they are framed in the simulation? As we saw in the foregoing critique of *The Oregon Trail*, women tended to focus more on maintaining community, than on hunting. Native Americans had a profoundly different relationship to the earth than did the Euro-American "tamers of the wilderness."

- What decisions do simulation participants make that may have consequences for social groups not highlighted in the simulation? And what are these consequences? Although the very existence of the Oregon Trail contributed to the decimation of Plains and Northwest Indians, simulation participants are never asked to consider the broader effects of their decision making. What may be an ethical individual choice may be unethical when multiplied several hundred thousand times. (In this respect, CD-ROM choice making both reflects and reinforces conventional ideas of freedom that justify disastrous social and ecological practices.)

- What decisions do simulation participants make that may have consequences for the earth and nonhuman life? Similarly, a simulation participant's choice to cut down trees for firewood may be rational for that individual, but may also have deleterious effects on the ecological balance of a particular bio-region.

- If the simulation is time-specific, as in the case of *The Oregon Trail*, what were the social and environmental consequences after the time period covered in the simulation? The wars between Indians and U.S. cavalry in the latter decades of the 19th century are inexplicable without the Oregon Trail as prologue.

- Can we name the ideological orientation of a particular CD-ROM? The question is included here simply to remind us that all computer materials—indeed, all curricula—have an ideology. Our first step is becoming aware of the nature of that ideology.

These are hardly exhaustive, but may suggest a useful direction to begin thinking, as CD-ROMs become increasingly available and as they come to cover more and more subjects.

Finally, let me use the example of *The Oregon Trail* to sketch out a number of ways that teachers can begin to foster a critical computer literacy:

- Once we have identified some of the social groups that are substantially missing in a CD-ROM activity like *The Oregon Trail*, we can make an effort to locate excerpts of their diaries, speeches, or other communications (to the extent that these cultures are print-oriented) and read these together.

- We might then engage students in a role play where, as a class, students face a number of Oregon Trail problems. For example, class members could portray women on the Oregon Trail and decide how they will attempt to maintain a community in transit. Or they might role play a possible discussion of Oglala people as they confront the increasingly disruptive presence of Wasi'chu crossing their lands.

- Students might be asked to list all the ways that African Americans would experience the Oregon Trail differently than Euro-Americans would—from planning to the trip itself. (It is unlikely, for example, that every White person on the streets of Independence, Missouri said a friendly "Howdy" to Blacks encountered, as each of them does to the implied but unacknowledged White male *Oregon Trail* simulation player.)

- In playing *The Oregon Trail* simulation, students could assume a particular racial, cultural, or gender identity, and note whether the choices or experiences described in the simulation make sense from the standpoint of a member of their group. For example, would a typical African American in Missouri in 1850 be allowed to choose which city to begin the trek west?

- As we share with students the social and ecological costs of the Oregon Trail, we could ask them to write critical letters to each of the pioneers they portrayed in the simulation. Some could represent Rogue Valley Indians, Shoshoni people, or even Mother Earth. For instance, how does Mother Earth respond to the casual felling of every cottonwood tree along the Platte River?

- A Native American elder or activist could be invited into the classroom to speak about the concerns that are important to his or her people and about the history of White-Indian relationships.

- We could encourage students to think about the politics of naming in the simulation. They could suggest alternative names for the Oregon Trail itself. For example, the historian of the American West, Frederick Merk (1978) aptly called the Oregon Trail a "path of empire." Writer Dan Georgakas (1973) named it a "march of death." Other names might be "invasion of the West," or "the 20-year trespass." Just as with Columbus's "discovery" of America, naming shapes understanding, and we need classroom activities to uncover this process.

- Students could write and illustrate alternative children's books describing the Oregon Trail from the standpoint of women, African Americans, Native Americans, or the earth.

- Now have them play *The Oregon Trail* again. What do they see this time that they did not see before? Whose worldview is highlighted and whose is hidden? If they choose, they might present their findings to other classes or to teachers who may be considering the use of CD-ROMs.

The Oregon Trail is not necessarily more morally obnoxious than other CD-ROMs or curricular materials with similar ideological biases. My aim here is broader than merely to shake a scolding finger at MECC, producer of *The Oregon Trail* series. I have tried to demonstrate why teachers and students must develop a critical computer literacy. Some of the new CD-ROMs seem more socially aware than the blatantly culturally insensitive materials that still fill school libraries and bookrooms. And the flashy new computer packages also invoke terms long sacred to educators: student empowerment, individual choice, creativity, high interest. It is vital that we remember that coincident with the arrival of these new educational toys is a deepening social and ecological crisis. Global and national inequality between haves and have nots is increasing. Violence of all kinds is endemic. And the earth is being consumed at a ferocious pace. Computer programs are not politically neutral in the moral contests of our time. Inevitably, they take sides. Thus, a critical computer literacy, one with a social and ecological conscience, is more than just a good idea—it is a basic skill.

ACKNOWLEDGMENTS

This chapter first appeared as an article in *Rethinking Schools* (Fall, 1995, Vol. 10, No. 1) and later in *Language Arts*. Permission to reprint by the National Council of Teachers of English is gratefully acknowledged.

REFERENCES

Applegate, S., & O'Donnell, T. (1994). *Talking on paper: An anthology of Oregon letters and diaries.* Corvallis, OR: Oregon State University.
Armstrong, D. (1996, February 23). Lucas getting into education via CD-ROM. *The San Francisco Examiner,* pp. E-1–E-2.

Beckham, S. D. (1991). *Federal-Indian relations: The first Oregonians.* Portland, OR: Oregon Council for the Humanities.

Bowers, C. A. (1988). *The cultural dimensions of educational computing: Understanding the non-neutrality of technology.* New York: Teachers College Press.

Davidson, J. W., & Lytle, M. H. (1992). *After the fact: The art of historical detection.* New York: McGraw-Hill.

Deloria, V. (1977). *Indians of the Pacific Northwest.* Garden City, NY: Doubleday.

Faragher, J., & Stansell, C. (1992). Women and their families on the Overland Trail to California and Oregon, 1842–1867. In F. Binder & D. Reimer (Eds.), *The way we lived: Essays and documents in American social history* (Vol. 1, pp. 188–195). Lexington, MA: D.C. Heath.

Georgakas, D. (1973). *Red shadows: The history of Native Americans from 1600 to 1900, from the desert to the Pacific coast.* Garden City, NY: Zenith.

Hill, W. E. (1989). *The Oregon Trail: Yesterday and today.* Caldwell, ID: Caxton Printers.

Johansen, B., & Maestas, R, (1979). *Wasi'chu: The continuing Indian wars.* New York: Monthly Review.

Kesselman, A. (1976). Diaries and reminiscences of women on the Oregon Trail: A study in consciousness. In R. Baxandall, L. Gordon, & S. Reverby (Eds.), *America's working women: A documentary history—1600 to the present* (pp. 69–72). New York: Vintage.

Lazarus, E. (1991). *Black hills/white justice: The Sioux Nation versus the United States—1775 to the present.* New York: Harper Collins.

Limerick, P. N. (1987). *The legacy of conquest: The unbroken past of the American West.* New York: Norton.

McLagan, E. (1980). *A peculiar paradise: A history of Blacks in Oregon, 1788–1940.* Portland, OR: The Georgian.

Minnesota Educational Computing Consortium. (1994). *The Oregon Trail II.* Minneapolis, MN.

Merk, F. (1978). *History of the westward movement.* New York: Knopf.

Pride, W., & Pride, M. (1992). *Prides' guide to educational software.* Wheaton, IL: Crossway Books.

Provenzo, E. F. (1991) *Video kids: Making sense of Nintendo.* Cambridge, MA: Harvard.

Schlissel, L. (1992). *Women's diaries of the westward journey.* New York: Schocken.

Unruh, J. D., Jr. (1993). *The Plains across: The overland emigrants and the trans-Mississippi West, 1840–1860.* Urbana, IL: University of Illinois.

Teaching Readings?

Bronwyn Mellor
Chalkface Press, Western Australia

Annette Patterson
James Cook University, Australia

BACKGROUND

Coming to terms with many of the recent changes in thinking about reading texts is difficult. Most teachers in the western world have trained in a quite different tradition, and the question, "What does it mean in the classroom?" is not addressed explicitly by most recent theory. The idea, for example, that a text might be thought of as a site for the production of multiple—and often contradictory or competing—meanings is a particularly challenging one in the context of the classroom. Moving from a conception of the text as a container of correct meanings for which readers must search, to one in which meanings are thought about as produced rather than discovered, and contested rather than agreed, has enormous implications in terms of assessment and power. Which meanings, after all, are to prevail?

Being able to ask questions about the meanings produced of texts seems to offer productive possibilities for practice because recent literary theory appears to suggest that through their taking up of multiple reading positions, readers might be able to reflect on the readings that they and others produce.

So that by encouraging students to read in a way that involved the construction of multiple readings of a text, we thought the likelihood of constructing readers who were critically conscious and aware appeared to be increased.

There are, of course, several competing strands to recent theory as it is propounded in the Australian context, whether applied to literary texts or popular culture, but initially, we took from it four principles:

- that a starting point for a discussion about texts is that they are made;

- that texts do not emerge from a timeless, placeless zone but are written and read in particular social contexts;

- that texts are sites for the production of meanings that may have nothing to do with what the writer intended; and

- that texts are sites for the production of multiple and frequently contradictory meanings.

Because we shared the concern about the production of particular readings of race, class, and gender in the classroom, we wanted to address these issues with students. At this point, we had discussions with a local primary school teacher, who kindly allowed us to work with her and her students over a number of weeks, using mainly folk and fairy tales to explore some of the questions about reading and textual study that we and she had. The state-funded school in which she worked was located in an established suburban area of an Australian city of more than 1 million people. The school had just over 200 students and a staff of approximately 12 full- and part-time teachers. It provided schooling for boys and girls ages 5 through 12 placed in year levels one to seven, with some split year classes. The students with whom we worked were in a split class; the 24 children ranged in age from 8- to 10-years-old and were studying curricula designed for Years 4 and 5. Although the class included eight children from South East Asian and Chinese families, English was their (at least equal) first language. The teacher, who had been teaching for 16 years, arranged her curriculum in terms of themes and subscribed to a whole language philosophy with regard to literacy education, but in practice she was eclectic, drawing at different times on genre-based strategies and activities. Highly organized and sympathetic, she was liked and respected by her students.

READING HANSEL AND GRETEL

Having explained to the students the sophisticated textual analysis that they would be asked to undertake, the first story we selected to read in class was a simple folk tale; *Hansel and Gretel*. The Brothers Grimm version we used was illustrated by Anthony Browne (1981), who adapted a translation by Eleanor Quarrie and updated the illustrations: The parents wear modern clothes, and in one scene, the mother, who dresses up in high heels and a leopard skin coat, sits watching the television, while her husband and the children sit at the table looking miserable. Apart from the interesting constructions of social class that might be read from the illustrations, we were intrigued by children's production of a reading in which the mother is viewed as bad, whereas the father, who also participated in the abandoning of the children, is invariably seen as nice.

The point of the reading activities we devised to accompany *Hansel and Gretel* was not, we thought at this time, to teach the students that their reading was wrong, but rather to analyze how and why this reading was produced. In other words, we were asking: In what circumstances could this text have this meaning? If it can be argued that both parents do the same thing (i.e., that both father and stepmother leave the children in the forest), how then is a reading produced that evaluates the stepmother as wicked and the father as nice, the victim of a nagging wife? What makes this reading possible? What might make an alternative or resistant reading possible? Our rationale for the reading activities was that by questioning dominant readings of *Hansel and Gretel* it would be possible to challenge dominant cultural ideas about gender because, we argued, it was these cultural ideas that made such readings possible and preferred by certain powerful groups at particular times.

Before reading *Hansel and Gretel* with the class of (mainly) 9-year-olds, we told them:

> You are going to read a story about a very poor family. The parents are so poor they do not have enough food to feed themselves and their children. One of them says, "Let's take the children into the bush and leave them there." The other parent is sad but agrees to do this.

Before reading the story, talk in your groups about the following ways of describing the parents. Choose the one you agree with. Be ready to explain why you picked the one you did.

- Both parents are very mean.

- Both parents are very nice.

- The parent who first had the idea of leaving the children is mean.

- The parent who first had the idea of leaving the children is sensible.

- The parent who felt sad about leaving the children is nice.

- The parents have no choice.

The students then were read (and shown) the version of *Hansel and Gretel* by Browne (1981). Despite quite lively debate prior to the reading, about the culpability of either or neither parent, after reading the story the stepmother was described by all the students as wicked and the father as not to blame and nice. Why, we asked the students, was it possible to see the parents so differently when they had done the same thing (i.e., left the children in the forest?). The students vehemently supported their reading of the father as nice by repeating that he was nice. To help the students consider this question a little more analytically than they at first could, we asked them to find examples of the father and the stepmother doing bad things and good things in the illustrations. It was noted that where the father looked unsmiling, he was judged to be sad and therefore nice, whereas the unsmiling stepmother was described as mean or nasty. In these ways, and others, we worked at making the students' production of their readings of the story seem strange. That is, we worked to make them question just how and why they produced—initially with total conviction that it was simply there in front of them on the page—a particular reading when other readings were more than possible, as indeed, we demonstrated by the provision of alternatives.

But we began to become worried about our use of the concept of multiple readings as the means by which students would become critical readers. Although the activities we had used were successful in encouraging children to ask some questions about the reading they were producing of *Hansel and Gretel*, and how and why they were constructing that particular reading over other possible readings of the characters and the story, the students were not particularly willing to construct alternatives.

We realized we had assumed that an adjustment of their initial reading would follow given their access to alternatives. The way students would do this, we thought, was by becoming conscious of sexism; once seeing the sexism of a particular reading they would choose another. Newly conscious and thus empowered to produce a resistant or critical reading, they then would be able to overcome both the potential for deception of the text and the power of dominant (sexist) readings. That is, conscious of the deceptions of particular conceptions of the text (as containing a correct meaning) and the power of dominant or preferred readings (which make always interested and partial meanings seem natural and neutral), the students would be free to produce critical readings. This did not seem to be the case. Although they appeared to benefit from the analytical activities that drew attention to the processes of their reading, they did not resist the dominant or preferred reading, nor did they adjust their initial readings in favor of an alternative construction.

Why were we worried about this? Surely the students had the right to stay with their initial reading of the stepmother as mean and the father as nice? But if we accepted that there was no one correct meaning, (no one correct gender?), did that mean that any reading (or gender) would do? We could think of meanings and genders (e.g., those associated with sexually violent and machismo models) that we would prefer not to accept, even in the cause of plurality and difference. At this point, we realized that not only were we not content with simply producing plural readings of the text, but that at times there were readings that we worked to adjust rather than simply analyze and even at times that there were readings (e.g., particular sexist and racist ones) that we did not want articulated in the classroom, often for quite practical reasons such as the possible embarrassing and hurting of some students. What we had been doing by using the strategy of multiple readings, we decided, was offering a falsely free situation in which children were invited to see the error of dominant or preferred readings (characterized as sexist or racist or class prejudiced) and to choose—apparently freely and consciously—an alternative reading from newly available reading positions.

We went on to question our use of the concept of *critical readings*. How, for example, would we recognize when our students had produced a reading that could be termed *critical*? To qualify as *critical* in a critical literacy classroom would a reading need to acknowledge gender, ethnicity, and class (depending on the requirements of the particular reading occasion) and do it in specified ways? That is, to be recognized as critical would a reading have to display certain features that included evidence of antisexist, antiracist understandings? We wonder now whether the concept of multiple readings offers the promise of conscious autonomy as proposed by many critical literacy theorists. It is used currently, we suspect, as a means of trying to get students to adjust their readings in favor of a required reading apparently through their own free—because conscious—choice. Usually, a required reading is thought of as being a dominant (and therefore a bad) reading (e.g., as in a reading required by oppressive, dominant forces such as patriarchy). But, in the case of critical literacy practices, the required reading (i.e., the critical reading) may well be a reading that many teachers would wish to support (e.g., an antiracist or antisexist reading). It is not usual to think of such a reading as required because generally it is proposed as the reading that the reader, who has had multiple subject positions made available to her or him, chooses freely. This is because power is theorized as repressive rather than productive (i.e., power in this mode of theorizing is seen as what blocks perception or "clear seeing"), but as Foucault (1977) argued, power is also productive of practices and knowledges (see also Gilbert, 1992; Janks, 1997). The implication for teachers of reading it seems to us is that the critical reading is as positively produced (i.e., taught), as the dominant reading.

The achievement of an antiracist or antisexist reading may involve the production of multiple readings, but this, we suggest, is in order to problematize and adjust the initial reading. The production of multiple readings does not, however, free students from the normative requirements of producing a specific reading—in this case, an antiracist or antisexist one. Choosing freely and consciously involves choosing correctly (i.e., in terms of particular requirements) in order to be judged free and conscious. The antiracist or antisexist reading, we now believe, is just as much a requirement (albeit a different one) as any other reading might be and is produced via the operation of the reading practices of a specific reading regime. The multiple genders and the multiple readings imagined by poststructuralist theory it seems are always conscious ones and therefore, it is assumed, will always be antisexist and antiracist. The possibility of a conscious racist or sexist reading is not acknowledged because the reading practices of critical literacy are narrativized in terms of the recovery or restoration of truth, rather than in terms of the normative production of certain knowledges or readings. This allows critical literacy pedagogy to claim to be both non-neutral (always on the side of good) and non-normative (always on the side of freedom).

To summarize, practical problems attend the encouragement of multiple readings. It is seldom acknowledged that there are readings that are not encouraged in the critical literacy classroom. Furthermore, they are not encouraged sometimes, we would argue, for good reasons. A highly racist reading, for example, may be one that a teacher (and many students) would not want to permit a student to express. However, it may not be much of a problem if only one student articulates such a reading. If 10 or 15 do in a multiracial classroom, the practical issues can be more challenging. If a teacher feels that she or he can handle the difficulties of open discussion, then perhaps that is fine, although we suggest that such debate, laudably undertaken in the name of democracy, still usually has as its aim the adjustment of certain points of view rather than just the expressing of them. The point, though, is that promises of plurality and difference—through which students will become empowered to resist deceptive texts and dominant ideologies—rest, on an inadequate acknowledgment of both the practical difficulties of encouraging truly multiple readings of texts in the classroom, and on a curiously self-serving theoretical analysis that allows us as teachers to attempt to adjust students' readings while apparently denying that we are doing so (Moon, 1994). So, why not acknowledge the difficulties? That is, why not explicitly acknowledge that some forms of plurality are more acceptable (and furthermore, required within particular reading regimes) and others are not? Interestingly, it is a question with which we feel uncomfortable even as we argue that it should be asked.

STUDYING STORIES

We wanted to explore some of these issues further in a practical context: We began by devising a series of activities in which we tried to get students to think about stories as something made, and about how they read them. Although the students did not necessarily believe that stories were true, they were accustomed to reading for a meaning that for the most part, they felt was unproblematically there in the text. Our experience with *Hansel and Gretel* already had shown that. The students tended to support their reading simply by repeating their reading, often with some exasperation because it was perfectly clear to them that the father was nice because he was nice, and the stepmother was mean because she was mean. How then, we wondered, could we teach a practice by which questions could be asked about the meanings produced of texts? We started with a story called *Goldflower and the Bear.* Whether the students were familiar with it or not, we thought we could rely on firstly, their recognizing certain textual *features* (as we termed them at this stage) and secondly, on their being able to make guesses and predictions about them. The story is a Chinese equivalent of *Little Red Riding Hood* (or vice versa), although the title has echoes of the tale of *Goldilocks and the Three Bears* for readers familiar with a European tradition.

We gave the students the following instructions:

> You are going to read a story called *Goldflower and the Bear.* Before you read it, or you listen to your teacher read it to you, talk with a partner for a few minutes about the title or name of the story. Try to make some guesses about what the story might be about and how the story might go.

> You could use these questions to help get you started:

> • Who or what do you think Goldflower might be?

> • What other characters do you think there might be in the story?

> • Where do you think the characters might live?

> • What do you think might happen in the story?

> • How do you think the story might end?

We then asked each pair to compare their guesses with another pair. This was to help any pairs that were having trouble making predictions. Before going on to read the story, however, the students were asked to share their ideas with the rest of their class in a whole-class discussion. This was both a supportive pedagogical strategy to provide predictions for any students who had not managed to produce any, but it also was designed to give students the opportunity to see the common strands to the class predictions. The teacher blackboarded a series of guesses from the students, which in the main drew on their intertextual knowledge of *Goldilocks and the Three Bears.* There *were* some students, though, who offered a different scenario.

There was one group that suggested Goldflower was a magic plant, and the Bear was a prince who had been changed into animal form by a wicked witch. Students working with the Goldilocks scenario did not think much of this, but again supported their predictions mainly by repeating their predictions, until one girl argued that if the Goldflower of the title *was* a plant and the Bear a prince, the title would be *The Bear and the Goldflower.* This caused a few seconds of profound silence, as we—and apparently the students—were struck by the sharpness of this argument. Although this was a momentary set-back for the magic plant supporters, they rallied and asked the teacher to begin reading. The very first sentence, however, brought vindication to Goldilock's side it seemed, but it was not to last. The first few paragraphs of the story are reprinted below:

Long, long ago, there was a clever and brave girl called Goldflower who lived with her mother and brother. They were very happy.

One day, her mother said, "Your Aunty is ill. I'm going to see her and won't be back tonight. Look after your brother and ask your Granny to stay with you tonight!" Then she left with a basket of eggs and a hen.

At sunset, Goldflower herded the sheep home. After penning up the sheep, she shooed all the chickens into the coop. Then, she and her brother climbed a small hill to call Granny. Usually, after one shout, there would be an answer, but today there was no reply after several shouts. Goldflower thought, "It doesn't matter. I'm not afraid." They went home and she bolted the door.

Lighting a wick, they sat by the fire-pan and she began to tell her brother a story. Suddenly they heard a knock at the door. Brother hugged her and cried, "I'm afraid!"

They heard a strange but kindly voice saying, "I'm Granny." Brother was very happy and shouted, "Sister, open the door! Granny has come!" Goldflower leaned against the door and asked, "Is that you, Granny? What's wrong with your voice?" (Zipes, 1983)

At this point, the students were asked, "What can be wrong with Granny's voice?", and then were given the following instructions: "Before turning the page, do you want to change any of your guesses about what might happen in the story? Do it quickly and then read on!"

By this time the students were keen to revise their first guesses and were pointing out similarities to *Little Red Riding Hood*. At the end of the story, the students were told that *Goldflower and the Bear* was a Chinese "version" of this tale and they were read some background information about it from Jack Zipes' (1983) fascinating collection of Red Riding Hood tales called *The Trials and Tribulations of Little Red Riding Hood*.

We decided it was time to return to the guesses the children had made prior to reading before their sense of producing the reading had become completely naturalized again. We wanted them to recall their sense of surprise at their ability to predict so much about not only a story they had not read but about a genre of tales, and to consider how so many predictions were similar, and why even those that were different, were recognizable. We asked the students to complete the following task:

You made guesses before you read *Goldflower and the Bear*. You could have guessed *anything* but you probably made many guesses which other people in your class did too.

Before you read the story did you guess that:

	Yes	No
Goldflower was a plant?		
Goldflower was a person?		
Goldflower was a girl?		
Goldflower was a boy?		
Goldflower was an alien?		
Goldflower might visit the bear's house?		
The bear might try to eat someone?		
Goldflower might eat the bear's food?		
The bear might be able to talk?		
Someone might trick the bear?		
Someone might need saving?		

The bear might be killed?

Goldflower might be killed?

The characters might live in the woods?

The characters might live in a spaceship?

We emphasized to the students that they had made lots of guesses about the story of *Goldflower and the Bear* before they read it, which were correct or could have been, and that without realizing it perhaps, they were able to draw on a great deal of knowledge that they had already built up by listening to, reading, and talking about stories. To make the task of talking about what they knew about stories more accessible, we broke down this knowledge into four suggestions that roughly relate to ideas about character, plot and genre.

You know a lot about what stories are like and about how particular kinds of stories might go:

- you can describe the sorts of characters in stories,

- you can describe the sorts of things that happen in stories,

- you can make guesses about what might happen next in a story,

- you can tell the difference between different kinds of stories,

We then asked the students to consider in terms of these suggestions just how they were able to make predictions about stories. They offered reasons to do with their having read and heard lots of stories and that stories were often similar and so on. Up to this point, although the students' contribution to the production of meaning had been acknowledged in a general sense (i.e., that they brought to the reading a lot of information and prior knowledge) the perception of the story being in the text had not been challenged.

READING FOR A STORY

An assertion of the necessity of considering how texts are read was followed by a short activity (adapted from Moon, 1990) that was fun and also powerful in that the students were gratifyingly surprised by it. The students were given a list of words beginning with the letter *A* and asked to try reading the list as a story and then to tell their story to a partner. This is the list:

Adolescent

Angry

Accelerate

Attention

Accident

Ambulance

We explained some of the words and talked briefly about ideas for reading this as a story and then asked them to try. Most pairs came up with little stories. How amazing, we said, that we can read a list of words, all beginning with *A*, as a story. Not so, the students said; "it is clearly a trick. You have put the words into order so that they tell a story—there it is on the page." So, the students were asked:

> Is it a trick? Is it possible to read the list as a story *only* because the words have been put in a special order to make a little story?

> Test it out! Change the order of the words. Experiment with putting the words in different orders. Can you still read the list as a story?

> Share the results of your experiments in your group.

Students wrote each word on a small separate piece of paper, which they could then move easily into different orders (alphabetical, random, etc.). The students were surprised by their continuing ability to read a story from the lists they put together (and for the purposes of the exercise we did not ask whether some orders were easier than others, or why). Again, we attempted to provide a way of thinking about how they were able to read the lists as stories by providing a framework. For those who feel this is too prescriptive, it would be possible not to give such a framework. A general question such as, "How were you able to read the lists as stories?" may be all that is needed.

But, one way of thinking about this question is that it is actually signaling what it is that we were trying to teach to students at this point, or indicating what it was that we wanted them to learn. The activities were designed to support that learning, but students may still need to be provided with a means of constructing a reading of those activities, unless we really are happy for students to answer "It's a trick, I haven't a clue" or "It's magic." At times, of course, those could be answers with which we might be happy, but in this case, we were not aiming to teach that reading was a matter of trickery, or totally mysterious or completely magical. We therefore suggested to students that they already had learned to expect particular things when reading stories, and so they were likely to supply them if they were missing. The aforementioned list did not have characters, or a plot or events, or an ending in the way we have learned to expect if we are reading a story. We asked them to think about their reading of the lists as stories in these terms:

> To read the lists you made as stories, you could have done some or all of these things:
>
> • imagined a character or characters and what they could be like,
>
> • imagined events and how they might happen,
>
> • made connections between events and characters,
>
> • thought about what characters might do,
>
> • thought about what might happen to these characters,
>
> • combined events in a particular order,
>
> • tried to bring the parts of your story together to make an ending, or
>
> • used words that you expect to read in a particular kind of story.

Again, we should say that these suggestions were not intended to reveal the true nature of texts or the reading process, but rather to give a way of talking about how readers might produce readings from texts in terms of particular requirements—in this case, to read a story from a list.

This was to prepare the students for the requirement to read a particular text in different ways, in order to teach an adjustment of the traditional reading of the tale in favor of a feminist reading. That is, we planned to use the strategy of problematizing the initial reading of a text in order to teach students how to produce an alternative reading. (This of course did not guarantee the success of such an objective; we have both taught the full stop and punctuation of speech openly and directly with mixed results.)

READINGS OF GENDER, RACE, AND CLASS

Traditional versions of *Scheherazade* now are a bit of a worry for many readers who have learned a feminist reading practice; the disposal of so many young women, before rewarding Scheherazade with his hand in marriage, does make the Sultan appear less of a catch than he was before feminist criticism. Nevertheless, an uninterrupted reading can achieve a stolid reaction from younger students who are familiar, after all, with reading "true love conquers all" as the leit motif of all kinds of texts. That the violence to a succession of unfortunate young women who lack Scheherazade's stand-up storytelling abilities is accepted without comment by students however, is, disrupted easily by swapping the genders of the protagonists. Rewriting the tale as the story of a wicked queen with a taste for nights with young knights—*ScheHISazade*—produces almost instant protest (He is nice; she is *so* mean). It is then possible to argue that a reading of the Sultan as deserving of Sheherazade is at the very least strange, and to use the reading of *ScheHISazade* to contest the traditional reading of *Scheherazade*—with a feminist one. In short, it becomes possible to shift the reading of the story to another reading regime or field of practice; one in which gender-related issues are problematized and adjusted according to certain social norms.

Another activity we have used to teach a feminist reading of the story is to stop the reading at the point where Scheherazade has succeeded in entertaining the Sultan with her stories for 1,001 nights, and then to provide two endings described as feminist alternatives to the traditional ending (Mellor & Patterson, 1996). These are analyzed in terms of the changes made from the traditional ending. The students are then read a story such as *The Thrush Girl* in which a prince who kills two princesses finally meets a princess who shows herself smart enough to stay alive in his company and is thus rewarded by marriage to him (they live happily ever after, of course). The students are taught to use the feminist endings from *Scheherazade* as models, to write a feminist ending to the tale.

This may be criticized as unacceptably normative practice. What might be less likely to meet with criticism is an activity that invites students to construct a range of readings from multiple reading positions made available by subjecting *Scheherazade* to critical scrutiny and then asking students to choose among the readings produced. We suggest that it is assumed by critical literacy pedagogy that once truly conscious, students will choose a feminist reading, which, we argue, is what is required. This, after all, is surely the point of problematizing the dominant or preferred reading by making available alternative readings? That is, the judgement that the dominant or preferred reading is in need of adjusting is the motive for producing a range of readings. Why problematize it otherwise? It is also interesting that an emphasis on students producing their own readings or interpretations (often argued to be the goal of critical literacy pedagogy; (Scholes, 1982, 1985) is suspended at this point; the initial readings produced by students are rarely accepted as their own readings. Rather, they are seen as unconscious readings produced when the students are at the mercy of dominant readings.

The proposal that teaching students how to produce multiple readings should be the focus of teachers' attention and not which readings are produced or selected by students is only tenable, we suggest, if we accept either the theoretical proposition that the availability of multiple reading positions will guarantee desirable readings; or if we are willing (and able) to tolerate (and manage) the practical implications of the articulation of sexist, racist, and class-prejudiced readings invited in the name of plurality, difference, and freedom in our classrooms.

We now see our aim of reading *Scheherazade* and other texts like it in different ways not as the unblinding of the student with regard to readings of male violence through the revelations afforded by the availability of multiple reading positions and the freedom to choose. Rather, the aim is to teach the production of a particular reading of a text in terms of the adjustment of particular social norms related to gender and violence. But this acknowledgement produces other problems.

A QUESTION OF EMPOWERMENT?

In Australia at least, current critical literacy models promote the empowerment of students to resist particular readings, thereby allowing the production of other previously silenced readings. Now, however, it seems to us, that we must think of empowerment not simply in terms of resistance and as something different from power, but in terms of the capacity to argue for specific readings (e.g., feminist and antiracist readings) and their production as alternatives to others. That is, we have come to feel that we have to acknowledge the normativity of our practice in arguing for the production of particular readings over others—admit, indeed, to the use of power, not simply to the resisting of others' uses of power.

We hope by now that it is clear that we are not arguing for a reading practice that aims for the production of plurality and difference in the hope of revealing the good reading hidden by the bad reading deceitfully posing as the single right reading of the text. Nor, however, are we arguing against multiple readings. In particular reading regimes or fields of practices, the production of multiple or alternative readings is a requirement. For example, the reading of a poem is regarded as always incomplete; there are always more readings to be produced of it (although a temporary agreement is reached for assessment purposes). Although it is possible to consider all texts—alphabetical lists, bus tickets, scientific formulae, road signs, stove installation instructions—as sites for the production of multiple readings, usually readers do not. There is a need, we argue here, to acknowledge that, at times, for reasons that may be more or less, mundane, we may want to teach a specific reading over others. It seems to us also that the teaching of multiple readings of Hitler's *Mein Kampf* might be dismissed in favor of teaching a specific reading of it as racist. Finally, we do not see these as arguments for normativity against the present freedom of the reading classroom. Our argument is that the reading classroom is already highly and inescapably normative, and that as teachers of reading, we need to declare this—both to ourselves and to our students. At the risk of being repetitive, then, we are not arguing against producing multiple readings but rather against the proposition that the practice of producing multiple readings frees students to escape the oppressions of normative readings. The other mundane point that bears repetition is that multiple readings are not encouraged for every text; although a bus timetable might be read in multiple ways, it probably is not that helpful if you want to catch a bus.

Of course, the problems do not disappear with an acknowledgment of the normativity of our practices. Recently, a pragmatic view—"So what if we're normative?"—has become apparent in discussion, and arguments have been made for the explicit teaching of the features of critical reading practices simply as requirements. However where the requirements of critical literacy intersect (as they must by definition) with ethical issues of ethnicity, class, and gender, the difficulties cannot be underestimated. Would racist students be willing to produce antiracist interpretations of texts simply to fulfil requirements? We are not sure, but invert that question—would antiracist students be willing to produce racist interpretations of texts to fulfill requirements—and the problems leap into focus. Although the reading lesson seeks to operate in ways that will allow students to choose freely, its critical aims are tied inevitably (and historically) to concepts of social good, which are highly normative. This need not mean that we must abandon the idea of a political project related to reading education. On the contrary, Meredyth (1993) argues that:

> the more prepared we are to acknowledge the historically-based argument that the classroom is a key site for the governmental production and adjustment of the 'norms of life', [or social norms] the more possible it becomes to regard these pedagogic norms of life as contingent, variable and adjustable. (p.229)

There is little reason to doubt, she adds that "this would assist equity-based educational and social reforms" (p. 229). However, such attempted adjustment of the norms of life, which include the teaching of antiracist, antisexist readings, cannot be done while denying our normativity and our use of power. Nor does the defiant embracing of a political radicalism, with its undertones of resistance and struggle, provide an answer in itself; although it may be attractive to many literacy teachers, for entirely predictable reasons, it does not solve the normativity problems. It seems to us that however historically uncomfortable it is, we will have to acknowledge that critical pedagogy is itself inseparable from the exercise of pastoral power (Hunter, 1994).

CONCLUSION

In many respects, the activities described previously work with students in that they encourage young readers to view reading as a practice or as the operation of sets of techniques for producing a specific reading or readings. We are not claiming to reveal the processes of reading. What we have done is describe some of the ideas that informed our wish to study texts with younger students and indicated some of our theoretical concerns and questions. A problem we faced in putting together and trying out the materials was how to give the students access to the kind of analysis we were proposing. In the vast majority of Australian schools, analysis is not usually seen as part of the game for younger students: There is the fear that it may diminish enjoyment and prove too difficult. In practice, these fears were not realized. The approaches we used begin with many children's expertise with folk and fairy tales, in most cases a genre with which they have become familiar through home and school reading. They rely heavily on reading activities to theorize the techniques involved and the practices deployed in producing specific readings. In reading these texts, students showed themselves to be confident about even quite complex textual theorizing.

REFERENCES

Browne, A. (1981). *Hansel and Gretel.* London: Little Mommoth Books.
Foucault, M. (1977). Truth and power. In P. Rabinow (Ed.), *The Foucault reader* (pp. 51–75). London: Peregrine-Penguin.
Gilbert, P. (1992). The story so far: Gender, literacy and social regulation. *Gender and Education, 4*(3), 185–199.
Hunter, I. (1994). Four anxieties about English. *Interpretations, 27*(3), 1–19.
Janks, H. (1997). Critical language awareness: Theory and practice. *Interpretations, 30*(1), 1–29.
Mellor, B., & Patterson, A. (1996). *Investigating texts.* Cottesloe, Australia: Chalkface. Urbana, Illinois: N.C.T.E. (2001).
Meredyth, D. (1993). Marking the immeasurable: Debates on ASAT. In D. Meredyth & D. Tyler (Eds.), *Child and citizen: Genealogies of schooling and subjectivity.* (pp.207–235). Brisbane, Australia: Institute for Cultural Policy Studies, Griffith University.
Moon, B. (1990). *Literacy terms: A practical glossary.* Cottesloe, Western Australia: Chalkface. Urbana, Illinois: N.C.T.E. (1999).
Moon, B. (1994). Rethinking resistance: English and critical consciousness. *Interpretations, 27*(3), 48–70.
Scholes, R. (1982). *Semiotics and interpretation.* New Haven: Yale.
Scholes, R. (1985). *Textual power: Literary theory and the teaching of English.* New Haven: Yale.
Zipes, J. (1983). *The trials and tribulations of Little Red Riding Hood: Versions of the tale in sociocultural context.* Massachusetts: Bergin & Garvey.

Critical Literacies
and Questions of Identity

Identity and Conflict in the Critical Literacy Classroom

Hilary Janks
University of the Witwatersrand, Johannesburg

This research on the development of Critical Language Awareness (CLA) materials for use in South African secondary schools took place from 1989 to 1991, during a turbulent period of South African history. When I began, at the height of the struggle against apartheid, there was little possibility of the materials being allowed into state schools; by 1991 the changes in the country enabled publishers to risk publishing them and teachers to risk trialling them. In 1993, six workbooks, designed to teach students about the relation between language and power, were published as the *Critical Language Awareness Series* (Janks, 1993a). Each workbook consists of 24 pages of critical literacy activities based on everyday media texts and valuing multiliteracies and linguistic diversity.

The pilot workbook, *Language and Position* (Janks, 1993b) focuses on different reading positions, in which *reading* is used broadly to incorporate the interpretation of print and non-print texts, both spoken and visual. Students are encouraged to provide a number of different readings and to think of meaning as plural and contested. This workbook was drafted in consultation with teachers who were involved in the research project. The materials were then redesigned on the basis of ongoing feedback from the teachers and feedback from the students once they had used the materials. What we learned as a result of piloting the first workbook informed the design of subsequent workbooks.

The findings reported in this chapter follow the teaching of *Language and Position* (Janks, 1993b) in seven schools in South Africa during 1991. Here I try to make sense of what happened in one of the classrooms in one of the research schools when these materials were used with students from across the divides created by apartheid. In order to do this it is necessary to provide an overview of the sociohistorical context in which the research took place.

THE SOUTH AFRICAN CONTEXT

The research on which this chapter is based took place from 1989 to 1991 during a significant period of South African history. In 1986, P.W. Botha, the State President, declared a countrywide state of emergency, which was renewed annually until June 1990. State of emergency regulations gave the Minister of Law and Order and the police wide powers to curb unrest. In South Africa *unrest* was the word used by the state and the media to describe any form of political insurrection or disturbance. Using these powers, the state closed down newspapers or seized specific editions; it banned 32 organizations, including many working in education; and by February 1989 the state was holding 3,707 people in detention without trial, causing the prisons to be overpopulated by 80% (Race Relations Survey, 1988/1989). Despite the emergency measures, "1988 was the most violent in South Africa's history," with 5,028 incidents of violence (Race Relations Survey, 1988/1989).

At the beginning of 1989, when this research began, South Africa was in its third successive year under a state of emergency and the antiapartheid struggle was at its height. The mass democratic movement, a loose alliance of antigovernment organizations, continued to organize resistance to the state. This reached a climax in the 1989 defiance campaign to protest the September general election in which Indians, "coloreds" and Whites voted for representation in the tricameral parliament, while the Black majority in the country remained unenfranchised.

By the beginning of 1989, there were signs that the state was vulnerable to both external and internal pressures. In November 1988, South Africa agreed to begin the process that would lead to Namibian independence on March 21, 1990. In April 1989, South Africa reactivated the 1984 Nkomati accord with Mozambique. It became clear that South Africa could no longer maintain hostilities with her neighbors.

Internally, a successful and prison-wide hunger strike by detainees, in February 1989, led to the release of most detainees and the collapse of detention as an instrument of repression. In August of the same year P. W. Botha resigned and F. W. De Klerk was elected as the new State President after the September general election. In his opening address to Parliament on February 2, 1990, De Klerk announced a number of changes aimed at paving the way for negotiations. These included the unbanning of the African National Congress (ANC), the Pan-African Congress (PAC) and the South African Communist Party (SACP); the unbanning of the organizations restricted by the state of emergency including many student and teacher organizations; the future release of political prisoners imprisoned for nonviolent activities; a stay of executions; and the lifting of all the media and education emergency regulations (Race Relations Survey, 1989/1990). On February 11, 1990, Nelson Mandela was released after spending 27 years in prison and, in June the 4-year-old state of emergency was lifted in all but one of the provinces.

From 1990 to 1994, negotiations took place amid ugly violence with perpetrators and victims across the political spectrum. The year in which this classroom research took place, 1991, was one of dramatic transformation that ended with a multiparty conference for a democratic South Africa that failed to reach agreement.

CRITICAL LANGUAGE AWARENESS AND ITS IMPORTANCE IN THE SOUTH AFRICAN CONTEXT

Because CLA focuses on the relation between language and power and is particularly interested in the way language is used to maintain and contest relations of domination, education in CLA can contribute to processes of resistance and transformation by denaturalizing dominant discourses. This denaturalization inhibits the manufacture of consent achieved by the distribution and circulation of these discourses. Critical reading of the media was important in South Africa because these were tightly controlled by the state. This control was particularly repressive during the successive states of emergency when newspapers were censored or banned and there was no independent television. CLA, which places language study in the context of power relations, can provide students with the means to see through the positions that shape the linguistic forms. In addition it can help them to understand how the linguistic forms are themselves used to shape perceptions.

CLA is the term coined by the Language-Ideology-Power research group at Lancaster University (Clark, Fairclough, Ivanic, & Martin-Jones, 1987; Fairclough, 1989, 1992) and refers to the same theoretical underpinnings and practices that go by the name of *critical literacy* in Australia. Both use concepts from critical theory such as *ideology* (Althusser, 1970; Eagleton, 1991; Thompson, 1984, 1990), *subject position* (Althusser, 1970), *preferred reading* (Hall, 1980), *intertextuality* (Kristeva, cited in Talbot, 1991), *naturalized conventions* (Clark et al., 1987), *myth* (Barthes, 1973), the *plurality of meaning* (Volosinov, 1973), and *determinism versus agency* (Giroux, 1983).

These concepts inform the workbooks in the series and are translated into exercises that students can recognize as part of their own lived experience. For example in *Language and Position* (Janks, 1993b) students are asked to think about how spectators at a football match might disagree about the referee's ruling according to where they are sitting; they are asked to think about issues that parents and children are likely to disagree about because of their different ages. The workbook builds student understanding of position by working from physical and then geographical positioning through social and historical positioning to an integrated exploration of the contextual determinants of meaning. The workbook as a whole aims to foster critical literacy (for a more detailed description of *Language and Position* see Janks & Ivanic, 1992).

THE RESEARCH SCHOOL

The discussion in this chapter focuses on the results obtained in one of the secondary schools used in the research project. This school is an independent school that opened its doors to students of all races before it was legally allowed to do so and that does not use race as a criterion for admission. More than half the student body is Black. Many of the students in the school receive bursary support and come from working-class homes. In South Africa, academic standards vary across schools and within and across racially divided departments of education, so teachers in the research project were asked to choose the level in their particular school for which they thought the materials would be suitable. In this school the workbook was used with grade 10 students, who were 15 to 16 years old. Grade 10 is the middle year in a 5-year secondary school program. In all the other schools the materials were taught in grade 11 or grade 12.

At this particular independent school students are treated as young adults. They are taught to question everything and to challenge anything including their teachers. Their views are taken seriously and they learn to be confident, outspoken, and vociferous. The school does not impose the strict discipline enforced by corporal punishment and a system of detentions then common in most South African high schools. Instead of a prefect system there is an elected students' representative council that has a voice in the governing of the school. In the South African context the school has a reputation of being somewhat alternative and unconventional. It was this understanding of the context that led me to believe that the materials would be most successful in this school but they were not.

What I had not taken enough cognisance of is that schooling teaches students that questions have right and wrong answers. This is most obvious in South Africa in the system of external matriculation examinations that teachers have to prepare students for. Poststructuralist theory teaches us that meaning is plural, not singular, that words, expressions, propositions, and so on, change their meaning according to the positions held by those who use them (Pecheux, 1975). Bakhtin (1981) taught us that meaning is dialogic yet our educational practices, which privilege rational deliberation, reflection, and debate, teach students to seek closure.

CLOSED MEANINGS IN SCHOOL

Student response to the pilot workbook was obtained by questionnaire and interview. I also interviewed the teachers. It is not my intention to report on the questionnaire in detail here (a full report on this research can be found in Janks, 1995). Suffice it to say that the questionnaire used a sampling procedure requiring students to respond to all the odd-numbered pages that an independent group of experts had judged to be representative of the workbook as a whole. The response to the first few pages was positive and then rapidly became more negative. What I do want to report on are the interviews that I conducted as it is this qualitative data that explains the students' negative responses in the questionnaire. These interviews were video-taped and subsequently transcribed. I interviewed all the students who were willing to be recorded, 10 out of 57 students (P), as well as both the teachers (T).

The students provided two main reasons for their disaffection with the materials. First, the students found the workbook boring because it labors the idea that meaning shifts according to one's position, physical, social, political, ideological:

P6: As it went on the content was different but the meaning was sort of the same.

P5: When you're repeating things you're just emphasizing on trying to get your message across. Emphasizing on the importance of how position affects your point of view.

Second, the workbook generated conflict in the classroom that the students and the teachers were unable to resolve. One such conflict-producing exercise occurred on page 6 of the 27-page pilot workbook. The page was headed *Standpoint or point of view*:

Work in pairs or in a group.

1. Who should look after the children? Do you think that men and women are likely to have the same or different positions about this? Why?

2. Give an example of an issue on which children and their parents are likely to disagree because of their different ages.

3. Do you think that people from a minority group in a population might have different views from people who are in the majority? If so, what about?

4. In 1926 English and Afrikaans became the two official languages of South Africa. How might people's standpoint on this issue be affected by the South African language that they speak?

The following page, page 7, states that this exercise showed us that our point of view may be affected by our gender, our age, our membership of a minority or majority group or by our membership of a language community. This page was headed *Positions based on who we are*, and included the following exercise:

1. In small groups list all the other factors you can think of that are likely to affect our standpoint on issues in our society.
   Combine the answers from the different groups in order to discover how many factors the whole class could find.
   Now that you have some idea of how many different things affect our points of view, you are ready to consider the next question. This is something for the whole class to discuss.

2. Can we choose to think what we think?

   OR

   Do the social circumstances in which we live make us think what we think?

   OR

   Is it a bit of both?

   It may help you to think about something specific. For example, how does living in South Africa affect people's attitudes to school? To race? To violence?

The intention was to get students to understand the concept of subject position and the balance between social determinism and human agency. In order to do this, students were required to stand back from the actual difference of views and generate the range of possible views from different subject positions. This is clear in question 1 on page 6, which has 3 parts. The first part focuses on the actual difference of views by asking "Who should look after the children?"; the second part asks students to examine the possibility of gender differences on this issue; and the third part, "Why?" asks students to account for such differences. Three interesting things happened: Firstly the students were unable to get beyond Part 1, the actual difference of views, secondly the students did not differ with one another only on the basis of gender but of race, and thirdly a few of the Black students chose this as an arena to contest dominant (for them, "White") practices in the school. In a nutshell, the White students, mainly girls, adopted a strong feminist position and the Black boys defended the idea that patriarchy was part of Black culture because:

> P5: Coming from an African family or society the woman is expected to look after the children and do chores like that.

> P1: The Black girls themselves didn't really fight didn't argue. It was like they seemed to accept that they must stay at home because that was their culture and the White girls got really upset.

> P2: And in our class the Black females in our standard don't do anything, they just sit there, they accept it.

The Black girls were very reticent and none of them was prepared to be interviewed. Unlike Pupils 1 and 2, the teacher believes that the Black girls did speak in this lesson.

> T1: The Black girls don't say a word.... For once the White kids were on the side of the Black girls against the Black boys.... We were saying why do they need to be educated? They were saying they need a certain amount of education but it's their role to look after the children. The Black girls were getting incited because the White girls were pushing them and me as well because [I] was getting involved because on the one hand you're asking for education and then you're limiting people because they're only fit for ... I was trying to get them to see that sexism and racism are the same thing but they refused to see it. They absolutely refused to see.

I: Any idea why?

T1:   They said it was their culture. After class the Black girls said they're right [the boys] that is what we are.

I: Did the Black girls say anything [in class]?

T1:   They did in class they took the boys on. They sit in front of them and physically turned around to argue with them. But that was in class. After class when they had lost the support of the White kids they actually said they are right that's what our culture dictates.

Before moving on to an analysis of what happened it is important to get a sense of how angry and heated this discussion or disagreement was:

P5:   Maybe you heard ... how sometimes the debates got so hot that people sometimes stormed out stormed out of the class angry with us, and sometimes we being angry with them because we think that they don't think they're just trying to be stupid sometimes.

P2:   Our class we just fought like you wouldn't believe.

P7:   For example for many of the Black students ... if anybody disagreed with them they would actually literally say "shut up" to you and "I'm not prepared to speak to you." Those were their exact words and when you've got people like that it was the attitude not the conflict that was problem causing.

P4:   When you put political things in ... [it] always ends up in arguments usually Blacks against Whites.

P3:   It just causes problems.

I: What kind of problems?

P4:   Racial problems and everyone starts accusing the other person of being a racist ...

P3:   and people get all argumentative ...

P4:   and that's the end of the lesson.

Nobody at any stage was able to stand back from the conflict and reflect on what was happening in the classroom in relation to the central idea of the *Language and Position* workbook. In terms of what the workbook is saying it is not at all surprising that students who because of apartheid have grown up in such different worlds should have such different positions. Despite the fact that students claim that the materials repeat the message about different meanings tied to different positions they are clearly not able to apply the message to their own lives. They appear to understand the point theoretically but politically and psychologically they need to defend their point of view and this produces serious conflict in the classroom.

This is confirmed by related work in the United States, reported in the *Harvard Educational Review* (Tatum, 1992). Tatum, who has many years of experience in teaching a course on the psychology of racism, maintains that insufficient attention has been given to the issues of process that inevitably emerge in the classroom when attention is focused on race, class, or gender. "The introduction of these issues of oppression often generates powerful emotional responses in students that range from guilt and shame to anger and despair. If not addressed these emotional responses can result in resistance to oppression-related content areas" (p. 2).

Weiler (1991), writing about feminist pedagogy, says:

> In settings in which students come from differing positions of privilege or oppression, the sharing of experience raises conflicts rather than building solidarity. In these circumstances, the collective exploration of experience leads not to a common knowledge and solidarity based on sameness, but to the tensions of an articulation of difference. (p. 469)

Ellsworth (1989), in an article entitled *Why doesn't this feel empowering? Working through the repressive myths of critical pedagogy,* raises important questions about the limitations of rational discourse and the extent to which myths of the ideal rational person and the universality of propositions have been oppressive to those who are not European, White, male, middle-class, Christian, able-bodied, thin, and heterosexual. She stressed that poststructuralist thought is not bound to reason but to discourse made up of partial narratives. "Partial in the sense that they are unfinished, imperfect, limited; and partial in the sense that they project the interest of 'one side' over others" (p. 305).

Where students have been schooled to believe that meaning is singular and that there are right or wrong answers it becomes important for them to convince the others that their position is right. There is a great deal at stake where, if one is not right, one is necessarily wrong. They fight about which culture is better and admitting defeat is betraying one's own culture:

> P5: That's what always happens we always have different point of views from the Africans according and the Whites. If I say Africans I mean like Black students. There's always a clash. We (the Black students) sometimes prefer … to drop it because it always gets into a hot debate about which culture is better.

This debate is not based on rational argument. Rather, it is psychological and political. It is psychological in the sense that students' identities are at stake and it is political in that the Black students' struggle is an attempt to win power for their meanings. There is evidence in the interviews that these students feel alienated in the school. It is as if the school is predicated on White meanings. The language of instruction is English, almost all the teachers are White, the textbooks and examinations were designed for White education, White values are hegemonic. Some of these students, no longer willing to accept the status quo that disempowers them, challenge the dominant practices and values, knowing that it will cause a clash and sometimes preferring to drop it. What they are really contesting is the way in which their schooling, in failing to recognize their meanings, is racist. Much of this is probably happening below the level of consciousness and the students may simply be responding angrily to their feelings of alienation.

On the surface what is happening in the classroom is an argument about who should look after the children. In the teacher's view it "wasn't a racial thing." In the heat of the moment, no one understands what is really at stake or why the argument is so angry and so painful. As a result the Black students' struggle to empower themselves within the school emancipates no one.

The *us* and *them* language of all the interviews reveals the opposing camps. This racial divide is also apparent from the way the students choose to sit in class. The teacher says that when she had the desks arranged in a U-shape, the White students sat opposite the Black students with nobody electing to sit in the desks joining the long-ends of the U. Now that the desks are arranged in an L-shape, the Black students sit along one arm of the L and the White students along the other "and never the twain shall meet" (Teacher). In the words of two White students:

> P8: [The school is] supposed to be integrated and all that but truthfully we don't integrate.
>
> P7: … Especially for a nonracial environment [the school] is particularly racial, it really is.

The Black students claim moreover that the teacher sides with the White students in the conflict:

P5: Like because the teacher once, once we started the debate she didn't realize it, she in a way took the sides of the other students like specially when we came to the thing of who's supposed to look after the children and in the end we were having everybody fighting but not realizing that that's the point of the book to try and teach us something about our point of views ...

This perception is confirmed by the teacher. Sharing the position of the White girls in the class, she was unable to mediate the discussion:

T1: The teacher also thinks that her culture is right.... Well it was probably happening with me as well. [I] can't help but getting upset and involved and then you look as if you're on the White kids side and they're right because you are.

The students and the teacher have multiple subjectivities. For the Black boys both race and gender are important. In order to contest their subjugation on the basis of race, they assert their cultural right to be patriarchal. If the teacher accepts this then she promotes gender domination. If she refuses this then she is promoting the White hegemony of the school. In fact if the teacher does the latter then it is further proof that the school supports western values and needs to be contested. Is there a way out of this problem that makes pedagogic sense?

To begin with we need to recognize some of the good that is happening. In 1991, Gaganakis, writing about Black students in open schools in South Africa in 1988 said:

Their mode of adaptation to the school is essentially conformist. This conformity, which is for Woods (1979) "a near or complete identification with the goals and means of the school" and "the meeting of organisational requirements without fuss or contradiction" (p. 19), manifests itself in the following beliefs and practices.... Their deference to the authority structures of the school ...; their acceptance of the schools' dominant ethos; ... and their perception of school knowledge as legitimate. (pp. 84–85)

Viewed against this background, the Black students in the open school in this study have come a long way. One of the significant differences is that in the open schools in Gaganakis' (1991) research only 5% of students were Black; this is an estimate based on figures from Freer and Christie

(1988). In the school I am considering, 50% of the students are African Black, and in this class it is even higher: 65%.

There is a good deal of evidence from the interview with the teacher that tensions already existed in the school. The focus on language and power provides a space for students to deal with these tensions. One of the clear findings of the research is that it is not easy to predict what text will ignite in different contexts. The contentious "who should look after the children" text was one of the most successful in an all-Black school in the research project. These students did not share the static view of culture held by the boys in the open school, who understand culture as "sets of beliefs and traditional values which are handed down to us in immutable form" (Gaganakis, 1991, p. 74). It is a view of culture that also sees blacks as a unified and undifferentiated cultural entity.

Since 1994, with a new constitution for South Africa that entrenches gender equality in law, there is a common moral reference for teachers and students that was not available when the materials were first used in schools. At the time, in 1991, one of the ways of helping students to rethink their unitary and static view of Black culture might have been to ensure that their reading included literature written by Black South African writers, to show that feminism is not exclusively White or Western. For the girls who were silent when confronted with a choice between their culture and those "women's meanings," which free them from the roles ascribed to them by patriarchy, there are many powerful Black women writers who can speak for them and to them. And the boys may have been more willing to hear these voices than the voice of their White teacher.

The students need to understand that domination takes many different forms. The Black students in the class need feminist novels that convey the effects of gender domination, and the White students need to understand the oppressive effects of White cultural hegemony. There are many postcolonial writers who articulate this struggle for cultural freedoms (Ngũgĩ, 1993).

CONCLUSION: THE IMPORTANCE OF OPEN MEANINGS

In a paper entitled *Critical Language Awareness and emancipatory discourse,* Ivanic and I (Janks & Ivanic, 1992) maintained that if one reads a text from a particular subject position, another reading may only be possible from another subject position. It is not always possible to put oneself in another subject position or sometimes even to conceive that another subject position exists. Groups made up of people from different social backgrounds, who do not share the same common sense, are unlikely to have the same reading of a text. They can therefore learn from one another. The range of perspectives available in the group serves to denaturalize all perspectives. Multilingual, multiracial, multicultural, mixed-gender classrooms provide an ideal environment in which people can test their own readings against those of others. If the group is socially heterogeneous enough then members of the group can be encouraged to articulate a range of meanings based on who they are and where they fit in to the whole social fabric. As it turned out this did not happen in practice. What we had not anticipated was the extent to which students might be invested in their own meanings; the extent to which students might feel the need in their class and in their school to win power and recognition for their own meanings and be unable to value the meanings of others. This research has produced evidence that where students perceive school meaning to be closed and excluding of their meanings, this contributes to conflict. What it also shows is that when classroom materials or other reading matter touches something sacred to a student, the student is not happy to have his or her own closed meanings opened out. Interview data from the other research schools suggests that sacred meanings are those that for the students, are constitutive of their identity and that therefore, "attack the fibre of their belief" (T5: Interview 15).

Because CLA can destabilize the discourses that construct students' multiple identities, it requires an environment in which it is safe for students to take risks. It is not enough for teachers to create secure contexts in their own classes. The environment of the school also needs to support communicative openness and transformative exploration. What is needed is openness that goes beyond the opening of doors; an understanding that meaning itself is open, and that attempts to close it are attempts to disempower other meanings. It is for this reason that a poststructuralist approach to reading, that teaches students to understand that meaning is plural and that different readings are tied to different social and historical conditions of possibility, may help students to understand the partial and interested nature of all discourse and all readings including their own.

REFERENCES

Althusser, L. (1970). Ideology and ideological state apparatuses. *Essays on ideology*. London: Verso.

Bakhtin, M. (1981). Discourse in the novel. In C. Emerson & M. Holquist (Eds.), *The dialogic imagination: Four essays by M. Bakhtin* (pp. 259–422). Austin, TX: University of Texas.

Barthes, R. (1973). Myth to-day. In A. Lavers (Ed.), *Mythologies* (pp. 109–159). London: Granada.

Clark, R., Fairclough, N., Ivanic, R., & Martin-Jones, M. (1987). *Critical language awareness* (Working paper series No. 1). United Kingdom: Centre for Language in Social Life, Lancaster University.

Eagleton, T. (1991). *Ideology*. London: Verso.

Ellsworth, E. (1989). Why doesn't this feel empowering? Working through repressive myths of critical pedagogy. *Harvard Educational Review, 59*(3), 297–324.

Fairclough, N. (1989). *Language and power*. London: Longman.

Fairclough, N. (Ed.). (1992). *Critical language awareness*. London: Longman.

Freer, D., & Christie, P. (1988). *The privilege of multicultural education*. Unpublished manuscript, University of the Witwatersrand, Johannesburg.

Gaganakis, M. (1991). Opening up the closed school: Conceptualising the presence of Black pupils in White schools. In D. Freer (Ed.), *Towards open schools: Possibilities and realities for non-racial schooling in South Africa* (pp. 73–93). Cape Town: Macmillan.

Giroux, H. (1983). *Theory and resistance in education—a pedagogy for the opposition*. London: Heinemann Educational.

Hall, S. (1980). Encoding/decoding. In S. Hall, D. Hobson, A. Lowe, & P. Willis (Eds.), *Culture, media, language* (pp. 128–138). London: Hutchinson.

Janks, H. (Ed.). (1993a). *Critical language awareness series*. Johannesburg: Hodder & Stoughton and Witwatersrand University.

Janks, H. (1993b). *Language and position*. Johannesburg: Hodder & Stoughton and Witwatersrand University.

Janks, H. (1995). *The research and development of critical language awareness materials for use in South African secondary schools*. Unpublished PhD thesis, Lancaster University, United Kingdom.

Janks, H., & Ivanic, R. (1992). Critical language awareness and emancipatory discourse. In N. Fairclough (Ed.), *Critical language awareness* (pp. 305–331). London: Longman.

Ngũgĩ wa Thiong›o. (1993). *Moving the centre: The struggle for cultural freedoms*. London: James Currey Heinemann.

Pecheux, M. (1982). *Language semantics and ideology: Stating the obvious* (H. Nagpal, Trans.). London: Macmillan. (Original work published 1975)

Race Relations Survey. (1988/1989). *Annual survey*. Johannesburg: Institute of South African Race Relations.

Race Relations Survey. (1989/1990). *Annual survey*. Johannesburg: Institute of South African Race Relations.

Talbot, M. (1991). *Critical language study and subjectivity, with a sample analysis of consumer femininity in two pages of a teenager's magazine*. Unpublished PhD thesis, Lancaster University, United Kingdom.

Tatum, B. D. (1992). Talking about race, learning about racism: The application of racial identity development theory in the classroom. *Harvard Educational Review, 62*(1), 1–24.

Thompson, J. B. (1984). *Studies in the theory of ideology*. Cambridge UK: Polity.

Thompson, J. B. (1990). *Ideology and modern culture*. Cambridge, UK: Polity.

Volosinov, V. N. (1986). *Marxism and the philosophy of language* (L. Matejka & I. R. Titunik, Trans.). New York: Seminar. (Original work published 1973)

Weiler, K. (1991). Freire and a feminist pedagogy of difference. *Harvard Educational Review, 61*(4), 449–474.

Woods, P. (1979). *The divided school*. London: Routledge & Kegan Paul.

10

Classrooms as Sites of Textual, Cultural, and Linguistic Reappropriation

Pippa Stein
University of the Witwatersrand, Johannesburg

In mainstream South African Schools, oral storytelling that draws on African theater and oral performance traditions is not a valued genre. The fact that the majority of Black students in urban schools use three or more languages in their daily lives is not generally regarded as a linguistic resource or incorporated into dominant pedagogical practice. Here I describe a project in multilingual storytelling practices that I conducted during 1994 with a class of 12- to16-year olds in a Black township school outside Johannesburg. The aim of the project was to explore the multilingual resources of a group of students who are learning all school subjects through English, which is their second or third language. What began as a project intending to focus on the uses of multilingualism in storytelling practices unexpectedly turned into an important project in the reappropriation and transformation of textual, cultural, and linguistic forms. Students started producing multimodal genres that had previously been infantalized or made invisible by the colonial and apartheid governments. They drew on a combination of African oral storytelling and performance traditions with contemporary film and television performance traditions in order to transform these genres for their own immediate purposes. I argue that the multimodal forms of the texts produced by the students provide evidence for the use of the classroom as a site for a pedagogy of reappropriation and transformation, but this process is dependent on innovative pedagogical practices that challenge dominant practices in schools.

BACKGROUND

South Africa is in its sixth year of democracy. Since the first democratic elections on April 27, 1994, the whole country has been engaged in massive processes of transformation, reconstruction, and development, from the macrolevels of government and policymaking to microlevels that affect the daily lives of ordinary citizens. In the educational arena, there have been far-reaching changes. The 17 education departments of the apartheid era, which previously divided school communities along the lines of race and language, have been collapsed in one unitary national education department; a new national qualifications framework has been drawn up; new school language policies, new curricula, and new assessment procedures are being implemented.

The project described here needs to be set against this shifting landscape of redefinition and change. I focus on possible ways in which the English classroom in South Africa can now become an important site for the institutional reappropriation and transformation of textual, cultural, and linguistic forms, which have previously either been marginalized, infantalized, or undervalued by the colonial and apartheid governments. The possibilities are now open, I think, to redefine or "redesign," to use the term of the New London Group Multiliteracies Project (Cope & Kalantzis, 2000) the relationship between mainstream and marginalized discourses in the language classroom. Drawing on the work of Roger Simon, Shirley Brice Heath, Bill Cope, Gunther Kress, Mary Kalantzis, Allan Luke and many others working in the field of literacy, language and pedagogy, I argue that what is needed in this moment of history in English classrooms in South Africa is a pedagogy of reappropriation and transformation. A pedagogy of reappropriation is a political project that seeks to make visible previously marginalized languages and discourses in the school context. However, reappropriation as a form of validation of marginalized discourses is only one part of this process: encouraging learners to freely draw on these languages and discourses in order to transform them for their own contemporary meaning-making or representational purposes, is another crucial part of this project. In multicultural classrooms, this process of reappropriation and transformation, if conducted with sensitivity

and awarenesss of all the interests at stake, can, I believe, lead to increased investment (Peirce, 1995) on the part of students in the language
learning process. This increased investment can lead to increased levels
of language learning. I believe that a pedagogy of reappropriation and
transformation can contribute toward building a critically reflective classroom community where all participants begin to share and re-evaluate the
relation between their histories, their engagement with popular cultural
forms and their language practices. At this time in our history, when we are
struggling with reinventing a new South African identity (or identities), this
process of re-evaluation, linked to developing a shared classroom discourse, is crucial.

I want to provide evidence for the implementation and benefits of such
a pedagogy from a case study of a year-long, classroom-based research
project I conducted in 1994 with a group of multilingual students in a
state-run primary school in a Black township area outside Johannesburg.
The project began a few weeks before the first democratic elections and
continued until the end of 1994. Similar projects based on this work have
been conducted subsequently in different sites. I shall discuss these im-
plementations later on in this article.

THE RESEARCH PROJECT

Working in the role of teacher-researcher, I was granted access to a Standard 5 class in a primary school run by the former segregated Black education department, the Department of Education (DET). The school is
well-run and situated on the border of a working-class and nouveau riche
Black township. Children from both communities attend the school.

The class consisted of 37 multilingual Black students, boys and girls,
ranging in age from 12 to 16. The average age for this level (Standard 5) is
13 years but there are many children in Black schools who have not had
regular schooling as a result of nationwide school boycotts and the
breakdown of schooling in the 1980s, hence the age range in this class.
The language of learning in this school is English, the home language of
10% of this class. All the other students are learning English as a second or
third language.

I began this project with a very broad question: What are the linguistic
resources that a group of students bring to this classroom in this specific
context at this time in our history? The motivation for this investigation was
to provide a body of data of the range of multilingual resources the students were using and bringing to the classroom in order to counter the predominantly deficit, and often linked to this, racist model about the
linguistic and cognitive capabilities of Black students in schools. This defi-

cit model has been part of state and educational discourse in South Africa for far too long.

Before the recent introduction of multilingual language policies in schools (e.g., the Gauteng School Bill, 1995), the extraordinary multilingual abilities of most South African children have not been recognized as a resource for learning or integrated into mainstream pedagogic practice. All the students in the school have the ability to interweave at least three languages and sometimes four or five into their everyday conversations and interactions. These languages include Zulu, Sotho, Venda, Xhosa, Swazi, and Afrikaans. The English-only model of teaching English predominates, even if, de facto, students use their home languages in group work and similar situations.

In implementing this research project, the central pedagogical question was how to structure the classroom context to give students opportunities to freely express their linguistic resources. Firstly, I decided to use the concept of story to elicit students' voices. I interpreted *story* in a very loose sense: autobiographical accounts, fictional representations, and narrative accounts of important experiences. Story and narrative are primary human activities. The way we narrate our lives to ourselves and to others is through story (Bruner, 1986; Bruner, 1994; Hardy, 1968; Rosen, n.d.). As Haas Dyson and Genishi (1994) showed, story and storytelling can be an powerful way of building a classroom community with students from diverse histories, backgrounds, and contexts. Part of this process of weaving a community through story is the way in which story has the capacity to develop empathy in students, an emotion that is crucial to the building of social relationships both inside and beyond the classroom. Heath (1994) demonstrated in her work with adolescents in inner-city neighborhoods in the United States that stories are a way of testing theories about social relationships in peer networks, as well as connections to the wider society. And from a language development perspective, story gives students an opportunity to develop and engage in sustained speech, to draw on available discourses and genres they already know. What was interesting, in the end, about the choice of *story* as a mediating concept for linguistic exploration was how the students extended the boundaries of what I understood to be story to include jokes, comic routines, songs, dialogues and stylized dramatized performances, as well as autobiographical and fictional narratives.

Once students were working with story, I decided to use a video camera to record the storytelling process. I believed, mistakenly, that student's would be captivated by the idea of seeing themselves on video for a few weeks, then things would settle down, and it would simply be regarded as another technology in the classroom. However, the opposite turned out to be the case. The video became a central mediating technology in the process of text production, and indeed, provided a crucial motivation for students in realizing their various story texts. A teacher-educator from the Gauteng education department has commented on the influence of the media in urban townships when she said recently, "There are more TV sets in Soweto than books." This provides one explanation as to why the students showed an ongoing preoccupation with the video and viewing of their work.

I started off this project by asking a research question related to the students' linguistic resources. After a few months of working, I came to realize that my focus on linguistic resources was far too narrow to encompass the rich range of multimodal texts, including the spoken, written, visual, gestural, and performance texts that the students were producing. Drawing on the work of Gunther Kress (1997, 2000) I changed my research question to focus on the students' representational resources: the multiple and complex ways in which they were using their bodies, their voices, their different languages, and their drawings, to make meaning or represent their stories to one another.

THE STORYTELLING PROCESS

I asked the students to think of any stories from their families or community networks that they would like to share orally with the rest of us as their audience. Out of 37 students, initially only 3 volunteered. The lack of response at this point was quite important, as well as surprising and could be attributed to a number of things, including the fact that students were possibly trying to work out what I, as "the White teacher" meant by *story* in an institutional context where the students are rarely, if ever, invited to draw on their community and family stories. The asymetrical power relationships may also have contributed to this hesitation—I am a White woman, an outsider. My research student, Patrick Baloyi, is Black and a master storyteller from Venda, a rural area. He managed to get the ball rolling very successfully by telling some stories he was told by his father as a young boy. As the project proceeded, and students could see that, as one student put it, "There was freedom of speech," students volunteered to tell more and more stories in front of the class and perform for the video camera.

The exact guidelines given to the students were as follows:

1. Divide yourselves into language groups where you all speak the same language/s.

2. Each person in the group tells a story. The story could be a story you have heard from someone in your family or community or it can be a

story that you make up yourself. TELL THE STORY IN THE LAN-
GUAGE/S IT WAS TOLD TO YOU. Use translation if needed, so that everyone understands.

3. Choose the best stories in the group to tell to the rest of the class.

4. The class listens together to the best stories from each group. Story-
   tellers should tell the story in the language it was told to them. If the
   story was not told in English, find someone to act as your translator or
   translate it yourself into English.

5. When this is over, the audience should comment on the story, ask the
   storyteller questions and generally discuss some of the issues or different meanings the story has for people. The storyteller could also
   talk about where and when she or he heard the story, who told the
   story and why she or he thinks the story was told.

By the end of the project, we had collected about 45 stories in oral, written, and video form as well as jokes, comic radio routines, rap songs, dialogues, and dramatized storytelling performances.

ORAL STORYTELLING AS A POPULAR CULTURAL FORM

What began as a fairly ordinary, rather loose language activity was transformed over a few months into a focused, engaged, and sustained project
in oral storytelling practices in which students drew heavily on popular
oral forms familiar to them and used in contexts outside the classroom.
These popular forms emerged in a number of ways.

Many of the stories students told form part of the genre of *dinonwane* or
traditional oral folktales or moral tales that have been an integral part of
community life in Africa since precolonial times. These included numerous trickster tales involving animals, principally Hare and Lion. The small
hare is the most successful trickster figure in African folklore and uses a
combination of guile and intelligence to outwit his more powerful opponents. Other stories included well known African tales such as *Tselane
and the Giant*, *The Wisdom Bird*, *Nwako and the Giant*, (an African version
of *Jack and the Beanstalk*), *Red Jersey and the Jackal* (an African version
of *Little Red Riding Hood*).

The stories that had the most powerful effect on the audience (causing
great mirth) were contemporary, politicized versions of traditional stories.
These political stories have as their central characters high-profile political
leaders who connive to outwit one another. These new, popular versions
of traditional animal stories have their origin in the local community and il-

lustrate what has been called *moving orality*, the fluid ways in which stories are shaped and transformed for new contexts and new historical moments. They also demonstrate ways in which communities transform or redesign meanings to work in new contexts and cultural sites.

Students introduced oral performance elements that are a fundamental feature of traditional storytelling events and one of the central resources of African cultural life. These oral performance elements are most evident in the performances for the video camera and show the powerful influence of television and radio on the style, gestures, and language of the students. They are not static forms but illustrate the dynamic ways in which genres across modalities, contexts, and media " transmute, quote each other, or cannabalise each other" (Barber, 1994, p. 8).

Traditional storytelling events, as a genre of popular culture, used to be social occasions that usually took place in the evenings around a fire while the evening meal was being prepared. The storytelling event often included jokes, riddles, proverbs, gossip, and conversation, in other words, a range of different oral genres besides the telling of the tale itself. The audiences were essential to the event and their participation were crucial to shaping the event. Audiences responded through joining in the songs, answering the riddles, and giving verbal affirmations of enagagement and interest. This alliance between audience and performer or storyteller made the occasion a highly interactive, living performance. However, according to oral literature researchers as well as popular views, with the rise of urbanization, forced removals of communities during the apartheid era and industrialisation in South Africa, many of these storytelling and performance practices have diminished and changed (Hofmeyr, 1993).

Although I agree that the storytelling event as a traditional cultural practice in rural communities has diminished and changed, I want to argue that these students' highly interactive, performance-based production of their stories provides evidence of resilient and hybrid storytelling practices that continue to thrive in urban communities. These urban storytelling practices draw on traditional storytelling events as one discursive domain for text production. They also draw on youth culture and oral language practices in their multiple forms (Stein & Heath, 1996). However, contemporary popular media culture, mainly radio and television, clearly provides another powerful and influential domain. It is interesting to note the increasing attention being paid by African scholars and media practitioners in the crucial role of the global media in the formation of popular consciousness in Africa. As the eminent African scholar, Karin Barber (1994), pointed out:

> The media in Africa do not constitute a distinct sphere and cannot be understood on their own. Print, radio, television, film and video interact with other popular cultural forms, including performances ranging from the great es-

tablished oral genres to the "innumerable little speech genres of everyday life," as Voloshinov puts it. Studies of popular culture in Africa have tended to focus on single genres in isolation, and relate these to a presumed ' popular consciousness' somehow located in everyday life or in ordinary language. But ... genres transmute, quote each other, or cannabalise each other ... materials circulate among media and genres in a movement that may be seamless or transgressively disruptive, sometimes reinforcing and sometimes undermining each other's sense. (p. 8)

AN EXAMPLE OF A STORYTELLING EVENT

I illustrate the aforementioned points by focusing on one of the contemporary political stories that was told in Zulu in an oral performance style by 13-year-old Nobayeni Ndebele. This story entitled, *Mandela, Gatsha and De Klerk* is a tale of trickery amongst political opponents and has many of the features of a traditional African animal folktale.

Nobayeni performed the story in Zulu for the class audience and for the video camera. She was accompanied by Justice Rapasha, her translator, who stood next to her, trying to intercept her narrative at key points to translate it into English. What you see then, on video, is a lively duet between the two performers, with Nobayeni rushing ahead in Zulu and Justice valiantly trying to keep up. In the end, he does not do justice to the story in English and the students boo him off the stage.

The following transcript of their interactions on the video text gives some indication of the performance features, but obviously cannot capture the full impact of the performance elements in this storytelling event. I ask you to imagine the exaggerated gestures, the nonlinguistic playful interaction between the participants as they signal to each other through gesture and eye contact when to stop and start translations, the murmuring of the adolescent audience as they listen intently and then burst out laughing at the mention of taboo topics, the ringing of the school bell toward the end, the faces of Nobayeni and Justice as they stifle their own laughter in the telling of the tale.

(A fuller translation of the Zulu text follows this transcript.)

> Nobayeni: (with a broad smile) Kwakukhona uMandela, uGatsha noDe Klerk.
>
> Justice: There was Mandela, Gatsha and De Klerk.[1]

---

[1]Nelson Mandela, the South African President; Gatsha Buthelezi, Zulu leader of the Inkatha Freedom Party; and F. W. De Klerk, ex-president of South Africa.

Nobayeni: (speaking rapidly) Manje uMandela bekehamba eya endlini kaGatsha. uGatsha bavumelana bathi uDe Klek sizomthola manje. Sizomfakela - (Justice indicates to her to stop talking with a polite hand gesture. She acknowledges him.) OK (laughing) Sizomfakela umuthi ekudleni.

Justice: (hesitantly) Er ... er ... Mandela and Gatsha decided to get Mandel –

Nobayeni: (whispers) De Klerk –

Justice: er ... De Klerk ... and put ... pour

Audience: Poison! (laughing)

Justice: And pour some poison in his food.

Nobayeni: Manje bahamba-ke. (smiling) Bavumelana bahamba baya endlini kaDe Klerk. Bafika bathi, 'Ayi namhlanje sididiyele kahle. (laughing) Sizodla manje.

Justice: They decided to go to De Klerk's house and they decided to say, 'Today we've got a lovely dinner.'

Nobayeni: Ayi, bahlala ... bahlala etafuleni. Ayi, uMandela wasika inyama. Wasika, wasika kahle, wasika kahle. Ayi, babeka kahle.

Justice: Mandela then ... er ... cut the chicken and put it ... er ... on the table and De Klerk didn't ... didn't eat the porridge.

Nobayeni: Manje uDe Klerk akalidli ipapa. Manje uMandela wathi, 'Ayi, asazi-ke ngoba wena awudli ipapa. Thina singamadoda sidla ipapa. Wena ngeke ube namandla. Wathi uGatsha, 'Akay, mina, ngizohamba ngiyothenga isikwa.'

Justice: Eh ... eh ... Mandela says (scratching his head) because you De Klerk you don't eat porridge, you'll ... eh ... you'll go to the shop to buy –

Audience: Bread!

Justice: Bread.

Nobayeni: Ayi, wahamba. Uthe nakefika e-shop uGatsha weza ne-
             slice esiyi-one, ene uMandela no Gatsha kade baphethe
             ipapa esitsheni esikhulu. (smiling broadly) Bazodla
             boyi-two. Ayi, badla, badla basigede. (Justice tries to stop
             her talking. She carries on at a rapid pace.) Bakugede
             ukudla lokha. uMandela noGatsha kade badlele
             esitsheni esikhulu (indicates the large size of the pot with
             her hands). Baphekele ipapa esitsheni esikhulu (laugh-
             ing, repeats the gesture for the large size of the pot, the
             audience is also laughing).

Justice: (Laughing) Mandela and Gatsha cooked the porridge in a
             big plate. (School bell rings. They pause.)

Nobayeni: Wathi uDe Klerk,' Mina angisayidli inyama. Sengidla
             lesinkwa lesi.' Wathi uMandela noGtasha bazodla
             lenyama leyo. Ngakusasa kuthe mabavukaekuseni,
             bavuka nahudile bonke. (Overcome with mirth, using
             large expressive gestures, she pretends to smear Jus-
             tice's body with the 'shit'. Justice is laughing, as is the
             whole audience at this point.) Wathi uGtasha, 'Hhayi
             indoda, mina ngiyofaka kulomuntu loyo.' uGatsha
             wakipha wonke amasimba wa wasulela ebusweni
             benyanga wathi, 'Hhayi ndoda, hhayi ndoda, nathi
             siyafuna lento lezi.' (Loud laughter from the audience.
             Justice opens his mouth to speak but the audience boos
             him off the stage.)

(Fuller translation of the story)

Once there lived Mandela, Gatsha and De Klerk. Mandela visited Gatsha in
his house and he and Gatsha agreed that they would add a potion to De
Klerk's food to win him over to their side. Off they went to De Klerk's house,
with pots of pap[2] and meat. On their arrival there, they said to De Klerk, "Today we have cooked deliciously. Let's eat together now." So they all sat down
at the table and Mandela cut the meat. He cut, cut, cut carefully and then laid
it out on the table artistically.

---

[2]Pap, a thick porridge made from maize, the staple diet of the majority of Black South
Africans.

But De Klerk was not used to eating pap. Mandela said to him, "Well we don't know what to do now because you do not eat pap. We, on the other hand, are men. We eat pap. You, I'm afraid, will never be strong."

Then Gatsha said, "OK, let me go and buy De Klerk some bread." And off he went. He bought only one slice of bread because he and Mandela had a huge pot of pap. They ate, ate, ate and finished all the food. They finished that food, eating it from that big pot. You see, they had cooked the pap in a big pot.

The De Klerk said, "I don' t want to eat this meat anymore. I am going to eat this bread only." And he told Mandela and Gatsha to finish eating the meat.

The next morning, when Mandela and Gatsha woke up, they found that their stomachs had been running. Gatsha said, "No man, I'm going to smear this faeces/shit on the face of that man." He did this to De Klerk, then wiped off all the shit. He then painted De Klerk's face with the marks of a sangoma[3] while saying to him, "No man, no man, don't forget that we also want what you've got!"

There are many ways of reading this story. My own reading is as follows: Mandela and Gatsha try to win De Klerk over to their political position by making him eat pap, the staple diet of Black South Africans. Eating pap will Africanize him, pap is associated with virility and manliness. But De Klerk outwits them and they are poisoned by their own food. However, their response is to take their problems to him, make him eat their shit, try to Africanize him again by giving him the marks of a sangoma, a traditional healer, and tell him they also want access to power. There is cunning on all sides here as the two Black leaders unite to get rid of the White leader. He succeeds in outwitting them but they have the last word. This oral story that draws on traditional trickster stories about Hare and Lion, was circulating in the community at the time of the elections and is, I believe, a political tale about the negotiation process.

This storytelling event is interesting from a number of points of view: I want to focus on the content of the story, the students' use of their home languages and the popular oral performance elements.

THE CONTENT OF THE STORY

This story is only one of a number of stories students produced that the school might call subversive and that is definitely not part of the main-

---

[3] *Sangoma*, a traditional healer.

stream curriculum. As the students felt more and more in control of the process, their stories became more and more interesting, touching on so-called taboo topics such as cannibalism, the scatalogical, the fantastic, the grotesque, and the satirical. To explain their interest in these taboo or subversive topics, I need to make a slight historical diversion, drawing on the research of Hofmeyr (1993), which explains this interest in these topics within a broader historical perspective.

As I said earlier, South Africa has a strong popular oral tradition that finds its expression in the traditional storytelling practices and folktales of the subcontinent. The history of how these tales came to be written down, however, is linked to the role of the foreign missionaries in the late 19th century who came to Africa to bring religion, literacy, and civilization to the natives. Part of this project involved introducing literacy and schooling to the local communities where they were working. One of the main problems confronting these missionaries was a lack of suitable reading material for students in the local languages. On the printing presses that they had imported in order to print the Bible in different local languages, they began producing series of school readers for children, which included local folktales—the dinonwane, as well as prayers, hymns, proverbs, and essays. But these traditional oral tales that the missionaries collected from the local people underwent a process of sanitization before they appeared in printed form. All tales that had scatalogical or cannibalistic references or any references to people that might be offensive to Christianity, were excluded. What suited the missionaries purposes perfectly were the animal stories, which with their anthropomorphic dimensions, could be used for educative and moral purposes. Subsequently, the missionaries' version of these tales became the official, institutionalized version of the dinonwane as they entered educational institutions via the English language and African language textbooks. These sanitized tales were thus appropriated by the dominant hegemony and became part of the official written canon—much celebrated—of the school textbooks in African languages. The effect on the meanings and definitions of these stories was profound: the most important feature with far reaching effects, was the infantalization of the dinonwane. The school primers established these stories as belonging to the realm of primary education and therefore of children. Later, these stories were only used in the first few years of school, which reinforced the view that dinonwane were only for small children. Although children were ostensibly the main audience of these tales in the community, adults often went to listen to the stories and participate in their production. As Hofmeyr (1993) said, "Today, there is an almost unshakeable belief that dinonwane are for children." (p. 54)

As I said previously, the students' interest and production of stories with elements of the scatalogical, the grotesque, cannibalism, and witchcraft, are far from the sanitized versions of tales appropriated by the missionaries for institutional use. The appearance of these taboo stories seems to suggest to me the presence of an alternative or competing canon of stories and tales that are thriving in communities and do not make their way in a public form into institutional spaces. Barber (1987), noted how, in repressive regimes in Africa, ordinary people's resentment and anger at their social and political powerlessness is often expressed through subversive means, in the forms of jokes, catchphrases, and anecdotes that circulate rapidly amongst communities. In this way, songs, jokes, and anecdotes become the principal means of communication for people who are denied access to the official media. The aforementioned story about Mandela, Gatsha Buthelezi, and De Klerk is an excellent example of a contemporary satirical tale, drawing on subversive elements, including the scatological and White fears of sangomas (African witchdoctors), as well as drawing on the trickster elements in some of the traditional South African animal stories.

THE USE OF HOME LANGUAGES AND POPULAR ORAL PERFORMANCE

Asking the students to tell the stories in the language or languages it was told to them was, I believe, a key to unleashing the stories as performance events. In performance, a student like Nobayeni, who was told many tales by her grandmother, became her grandmother, using the language, inflection patterns, and behavioral gestures of her grandmother, and in the retelling, her own storytelling skills were born. Because students were not primarily focused on language form or a model of language correctness, they were freed up to focus on other important features of the event, like their gestural behavior, their intonation, and their inflection patterns and the need to quickly establish an interactive relationship with the translator and the audience. It is interesting to note that in the aforementioned transcript, Justice has some difficulty in finding the correct English words to translate the Zulu text, and the audience, after prompting him on several occasions, quickly loose interest in his faltering speech. His focus on language form—and his anxiety about correctness—actually prevents him from establishing and maintaining a direct connection with his audience.

IMPLICATIONS FOR CRITICAL LITERACY

The storytelling project described is primarily concerned with developing students as multimodal text producers: students are asked to use their linguistic, cultural, and textual resources to create a body of texts that has the potential to challenge the hegemony of existing texts used in mainstream classrooms. Thus the production of countertexts by the students can be viewed as part of a project to subvert the existing canon and reconstitute an alternative canon. This reconstitution involves the reappropriation by the students themselves of previously marginalized, sanitized, and taboo cultural and linguistic forms.

In terms of a critical literacy project, I think the first stage is the creative process that focuses on the production of a body of texts, some of which might constitute an alternative canon. The next stage in this project involves students analyzing the texts they have produced using critical reading practices. These can focus on a number of key areas:

- Helping students to become aware of the ideological nature of text production: that the stories they have produced are not neutral, autonomous texts that have been passed on from generation to generation in a seamless oral tradition but that these texts, particularly the African folk tales or dinonwane have been appropriated by different interest groups in South African history to serve a range of ideological and political purposes.

- Analyzing the texts themselves from a critical linguistic perspective, looking at the relation between language, power, and ideology in the contemporary political stories, for example. Whose interests do these political stories serve?

- Critically analyzing the relationship between the storyteller, the translator, and the translation: in what ways does the translator produce a new text? What is foregrounded and backgrounded? What is omitted from the original text and why? This could form the basis of a fascinating discussion on the highly political role that translators and interpreters have played in the law courts in South African history.

- Encouraging students to produce multiple readings of their own texts and to reflect on the shifting meanings the stories might have had for different audiences over time in varied locations.

CONDUCTING A SIMILAR PROJECT IN DIFFERENT SITES

Oral storytelling and performance projects, similar to the one described, have been subsequently carried out in the Johannesburg area by five different teachers in different sites: a technical high school in Soweto, a state high school in Soweto, two multicultural high schools in northern Johannesburg, and a second-year university class studying a course in text and genre.

Donald Masasanya, an English teacher from a state high school in Soweto, wrote about the storytelling project he did with his final year high school class in a personal communication with the author. In his account he critically reflects on his own difficulty around handling the taboo topics in his students' texts and questions his role as a censor in his classroom:

> For the first time this year, I dedicated a one hour period to storytelling. Pupils' immediate reaction when I introduced the subject was that of surprise. They view storytelling as a practice that is only relevant to pupils in primary school. "What stories do you want?", they asked. "Are you interested in primary school stories? Can they be in the form of jokes?" were some of the questions asked. These questions were not that surprising to me because storytelling is one area that I had previously neglected and is also a rare practice in my school.

> Telling stories in groups enabled pupils to be free amongst themselves and narrate stories that I could have condemned and dismissed as inappropriate. One story had reference to sexual organs and I was in a position where I could not handle that. I pretended not to know what the insinuations were about. The problem to me then was to what extent I should censor the stories and how to do so. However, I used one of the other stories told called 'Two possibilities' in my subsequent lesson where I taught a short story. The story helped me to promote "multiple readings" of texts using the notion of "possibilities" which was so thoroughly enjoyed in the storytelling class.

> The session stimulated remarkable interest in everyone in the class. I could see groups getting involved as the stories were told. To my surprise and theirs, pupils were entertained by stories from their peers and I discovered that storytelling continued even after my lesson had ended in class. (1997, p.3)

Andrew Brouard, a high school English teacher from a multicultural state school in the heart of Johannesburg's richest suburbs, tried a similar storytelling project with his Standard 7 class of students ages 14 to 15. In his account, he reflected on how the project gave space to some of the Black students in his class "who are very quiet and never offer an opinion" to tell their stories:

> I decided to use storytelling as a means of drawing out pupils, especially the four Black students.... My first interesting observation was made in the preparation phase of the exercise. Many of the White pupils as well as one of the

Black pupils who did not belong to the group of four Black students came to me repeatedly to clarify what I meant by "stories." I noticed that none of the four came to me to discuss any problems; when I approached them they told me they knew what they wanted to say. (1996, p. 1)

Andrew went on to reflect on the multilingual aspects of the activity and comments on the diverse genres of story produced by his students:

My second observation was made when the stories finally were told. It was a fascinating exercise as English, Portuguese, Italian, Zulu, Tswana and many other languages were heard and translated. There was a distinct difference in the types of stories told. Those pupils who were English or predominantly English speaking at home recounted holiday experiences, frightening incidents and so on. The four black pupils told stories which had a mythic element to them. Sizwe spoke of a man in jail who predicted that it would rain grapes; another told of a statue that would come alive; Tshegofatso enacted a tale of a young girl and an evil spirit that could take different shapes; while Thabo told a more urban legend of an unfortunate man who hid his money in a hollowed out loaf of bread only for a greedy individual to eat it. These stories, although banal in print, had a magical quality about them in the telling. And they were told with confidence and ease in the respective mother tongues. (1996, p. 3)

A PEDAGOGY OF REAPPROPRIATION AND TRANSFORMATION

What these two accounts reveal is that all students have stories to tell but are not often given the chance to tell them in our schools. Teachers and students seem surprised at the range of representational resources that students bring from their homes and communities to classroom spaces. They seem to be also surprised at the fun they can have listening to and discussing the meanings of their different stories.

In mainstream South African schools, oral storytelling that draws on African theater and oral performance traditions is not a valued genre. The fact that the majority of Black students in urban schools use three or more languages in their daily lives is not generally regarded as a linguistic resource or incorporated into dominant pedagogical practice. Drawing on oral storytelling as a pedagogical practice is only one way to tap into the representational resources of students whose linguistics, textual, and cultural resources have been marginalized or infantalized. In conclusion I suggest that it is an appropriate time in South Africa to introduce a pedagogy of reappropriation and transformation. By this I mean an educational intervention that attempts to reappropriate and allow for transformation of previously marginalized, infantalized, or invisible cultural forms into institutional spaces, for example, the English classroom. It is a political project that applies to the South African context and arises out of a specific moment in South African history and context.

In practice, in the English classroom, it means:

- creating opportunities for marginalized genres and discourses, for example, popular cultural forms, to become part of the mainstream classroom;

- valorizing students' multilingual resources: seeing students as language experts;

- encouraging learners to freely draw on these languages and discourses in order to transform them for their own contemporary meaning-making or representational purposes;

- validating students' oral languages uses and experiences beyond the borders of the classroom, in their homes, and in their communities;

- redefining the relation between orality and school-based literacies;

- re-evaluating existing assessment procedures, for example no marking;

- perceiving students as multimodal text producers rather than text receivers;

- reconceptualizing students' text production and reception within a critical orality or literacy paradigm in which students and teachers critically explore the social production of their texts within an historical, social, and political context.

Some cautions for such a project, however, need to be considered.

There is a real danger when working with theories of culture and popular cultural forms of homogenizing people from different and varied communities and contexts. In South Africa, we have to be particularly vigilant of stereotypes and the old apartheid way of categorizing people into different cultures, languages, and identities (e.g., classifying Black people as "the oral people" and White people as "the literate people.") There is a need for specificity and localized exploration of cultural forms and processes.

Participants in such project need an understanding that cultural forms and processes are fluid, that they change in time and are transformed by history, power, and different contextual needs. Any exploration of popular forms should involve a critical interrogation of the traditional (e.g., to explore the gendered nature of oral storytelling practices and how different interest groups have appropriated this tradition for their own interests and purposes). During this crucial time of transition and change, when South Africa is struggling to reinvent itself as a nation, I believe that the English classroom can offer a creative and critical space for South African young people to begin to understand the evils of the past. These critical explorations that lead to redefinitions of ourselves as individuals and members of a new nation are essential to the process of taking responsibility for the past and being prepared to imagine a hopeful future.

ACKNOWLEDGMENT

I would like to thank Patrick Baloyi, the staff and 1994 Standard 5 class at Igagasi Primary School, Spruitview, Gauteng for their participation in the study and Isabel Hofmeyr and Hilary Janks for their helpful advice on some of the ideas in this chapter.

REFERENCES

Barber, K. (1987). Popular arts in Africa. *African Studies Review, 30*(3), 1–78.

Barber, K. (1994). Concluding remarks. *Passages, a chronicle of the Humanities, 8,* 8.

Brouard, A. (1996). *Storytelling project at Sandringham School* (Personal communication with author).

Bruner, J. (1986). *Actual minds, possible worlds.* Cambridge, MA: Harvard.

Bruner, J. (1994). Life as narrative. In A. H. Dyson & C. Genishi (Eds.), *The need for story: Cultural diversity in classroom and community* (pp. 28–37). Illinois: National Council for Teachers of English.

Cope, B., & Kalantzis, M. (Eds.). (2000). *Multiliteracies: Literacy learning and the design of social futures.* London: Routledge.

Dyson, A. H., & Genishi, C. (Eds.) (1994). *The need for story: Cultural diversity in classroom and community.* Illinois: National Council for Teachers.

Gauteng School Bill. (1995, May 12). Gauteng School Bill. *Provinical Gazette Extraordinary,* 17–18.

Hardy, B. (1968). Towards a poetic of fiction: An approach through narrative. *Novel: A Forum on Fiction, 3,* Brown University.

Heath, S. B. (1994). Stories as ways of acting together. In A. H. Dyson & C. Genishi (Eds.), *The need for story: Cultural diversity in classroom and community* (pp. 206–220). Illinois: National Council for Teachers of English.

Hofmeyr, I. (1993). *We spend our years as a tale that is told: Oral historical narrative in a South African Chiefdom.* Johannesburg: Witwatersrand University Press.

Kress, G. R. (1997). *Before writing: Reinventing the paths to literacy.* London: Routledge.

Kress, G. R. (2000). Design and transformation: New theories of meaning. In B. Cope & M. Kalantzis (Eds.), *Multiliteracies: Literary learning and the design of social futures* (pp. 153–161). London: Routledge.

Masasanya, D. (1996). *Notes on a storytelling project in Soweto High School* (Personal communication with author).

Peirce, B. N. (1995) Social identity, investment, and language learning. *TESOL Quarterly, 29*(1), 9–31.

Rosen, H. (n.d.). *Stories and meanings.* United Kingdom: The National Association for the Teaching of English.

Stein, P., & Heath, S. B. (1996). *What we don't accept and can't teach: reminders from South African street children.* Unpublished manuscript, University of the Witwatersrand, Johannesburg.

11

"Dickheads, Wuses, and Faggots": Addressing Issues of Masculinity and Homophobia in the Critical Literacy Classroom

Wayne Martino
Murdoch University, Perth, Western Australia

This chapter explores how various forms of masculinity influence the ways in which a group of Australian boys read and the implications of this for developing specific strategies for targeting masculinity and homophobia in the critical literacy classroom. The focus is on adolescent boys' responses to two texts. These data are used to draw attention to the role of masculinities in influencing and shaping the literacy practices of these boys. Although solutions are not provided to the problems associated with boys' acquisition of literacy, I attempt to signal what I think are some of the implications of my work for developing and facilitating effective and critical literacy practices for boys. In this way, I hope to raise issues around how we might work toward developing reading practices that not only enhance boys' involvement and interest in reading but also encourage them to reflect critically on the role of masculinity in their own lives. In light of these concerns, I attempt to address the following questions in this chapter:

- What appear to be the links between masculinity and boys' literacy practices?

- What are some of the implications of current research into the links between masculinity and learning for developing our understanding of boys' literacy practices?

- How can literacy educators equip students with the kinds of sociological and political knowledges that will enable them to develop self-reflexive and analytical capacities for reading masculinity?

- What possible kinds of strategies, reading practices and approaches can be developed for enhancing boys' acquisition of literacy?

In trying to address these questions, I hope it is possible to examine the extent to which boys' acquisition of literacy is implicated in a network of wider social, cultural, and political practices through which boys enact their masculinity (Martino, 1994c).

EXPLORING THE LINKS BETWEEN MASCULINITY AND BOYS' LITERACY PRACTICES

In this section I briefly draw attention to some of the research that has been conducted into the links between masculinity and boys' literacy practices. This will help us to understand why many boys reject reading and the subject English. However, in drawing attention to the impact of masculinity on the literacy practices of boys, I do not intend to invoke what Cox (1995) termed the *competing victim syndrome* or what Wearing (1994) referred to as the *poor boy* approach. As it is, concerns related to boys' acquisition of literacy have been specified in the public media in Australia within such a frame of reference that collapses into drawing comparisons between boys and girls on the basis that they are equally disadvantaged. In short, boys are cast into the victim mould. As I have argued elsewhere, any attempt to address such problems must be situated within a gender equity framework that does not draw comparisons between boys and girls on the basis that they are equally disadvantaged (Clark, 1995; Gender Equity Taskforce, 1995; Martino, 1994a, 1995a). The point I want to emphasize at the outset is that I do not think it is very productive to frame the problems that boys experience in these terms. I believe that attempts to address the literacy practices of boys must be situated within an alternative framework that draws attention to the effects of a restrictive gender system in

which masculinity and femininity are structured as oppositional categories (Connell, 1994); and it is within such a frame of reference that I want to
explore further the effects of dominant models of masculinity in relation to
how they impact on the literacy practices of boys.

What emerged from earlier research that I conducted into the links between masculinity and boys' engagement with literacy, was a pattern in
the way that some boys and girls perceived the subject English in terms of
its sex-appropriateness (Martino, 1994c). In other words, gender appeared
to play a major role in the attitudes that many boys and girls expressed to
studying English. In fact, the data supported claims made by Kenway
(1986) and Curtis (1992) that boys perceived English as a girls' subject and
rejected it on this basis: Boys were caught up in a gender bind in which
they perceived the subject English as a feminized learning practice that
conflicted with their tenuous masculinity.

Many boys surveyed in this study found reading boring and this ham-
pered their engagement with officially sanctioned literacy practices. Some
boys tended to explain their lack of motivation for reading in terms of girls'
predisposition for this kind of literacy practice. Thus, on the basis of this
study it would appear that the acquisition of literacy seems to be hindered
by a set of cultural practices through which boys learn to establish their
masculinity. It is not that boys do not have the ability to develop such capacities for reading print texts. Rather, they find it boring and, hence,
choose not to engage in a literacy practice that does not in some way vali-
date a form of masculinity that they find desirable (Nichols, 1994).

Such research helps us to understand the gender dynamics involved in
boys' resistance to English and their lack of interest in reading. If reading and
English are perceived to be feminized practices and if boys establish their
masculinity on the basis of a denigration and inferiorization of the other,
then it is possible to understand why they might refuse to engage in such a
practice (Davies, 1995). However, as the following survey responses indicate, boys will engage in a literacy practice if it validates a form of masculinity that they find desirable. I do not mean to imply that the way to enhance
boys' involvement in reading is to choose texts that merely cater for their interests. This would only serve to reinforce the detrimental and limiting effects of dominant models of masculinity. But, if Jordan (1995) is correct in
claiming that gender categories are firmly established by the age of 2, it
would appear that an attempt must be made from an early age to model for
boys and to teach them ways of thinking, being, and relating that are not tied
to defining masculinity in oppositional terms (Clark, 1990; Martino, 1994b).
This, it seems to me, is vital in building on the work that currently is being undertaken to develop strategies for making available alternative versions of
masculinity. (Gender Equity Taskforce, 1995; Martinez, 1994; Martino &

Mellor, 1995; Mellor, O'Neill, & Patterson, 1991; Mellor & Patterson, 1996; Pallotta-Chiarolli, 1994a; 1994b).

TARGETING MASCULINITY IN THE LITERACY CLASSROOM: READING THE GUN

I now want to focus on some of my current research into the reading practices of adolescent boys at one particular school as a basis for considering possible ways of targeting masculinity in the literacy classroom. The students surveyed in this study attended a middle-class coeducational Catholic school in metropolitan Perth, Western Australia. Many students attending this fee- paying school were from privileged backgrounds, with at least 50% meeting the requirements for university entrance. Although some students' parents were born in Malaysia or Indonesia, the dominant cultural group comprised White anglo-Australians. Fifty-six Year 10 students (32 boys, 24 girls) age 15 were asked to write a response to a story by Ruben Fernandez (1994) entitled *The Gun*. It is a first person narrative about an adolescent boy, 13-years-old, who is talking to a psychiatrist about his problems. He tells the story about his experiences with the gun his father gave him for his birthday. At first, the boy treats the gun with great care and even tucks it under his pillow but then his father encourages him to use the gun and questions his masculinity for not doing so:

> My father came into my room a couple of days after he'd given me the gun. I thought he was going to beat me up for flunking maths or something but he just asked me how come I never used the gun. "That's what guns are for, you know?" he said. "You're supposed to fire them, not talk to them and pamper them like a doll! Why don't you just go and shoot some cans or something, boy?" (p. 133)

So, he ends up by going down to the river and shooting a thrush who was feeding its chicks in a nest. And this is the beginning of a shooting spree:

> But I wanted more, so I aimed at the chicks. I loaded the gun again and shot, and again, and again, and again. I think I only missed once. There they were, twisted and pulling weird faces on the ground. And then it sorta struck me I didn't know what the hell to do with them, so I chucked them in the river. I shot about twenty of them birds before I realized it was almost eight thirty and I was late for school, so I ran my butt off back home. (p. 135)

He proceeds to talk about how he became obsessed with the gun after this and started spending more time by himself rather than with his friends. He mentions how he would hang live frogs upside down, burn, and then shoot them. Detail is also provided about how his father beat him when he flunked all of his subjects at school. He ends up by shooting his brother who had "egghead glasses" from his bedroom window and achieved the best grades at school. He even had a girlfriend. But the boy is adamant that he did not really want to hurt his brother:

> But I never wanted to hurt him. I swear. I just wanted to make him feel the way I felt sometimes, threatened and screwed up. I just wanted to hit the sign. But I'll never do it again. He's alright now anyways, and I think I'm better now too. (p. 138)

I chose this story because I felt it could be used to raise questions about the link between a particular type of masculinity and a whole range of behaviors and attitudes. For instance, it creates a space for exploring:

- the links between power, violence and masculinity;

- the role of fathers in establishing a model of dominant masculinity for their sons;

- the kinds of struggles, pressures, and expectations that some boys experience as a result of the imposition of a dominant model of masculinity; and

- the need for boys to develop capacities to understand, express, and deal with emotions.

As the students were reading this story there was total silence. I do not think I had ever experienced such silence in this class. They appeared to be really involved and engrossed in their reading and this was confirmed by the comments some of the boys made in their interviews. Overall, what was interesting about many students' responses to this story was that they did not read the boy's behavior as related in any way to the effects of a dominant model of masculinity. In other words, they did not read for gender, and, in this case, specifically for masculinity. Such a reading practice did not appear to be a readily available to them on this particular occasion. Perhaps they had not been subjected to such training on a regular basis. Rather, they tended to read this boy as having psychological problems and rejected him outright as a sick human being:

> I respond to this boy in a negative way as soon as he receives the gun for his birthday. When he goes out shooting and kills the brother and then the baby

birds, I respond to him as a thoughtless person who doesn't care about life. This is illustrated again with the burning of the frogs and then shooting it and then he says 'get a real kick out of it'. I see him as a sick human being who needs help, and this is what he is receiving when he is telling this story. (Brad)

The story *The Gun* by Rubin Fernandez is about a boy and his experiences with a gun his dad gives him. The boy is ruthless and we reject the things he does.... He is brutal and this is shown by his experience with the gun and animals. He shoots the animals just for fun and details like him burning the frogs emphasises the brutality of the boy.... I think the boy is psycho and violent. (Aaron)

Both students frame the boy's problem in psychological terms. Aaron for example constructs the boy as violent and brutal in his killing of the animals and reads him as engaging in such practices for pleasure. On this basis, he rejects him as a psycho. Masculinity does not appear to be an issue for these students in their reading of the boy's behavior. It is possible to argue that they do not explain the boy's behavior in these terms because they are not explicitly required to read the text in this way. Moreover, such a reading practice may not have been made readily available to them as part of their prior literacy training in schools. This is also evident in the following two responses:

I think the boy in this story is a kid with a problem. He is obsessed with his gun and doesn't value the lives of some animals and doesn't value life itself ... I think he's a dickhead for thinking its fun. The boy is clearly a bloody wierdo. (Matt)

I think that the boy in the story was screwed in the head because he was doing all these sadistic things like torchering frogs and other animals. He seemed to get a big high when he shot the gun and other stuff like that. I definitely wouldn't be his friend because he could shoot you because he shot his brother. I think that the only thing he did right in the story was go and see a doctor because he definitely needed some serious help. In other words, what he did just screwed his whole life up, totally. (Joel)

Both these students read the boy as a psychologically disturbed individual and Joel emphasises that he quite clearly needs psychiatric help. But, once again, they make no comment about the role of masculinity in shaping these kinds of behaviours. They do not even mention the father's treatment of his son. I do not think that these students are merely choosing to read the character's behavior as deviant or abnormal. Alternative ways of constructing the boy's actions are not available to them because they have not been taught explicitly to read for masculinity in such a way that would enable them to interpret the character's struggles in terms of grappling with the imposition and effects of a dominant model of masculinity. And more importantly, it may be that the workings of masculinity in their own lives are so naturalized that their effects remain invisible for these boys. It is in this sense that boys not only need to develop capacities for reflecting on the effects of masculinity, but they also must learn to apply this understanding to their own lives.

The following response is more elaborate than the previous ones in that it does target the father as partly responsible for the boy's problems:

> The boy in the story is constructed as obsessed with his air gun his father gave him for his birthday. He's portrayed as somewhat destructive and totally disregards the value of life. The relationship between him and his gun is out of control and very disturbing. The heartless and senseless acts towards the animals and his brother incriminate him even further and only someone who has no respect for others could do something like that. I think he's a f...ing wierdo, what person would go around shooting animals and put them through torture just for personal satisfaction. However, the boy's father is responsible for some of his actions. Not teaching the boy to think logically with a gun and encouraging him to shoot something totally goes against my beliefs. I think the best thing he did in that story was seek professional help and deal with his obsession. (Chris)

Chris clearly disapproves of the boy's actions and at the point where he mentions the father, a possibility is opened up for discussing the effects of the dominant model of masculinity that the latter imposes on the former. It is not that Chris refuses merely to take up such a reading position. It is more likely that he is unable to do so and returns to his former reading position of framing the boy as a psychologically disturbed individual who needs professional help. In short, the assumption that the boy's behavior is deviant and unrelated to the effects of masculinity, still remains at the basis of this student's response.

Other boys, however, some of them tending to concentrate on the father's treatment of the boy, were able to take up a very sympathetic reading position and demonstrated a sophisticated capacity for understanding the motivations of the latter:

> The boy in the story sounds lonely and depressed. We tend to think this because he was not treated the way his brother was, he was belted, and treated

unfairly. This makes me feel sorry for him and he used to take his anger out on the birds and frogs. (Nick)

The boy in the story seems quite lonely and outcast. His family seems to favour his brother and maybe because of this he turned to his gun. At first he starts shooting birds and frogs and builds himself up to shooting at people. Even his own brother. He shot at his brother because he was jealous and angry at him for being smarter and his relationship with his dad was bad and could have influenced his actions. (Josh)

Some boys, however, did read for masculinity or signalled a reading that targeted masculinity as an issue related to the boy's behavior:

The character in this story is male and he is trying to prove that he is a man by using his gun, he thinks he has power and authority when he has that gun. (Glenn)

The main character is trying to prove he's a man. By using the gun, he thinks he has power and is an adult. (Terence)

He thinks that because he has a gun he has power.... Because he has the gun he thinks he is a man and tries to be like one. The text says "I could break it and shoot it with my right hand, just like a man." (Peter)

I think the boy in the story The Gun is a young confused boy who is discovering life ... I believe that the boy is lost between two worlds, one of being a young innocent child, the other a violent man. (Michael)

What is particularly noteworthy about all of these responses is the level of engagement and involvement of the boys in reading this text. In fact, based on these boys' responses to The Gun, it would seem that deploying such a text within a reading practice, designed to target masculinity and its effects, could have beneficial results. In this way, the text could be used to encourage boys to consider "the negative consequences of masculine power at the hands of adult men and older boys" (McLean, 1995, p. 23). Moreover, through encouraging boys to empathize with experiences of injustice and to reflect on such experiences in their own lives, resistance to addressing the effects of dominant masculinity can be diminished significantly. This is also demonstrated in the next section in which I use a text that explores the effects of masculine power in relation to the homophobic harassment and bullying of an adolescent boy on his first day at a new school.

ADDRESSING HOMOPHOBIA: "THE LANGUAGE OF VIOLENCE"

The Language of Violence is a rap song by the Disposable Heroes that deals with a boy, age 15, who on his first day at a new school is called names like *faggot, sissy, punk, queen, and queer* and is harassed for no apparent reason by a group of boys. We learn that these boys were abused by their fathers at home and their behavior is explained in terms of proving to each other that they were not "homos." The victim of the homophobic name calling is bashed to death by this group of boys and one of them ends up by going to prison to receive the same homophobic treatment that he meted out to the boy he killed. The song is very powerful and has proved quite successful in raising issues around homophobia. As I have argued elsewhere, I believe that dealing with homophobia is central to any work with boys or literacy practice designed to target the effects and impact of dominant models of masculinity (Martino, 1994a, 1995b; McLean, 1995). Such models of masculinity will remain intact until boys and men cease to engage in homophobic practices.

The song was played to two classes, my Year 10 English class of 1995 (Class A) and another class of students (Class B) whom I had never taught. I played the song to both classes and then asked them to write a response to the song, focusing on what they thought about the people and the situation referred to in the text. I also asked them to comment on whether they thought the situation related to the way some people are treated at their own school. Only two of the boys in Class B refused to engage with the song, whereas no boy in my class displayed any overt form of resistance. Before referring to these students' responses in greater detail, I map out patterns in the way the boys responded to this text overall. Their responses are significant because they point to the potentialities of using this text to help boys to:

- develop an understanding of the links between masculine power and the practice of bullying;

- learn to identify and empathize with experiences of injustice that are perpetrated through homophobic harassment;

- explore effectively the role that homophobia plays in the construction of dominant models of masculinity; and

- reflect on how they construct their own masculinity.

Most of the boys rejected the bullies and positioned themselves empathically in response to the victim. In fact, they demonstrated a capacity to identify with this experience of injustice and to reflect on such experiences in their own lives at school:

> The situation presented by this song is that people try to prove that they're not "wooses" and "homos" and show it by bashing up helpless young teenagers to death. They're showing that they are strong and powerful but I think they are just idiots and foolish. At this school there are not people getting bashed but people getting bullied because of the way they might look like, the way they talk, or the way they walk. People do things like this to show off in front of their friends or to feel tough (the best). In the end the bullie deserved what he got and I have no sympathy for him. (Justin)

> The bullies are presented as cowards by the way they fight 10 against 1 or 5 against 1. The bullies pick on someone younger than them by starting out calling them names. The lyrics said "And when they provoked him, it became open season for the fox and hunter, the sparks and the thunder that pushed the boy under." This means that the name calling hurts people and they lose their confidence. It says "Brutality and dominance, they didn't hear him screaming, they didn't hear him pleading, they ran like cowards and left the boy bleeding in a pool of red." This depicts the bullies as wimps because they hunt in packs instead of just facing them 1 on 1, like real men ... I think that this thing happens in this school but just on a smaller scale. Although there is not as much fighting as what goes on in the song but there is still name calling and it still hurts people. (Sean)

Both these boys are able to consider the effects of masculine power and to reflect on instances of it in their immediate context. Justin, for instance, demonstrates a capacity to reflect on the effects of masculine power in the form of machismo practices and displays of bravado within peer group relationships, whereas Sean draws attention to its debilitating effects on an individual's self-esteem. These responses point to the value of using such a text to interrogate dominant constructions of masculinity. The following student's response also documents the impact of homophobic practices and abuse on the life of a boy who is desperately calling out for help:

> To me the story is about a teen who goes to his first day of high school, he is tormented called a faggot, sissy, punk, queen and queer. He is verbally and mentally abused ... and has to put up with the mental torture until one night a group of bullies bash the teen to death.... The teen had to go through a lot until he was finally put out of his misery.

I know what it's like to be tormented and bullied, I have to put up with it every day of my high school life, until I leave or have to put up with it I complete school. Some days are easier than others, some days only one comment others thousands. I hate most of all the stares and looks I get from people who don't know ME, not the true me. Some days I want to curl up in a ball and die, but I can't. (Ryan)

Through this response, we are able to gain access to a student's private world of anguish and experiences of victimisation. Ryan's identification with the boy as victim in the song, and which is signalled by his use of language such as "tormented" and "mental torture," provides a threshold for him to reflect on his own experiences of homophobic harassment. And most of the boys were able to engage in this kind of reading practice involving a progression from reflection on the text to reflection on self:

The story tells an emotionally graphic story of a bully who murdered a young boy that was starting a new school. For his crime he was sent to jail and the tables were then turned and he was now the victim starting a new life in jail. The giant reduced to Jack Horner tells us how the bully was confronted by a group of inmates and was raped and became the victim. It focuses mainly on violence getting out of hand. I think the act towards the victim at school was cruel and unfair and it occurred because the bully needed to make him feel good or because he's a new kid at school. However I thought the kid got his just desserts, because of his heartless act I feel no sympathy towards the bully turned victim.

This sort of thing happens in schools today, I should know it's happened to me (except the killing of course). People do this to make them feel big or because the victim is different. (Chris)

This response also demonstrates that Chris is able to engage in a literacy practice that encourages him to move from the text to reflect on his own experiences. What is important to note, however, is that the boys were encouraged to read in this way as a result of the questions they were asked in response to the text. Moreover, these questions were structured in such a way as to direct students to move from the text and then to reflect on their own experiences or knowledge of bullying at school:

- Listen to and read the lyrics of the song *The Language of Violence*.

- Write a response in which you outline what you think about the people and the situation referred to in this song.

- Please include any other comments to explain the way you think and feel about what happens in this text.

- Do you think that the situation in this text relates to the way some people are treated at this school? Explain how.

However, the following two boys from Class B refused to engage with this song because they read it as endorsing homosexuality:

> All I know is that the song was about a bunch of gay faggots and people getting the shit bashed out of them. I think this is a pointless exercise and I'm not doing any more. No I don't think so [that the song relates to way people are treated at school] because we don't welcome gays in this school. (Warren)

> I think this song is about people getting the shit smashed out of them because they are gay home boys. If I was getting hit I would kill them all. This proves societie has its own laws and takes the law into its own hands. I'm not a 'hommie' so I think you should burn this crapy song and never pollute my ears with it again. Got it You better. P.S. I think this is the biggest load of crap I've ever had to do in English it just shows how crap this school is. HOMMIES SUCK CRAP. No it doesn't relate to people in this school except to people who are gays like Ryan or to home boys we all hate. (Adrian)

The violence of these responses and the level of these boys' resistance do raise issues about the difficulty of encouraging some boys to engage with such issues. However, I did not know these students, and the boys in my classes did not respond to the text in this way. I believe that before such issues can be dealt with effectively in the literacy classroom, it is important to establish relationships with the students based on mutual respect and an expression of genuine concern for their well-being.

Although the other boys did not respond to the text in this way, some of them still read the text as dealing with discrimination against gay people. In other words, they assumed that the boy who was bullied was gay:

> The kid was a faggot at a new school and bullies pick on him. The main bully eventually kills him because he is homophobic.... It is good how the bully got some of his own medicine.... I think gays get beaten up because nobody likes gays. It happens at most schools but at a much lower level. (Mark)

> The song is telling a story in two parts. The first, about a gay boy on his first day at school. (Ben)

The boy on his first day of school was killed by the bullie only because he was different or queer. In this school it doesn't happen in such a manner of killing a person but people still crap to other people for doing stuff or having a poofy voice or something like that. This song presents how gays are treated differently 'not killed' but bashed because people are scared of the thought. (Frank)

Although these boys do not produce homophobic readings of the text, their responses are still based on certain normalizing assumptions that I would want them to reflect on (Martino, 1995b). In questioning these boys about their responses in later interviews I conducted, they were able to reflect on their readings and re-evaluate the assumptions leading them to respond in this way.

In this chapter I investigated what I think are some of the possible ways of encouraging boys to engage in a literacy practice that targets the construction of masculinity as a particular object of study. I have steered away from comparing boys' responses with those of girls because I did not want to use the latter responses as a benchmark for evaluating the former's reading of the text. This is not to say, however, that the work undertaken with the two texts that I refer to in this chapter has no relevance to girls. This denigration and inferiorization of the other, which is built into the homophobic practices of boys, also relates to the way girls are treated and positioned within such a gender system in which masculinity and femininity are defined as oppositional categories (Martino, 1994b). I think that the approach to working with boys that I am signaling in this chapter requires relating to boys in ways that are not based on authoritarian disciplinary mechanisms of power (Kennedy, 1996). I hope the implications of working with boys in this way for framing a critical literacy practice and for creating a climate conducive to boys' commitment to literacy has been illustrated through the analysis of data provided in this chapter.

TOWARD A WHOLE-SCHOOL APPROACH

Because dominant masculinity is also the object of a critical literacy agenda designed to enhance the formation of literate capacities for boys, it is important for all members of the school community to understand that gender is socially and culturally constructed. English teachers cannot work in isolation—a whole-school approach is necessary. The wider school community needs to develop an understanding of the processes by which students become gendered in schools through curriculum, teaching situations and approaches to disciplining students as well as through informal social situations and practices. In other words, through both formal and informal social practices in schools oppositional categories of gender are established and reinforced (Blackmore & Kenway, 1993; Curtis, 1992; Davies, 1989, 1992; Gilbert & Rowe, 1989; Gilbert & Taylor, 1991; Kenway, 1986; MacDonald, 1980; Martino, 1993, 1994b). Oppositional ideas of masculinity and femininity are still clearly reinforced through an interweaving social network of practices in schools within which students and teachers and administrators, are implicated (Alloway, 1994; Connell, 1989; Danby, 1994; Kamler, MacLean, Reid, & Simpson, 1994; Kessler, Ashenden, Connell, & Dowsett, 1985). Differences between boys and girls are reinforced in the assumptions that are made about their behavior, attitudes, responses, and practices by those working in schools and this leads to boys and girls being treated in discriminatory and stereo-typed ways (Mac an Ghaill, 1994; Mahony, 1985; Wolpe, 1988).

The point is that if literacy intervention programs for boys are to be successful it is important that the whole school develops an understanding of and a commitment to the need to elaborate alternative versions of masculinity and femininity that are not tied to a system of oppositional gender categories (Davies, 1995; Martino, 1994b, 1995b).

Professional development and training will be necessary on a whole-school basis to provide the opportunity for all school personnel to develop an understanding of gender as socioculturally constructed.

CONCLUSION

In this chapter I have addressed some of the issues that I think are important in exploring the literacy practices of boys. I do not believe that it is possible to discuss boys' acquisition of literacy without considering the wider social network of cultural and political practices in which these boys' experiences are formed. Although one of my aims in this chapter has been to draw attention to the role of masculinity in the literacy practices of boys, I have also attempted to signal what I think are some of the implications of my research. As English teachers and educators, I believe that we have to continue to think of ways of enhancing boys' commitment to literacy, which cannot be separated from developing strategies for encouraging them to reflect on the effects of masculinity in their own lives and those of others. I believe that in developing such a literacy practice, literacy educators need to use texts in a strategic attempt to teach boys to read for masculinity and to reflect on the effects of masculine power in their own lives (Martino & Mellor, 1995). Strategies for working with boys that are based on an acknowledgment of their feelings, values, and opinions must inform the implementation of any literacy practice designed to encourage boys to reflect on the workings of masculinity in their own lives. And I believe that targeting masculinity in this way has the potential for enhancing boys' acquisition of literacy. But this cannot be seen as just the business of English teachers. A whole-school approach that is committed to interrogating the workings of masculinity at all levels and across all departments of school life is necessary if we are serious about promoting alternative models of masculinity within a framework for addressing gender equity.

ACKNOWLEDGMENTS

This chapter is based on a paper presented at the Gender Networking Conference which was organized by the NSW Department of School Education to inaugurate the launch of their Gender Equity Strategy for schools. It is also is based on my doctoral research into the links between masculinity and learning. I would like to thank Bronwyn Mellor for her useful comments and terrific support. Also, I would like to acknowledge the students who so willingly responded to my questions. Without their cooperation and trust I would not have been able to produce this chapter.

REFERENCES

Alloway, N. (1994). *Foundation stones: The construction of gender in early childhood.* Melbourne, Australia: Curriculum Corporation.

Blackmore, J., & Kenway, J. (1993). *Gender matters in educational administration and policy.* London: Falmer.

Clark, M. (1990). *The great divide.* Melbourne, Australia: Curriculum Corporation.

Clark, M. (1995). Gender equity: Reworking the discourse. *South Australian Education of Girls and Female Students' Association, Inc. Journal, 4*(3), 4–14.

Connell, R. (1989). Cool guys, swots and wimps: The interplay of masculinity and education. *Oxford Review of Education, 15*(3), 291–303.

Connell, R. (1994, April). *Knowing about masculinity, teaching boys and men.* Paper presented at the Pacific Sociological Association Conference, San Diego.

Cox, E. (1995). Boys and girls and the costs of gendered behaviour, *Proceedings of the Promoting Gender Equity Conference* (pp. 303–311). Canberra, Australia: Department of Education and Training.

Curtis, M. (1992). The performance of boys and girls in subject English. *Interpretations, 25*(1), 43–60.

Danby, S. (1994, November). *The gendered practices of young children in a preschool classroom.* Paper presented at the Australian Association for Research in Education Conference, Newcastle, Australia.

Davies, B. (1989). *Frogs and snails and feminist tales.* Sydney, Australia: Allen & Unwin.

Davies, B. (1992). *Shards of glass: Children reading and writing beyond gendered identities.* Sydney, Australia: Allen & Unwin.

Davies, B. (1995). What about the boys? The parable of the bear and the rabbit. *Interpretations, 28*(2), 1–17.

Fernandez, R. (1994). The gun. In P. Moss (Ed.), *Voicing the difference* (pp. 133–138). Kent Town, Australia: Multicultural Writers' Association and Wakefield.

Gender Equity Taskforce, (1995). *Gender equity: A framework for Australian schools.* Canberra, Australia: Ministerial Council for Employment, Education, Training and Youth Affairs.

Gilbert, P., & Rowe, K. (1989). *Gender, literacy and the classroom.* Melbourne, Australian Reading Association.

Gilbert, P., & Taylor, S. (1991). *Fashioning the feminine: Girls, popular culture and schooling.* Sydney, Australia: Allen & Unwin.

Jordan, E. (1995). Fighting boys and fantasy play: The construction of masculinity in the early years of school. *Gender and Education, 7*(1), 69–86.

Kamler, B., MacLean, R., Reid, J., & Simpson, A. (1994). *Shaping up nicely: The formation of school girls and school boys in the first month of school.* Canberra, Australia: Department of Education, Employment and Training.

Kennedy, G. (1996, October) *Taking the tide: The successful implementation of aspects of poststructuralism, critical literacy, and feminism in literacy practicies with year 10 non-academic boys.* Paper presented at the National Conference for the Australian Association for the Teaching of English, Melbourne, Australia.

Kenway, J. (1986). Is gender an issue in English teaching? *Interpretations, 20*(1), 17–30.

Kessler, S., Ashenden, D. J., Connell, R. W., & Dowsett, G. W. (1985). Gender relations in secondary schooling. *Sociology of Education, 58,* 34–48.

Mac an Ghaill, M. (1994). *The making of men: Masculinities, sexualities and schooling.* Buckingham: Open University.

MacDonald, M. (1980). Schooling and the reproduction of class and gender relations. In L. Barton, M. Roland, & S. Walker (Eds.), *Schooling, ideology and the curriculum* (pp. 29–50). London: Falmer.

Mahony, P. (1985). *Schools for boys: Co-education re-assessed.* London: Hutchinson.

Martinez, L. (1994). *Boyswork: Whose work? The changing face of gender equity programs in the 90s.* Brisbane, Australia: Department of Education.

Martino, W. (1993). *Boys' underachievement and under-representation in subject English.* Unpublished MEd Honors thesis, Murdoch University, Perth, Australia.

Martino, W. (1994a). Editorial. *Interpretations, 27*(2), i–vi.

Martino, W. (1994b). The gender bind and subject English: Exploring questions of masculinity in developing interventionist strategies in the English classroom. *English in Australia, 107,* 45–52.

Martino, W. (1994c). Masculinity and learning: Exploring boys' underachievement and under-representation in subject English. *Interpretations, 27*(2), 22–57.

Martino, W. (1995a). Critical literacy for boys. *Interpretations, 28*(2), 18–32.

Martino, W. (1995b). Deconstructing masculinity in the English classroom: A site for reconstituting gendered subjectivity. *Gender and Education, 7*(2), 205–220.

Martino, W., & Mellor, B. (1995). *Gendered fictions.* Cottesloe, Western Australia: Chalkface.

McLean, C. (1995). What about "what about the boys"? *South Australian Education of Girls and Female Students Association Inc. Journal, 4*(3), 15–25.

Mellor, B., O'Neill, M., & Patterson, A (1991). *Reading fictions.* Cottesloe, Australia: Chalkface.

Mellor, B., & Patterson, A. (1996). *Investigating texts.* Cottesloe, Australia: Chalkface.
Nichols, S (1994). Fathers and literacy. *The Australian Journal of Language and Literacy, 27*(4), 301–312.
Pallotta-Chiarolli, M. (1994a). Connecting landscapes of marginality: AIDS and sexuality issues in the English classroom. In W. Parsons (Ed.), *Landscape and identity: Perspectives from Australia* (pp. 111–126). Blackwood, Australia: Auslib.
Pallotta-Chiarolli, M. (1994b). Butch minds the baby: Boys minding masculinity in
  the English classroom. *Interpretations, 27*(2), 96–111.
Wearing, B. (1994). Poor boy, power and gender: The masculinist response to feminism. *Interpretations, 27*(2), 1–21.
Wolpe, A. (1988). *Within school walls: The role of discipline, sexuality and the curriculum.* London: Routledge & Kegan Paul.

12

Ta(l)king Back: Dialogizing Authorship

Leora Cruddas
Local Education Authority, London

Patricia Watson
University of the Witwatersrand, Johannesburg

During 1995, we participated in the production of 18 English Readers for Speakers of Other Languages. The English Readers were developed for a nongovernmental organization working in the broad area of adult basic education in South Africa. The project emerged out of a specific set of political, historical, and institutional circumstances that shaped and constrained the production of the Readers. It was implicated in a complex set of interconnected struggles among actors differently positioned in various social practices and institutional sites. Therefore, we locate the project within the context of the new South Africa.

In the last 5 years, the new South Africa has sustained the optimism associated with the honeymoon period of liberation, fueling the process of dismantling apartheid. This political process is marked by the unbanning of the African National Congress in 1990, as well as other liberation movements, and multiparty negotiations that culminated in the first democratic election and the inauguration of Nelson Mandela as the president of the Government of National Unity in 1994. These historic political events were pivotal markers of the move from minority nationalism founded on the politics of racial segregation, to constitutional democracy based on the politics of inclusion, and the redress of inequalities associated with race, class, and gender.

The question of redress also extends to rural inclusion, in which the apartheid divisions between the rural Bantustans and urban centers are being dismantled. The rural Bantustans accommodate a large proportion of the Black population who were forceably removed from urban centers by the apartheid government. The people living in Bantustan areas have been historically excluded from access to resources, the economy, and political action. The rural–urban divide is partly reflected in the current state estimates that put the figure of illiteracy and innumeracy amongst the Black population at 11 million people of a population that totals 40 million. This alarming figure reveals the impact of apartheid that disenfranchised Black South Africans, and highlights the extent to which the current government is hard pressed to meet its commitment to ensuring the provision of equity for all.

EDUCATIONAL CONTEXT

The context of education in the new South Africa is still framed by the slogans of resistance that characterized the educational boycotts of the 1980s: Restore the culture of learning!; The doors of learning shall be open to all!

Such slogans signal, in the broadest sense, the educational stakeholders' ongoing commitment to overcoming the destructive history of apartheid education. It was not in the interests of the apartheid state to produce literate Black workers. In fact, Black people were systematically excluded from education insofar as Black childrens' education was not free or compulsory. MacDonald (1990), in her seminal investigation of the learning experiences of Black primary school children, found that the state's trilingual primary school language policy cognitively overburdened young learners' abilities to engage meaningfully with the curriculum. Consequently many children dropped out of the formal school system, only to return in later years to adult literacy night classes. Adult basic education, for the most part, fell outside the state's formal delivery of education. It therefore became the responsibility of nongovernmental organizations and the corporate sector, who have tended to view access to literacy as access to English literacy. These adult literacy programs suffered from pernicious legislation, censorship, and the constant threat of closure.

The Government of National Unity has expressed its commitment to implement the ideals of the 1995 Freedom Charter, which called for a mass state plan to put an end to adult illiteracy and to open the doors of learning and culture to all. Following recent trends in British and Australian education, South Africa is in the process of implementing a National Qualifications Framework (NQF) that intends to standardize certification procedures across different sectors responsible for educational provision at all levels. The NQF is a competency-based model of education that constructs learning in terms of the aquisition of basic skills. According to Collins (1993) and others: "the language of remediation, phrased as a basic skill, is a language of exclusion, a definition of the newly-arrived as not-yet-ready" (p. 183). Thus, although the new dispensation has embraced literacy as one of the essential ways of building a democratic society, it continues to construct a deficit model using the language of crisis and remediation to interpret people deemed *functionally illiterate*.

PUBLISHING: WHOSE STORIES ARE HEARD?

An important part of sustaining adult literacy, once it has been achieved, involves the generation of reading materials that are relevant to an adult audience. In the past, adult learners have lost mastery over reading and writing because these skills have either little social and material purpose or are not sustained through a popular reading culture. One of the contributing factors is that South African publishing houses have neglected the reading needs of novice adult readers. According to Kromberg, Govender, Birrel, and Sibanyoni (1993) this is because publishers have tended to invest in the production of textbooks that have the potential to be prescribed for schools en mass. They have also promoted children's fiction and as a result, either lost or infantilized the novice adult reader. Against this backdrop, the organization was well positioned to motivate for the development of easy reading materials that would support a reading culture amongst newly literate adults.

Publishing has historically been an area from which Black writers have been excluded. During the severe censorship of the 1970s and 1980s, Black writers found forums for publishing in alternative publishing houses and lived under the constant threat of detention. With the dismantling of apartheid, capital has shifted in the interests of an emerging Black bourgeoisie and education has been targeted as a prime market. Publishers have begun to see an emerging market in the field of adult literacy and African languages and have been quick to stake their claim.

Part of publishers' renewed interest in African languages and literature is due to the revision of South Africa's language policy, which provides all of South Africa's nine indigenous languages, including English and Afrikaans, with official status. This is the first language policy in the history of South Africa to elevate African languages to the same status as English and Afrikaans. However, the African languages have not been developed to the same extent as English and Afrikaans. Consequently, the language profession is under pressure to address the developmental needs of African Languages. In this regard, publishing houses are in the process of producing new series of African language readers for the emergent African languages readerships. However, writing in and for this new market is constrained by the ideological values attached to certain languages, especially English. Standard English carries a lot of material and symbolic value amongst African language speakers: It is associated with the accruing interests of capital, class and education. According to Bourdieu (1991) the symbolic value of English is also associated with certain dominant modes of expression. The forms and conventions of writing are inscribed within patterns of proscription, which are often not transparent but have to be learned in order to be able to write with or against them. This collaborative writing project intended to give historically disdadvantaged writers access to these conventions, in order that they could use English, the language of symbolic power, for their own purposes. Thus, although this series of English Readers is in the language of the colonizer, the content of the English Readers does not reflect its ideological interests per se, because the content is local and reflects the political and historical interests of the colonized.

FUNDING OF NONGOVERNMENTAL ORGANIZATIONS WORKING IN ADULT BASIC EDUCATION AND TRAINING (ABET)

Since the early 1990s, the funding arena for ABET nongovernmental organizations has been compromised. There are a number of reasons for this. Firstly, these organizations are no longer perceived by the donor community to be holding a crucial position of resistance against the apartheid state. Secondly, funding has been increasingly difficult to obtain as donors are encouraged by the state to channel their money through the government's National Reconstruction and Development Program. Donor sponsorship has become difficult to access because there are few existing infrastructures through which the money can be routed. The crisis in funding has resulted in the closure of many of the organizations working in the field of adult basic education and training. A number of projects producing magazines and newspapers for newly literate adults have closed down. The result is a dearth of popular reading material for newly literate adults.

Thirdly, many of these organizations have been hard pressed to articulate a new political vision that is in kilter with the political processes of transformation and reconstruction. Nongovernmental organizations have been forced to show a commitment to becoming self-sufficient in order to secure what funding is available for them. Projects have also had to show income-generating potential and a willingness to seek synergetic partnerships with the corporate sector.

Another of the funding criteria is the demand for an affirmative action element to be built into all projects. In South Africa, affirmative action has entailed the demand for inclusion of Black people, of rural people, and of women. Although affirmative action on these terms is long overdue, it is important not to assume that members of a group are best positioned to produce for each other. This assumption homogenises experience (whether racial, rural, or gendered) and divorces it from issues of class. This is partly because it assumes that culture is a given, and that members of a particular group will all have the same access to the dominant cultural constructs of that group and a commitment to reproducing them.

The proposal to produce 18 English Readers for Speakers of Other Languages emerged out of this culture of production. Consequently, the project aimed to fulfill the following goals:

1. Employ novice writers who showed potential to produce vibrant and authentic stories from their experiences of communities in South Africa.

2. Make a concerted effort to include and provide support for novice writers in the rural periphery, especially those who are unfamiliar with literary market place expectations and what is economically and technically feasible.

3. Avoid the language of exclusion and deficit by viewing reading not so much as a skill but rather as a dynamic, interactive process between writers and readers by including readers in the writing process.

4. Produce relevant reading material that reflects the dreams, concerns, and aspirations of African adult readers.

5. Generate income for the nongovernmental organization as a pilot project.

6. Forge a synergetic partnership with a commercial publisher so as to secure financial investment and publishing expertise for the post production and distribution of the 18 English Readers.

These goals seek to contest the received myths about literacy and reading that often are conceived of as individual, psychological skills. The project aimed to present an alternative way of generating texts that included those groups that have been historically excluded from education, writing, and publishing. Writing is viewed as a political action, closely linked to issues of language and power. It speaks through many voices and registers and tries to confront issues of resticted access for novice writers to the publishing arena. It also raises questions about the recognition of those nonstandard voices and registers. This project allowed writers to reposition themselves and to challenge the dominance of the English language and literacy traditions. The project foregrounds stories that are products of specific cultural contexts and that are determined by certain institutional conditions and political interests.

On the basis of these goals, the project was able to secure funding for the preproduction and production phases of the readers. The organization was therefore able to afford to sustain the collaborative process of story development among writers, artists, communities, and mentors. The collaborative process was seen as an important way of redressing the fact that reading materials for adult learners have a reputation for being either inaccessible or patronizing.

THE CONTEXT OF PRODUCTION

A description of the social and material processes involved in generating the 18 English Readers will reveal how the project attempted to collapse the written reader binary by using potential readers to generate stories through consultative workshop processes. Superimposing the initial culture of reception onto the culture of production means that the match between texts and readers is more predictable. In a sense, the project operated in the intertext: "The associative networks of textual memory from which our sense of culture is woven" (Jones, 1990, p. 165). This chapter is an attempt to socially situate this writing project within the culture and context of production, and to critically reflect on the collaborative aspects of the project, in particular the story generation workshops and the writer–mentor editing workshops.

The organization that commissioned the writers was committed to setting up a consultative workshop process to generate stories using adult-learner and community groups. It was concerned to employ writers who, by privilege of their contexts, would be able to generate stories from a wide range of communities in the country. A possible problem with an experience-based approach to writing is that it can lead to writing that is too narrowly focused on the ahistorical, on the here and now (i.e., on the sensible rather than the analytical). Collins (1993) warned of the dangers of this approach, claiming that it often leaves writers with no framework for talking about how experience is historically structured: "Experience-based process writing always risks representing the source of writing as an unmoored subjectivity with no larger historical or institutional text to write with or against" (p. 179). The English Readers project attempted to address this concern by using different groups to engage the experiences of race, class, and history (among other issues) as part of the process of story generation. The organization advertised for writers in *The Mail and Guardian*, one of the national papers in South Africa. Applicants were asked to submit a piece of writing along with a curriculum vitae. The writers were selected on the basis of community work experience and written submissions. The writers selected were drawn from a wide variey of geographical and social contexts: Gauteng, Eastern Cape, Western Cape, KwaZulu Natal, and the Northern Province. The organization also attempted to select a group that would be representative in terms of class, race, and gender.

The project operated in the double-sidedness of reading and writing. The processes of story generation superimposed the culture of production onto the initial culture of reception in two important ways: firstly through collaborative story generation workshops and secondly through collaborative writer–mentor editing workshops.

The story generation workshops used the models that readers usually bring to texts and engaged in the transactional nature of reading and writing relations. The culture in which the text is produced is simultaneously the initial culture in which it will be encountered, although the stories obviously have a much wider potential culture of reception after publication. The writer works collaboratively with an audience rather than trying, in isolation, to invoke a hypothetical community of readers. In this way, the writer's imagination renews and transforms the resources of a community's culture and visa versa.

Heller (1994) proposed that writing can be the foundation for a transformative community. She claimed that workshops serve several important functions: forming definitions of oneself and engaging in complex examinations of language, history, race, and gender; sharing life histories, experiences, and information; boosting identity and self-esteem as people and as public presences; raising consciousness and political awareness; bonding and building an internal community; supporting each other to take action in the world by imagining and acting out alternative possibilities.

Simmonds, one of the writers, reflects on the process of generating a story with a group of adult learners:

> I wanted the voices of the students to form the core of the book, to give it au-
> thenticity. The workshops were therefore recorded on cassette and tran-
> scribed ... I was concerned that I might be pushing my own political agenda
> and influencing the outcome of the story too much. Fortunately there was a
> strong congruence of opinion between myself and most of the students....
> The students could find out more about themselves. They could learn more
> about the history of their country and locate their own experiences within a
> context. Through a dialogic process, the students could explore their experi-
> ences and give meaning to them. They also became more aware of how
> their individual decisions are influenced by what happens at a macro
> level.... The process, particularly the workshops, were positive in that they
> gave students a voice which was taken seriously.... I am hopeful that giving
> students an opportunity to be heard will break the "culture of silence" which
> Paulo Freire has spoken of in his writings. This kind of process is also relevent
> if we are truly to democratise education, right down to the actual process of
> creating texts for use in classrooms.

The writer's function in the production workshops was to capture the
narratives generated by participants and especially the images and metaphors used to describe the situations in the story. The writer's brief was
to listen carefully to the idiom of the language and to try to reproduce it in
the formalizing of the story. This involved capturing the varieties of popular speak, colloquialisms, and code-mixing patterns used by participants. In this way, the semantic content of the stories is likely to be more
closely aligned with the reader's background knowledge of the world
and use readers' potentials to make meaning that compensates for weak
syntactical control of the target language. As a result a contextually vivid
story can be longer in length and carry more tenses and more complex
language structures, without losing the reader. The compromised independence of the writer in this process was tenuously restored in two
ways: through memory and imagination. For Jones (1990), memory is
the sedimented knowledge of our participation in a common history and
imagination is the capacity of the human mind to elude conventions, to
think in metaphor, to fuse and to reconnect the elements of language and
experience "it is imagination that renews and transforms the resources
of a culture" (p. 160).

Thus far, we have been making claims for the relational character of
knowledge, the negotiated character of meaning, and the experience
driven nature of writing. In effect, the story generation process we have described involves a shift from the centrality of writing as a cognitive process
to the centrality of writing as a social process. These situated communications are part of a larger theory of situated learning.

THE SHARING OF CULTURAL CAPITAL: AN EXAMPLE OF NEGOTIATING STORY IN THE DIALOGIC SPACE

The organization was concerned to include African, rural-based writers in the project, although these writers found it difficult, in literary market-place terms, to transform their oral stories into written ones that conformed to the conventions of the genre. The solution was to engage the editors (Watson & Cruddas, 1996) to mentor the writers in the drafting of their stories. Thus, the second way in which the culture of production is superimposed onto the culture of reception is through collaborative writer–mentor editing workshops. Writer–mentor editing is about the editor giving up the red pen and the cap of expert. When the editor gives up the autonomous right to control changes to the story, she becomes a mentor and shares in the dialogic space. Collaborative writer–mentor editing occurs when the mentor and the writer share in the editing process as dialog partners. This approach develops the writing and editing skills, and the confidence of the writer who is not necessarily proficient in the writing and editing of English single-handedly.

Our major contribution was to initiate this process, give definition to it and to mentor the inexperienced writers. We had been involved in many of the production processes in various roles and had observed others. We were therefore ideally positioned to contest the appropriacy of conventional editing and develop the process of writer–mentor editing out of the problems that arose with regard to writers who were not optimally proficient with writing in English or who were inexperienced in literary market-place terms. Writer–mentor editing developed out of our shared understanding of the problems associated with conventional editing, our interaction with the writers and our commitment to publishing the stories which we received.

In order to show the movement from one of the African, rural writer's first drafts, to the negotiated second draft, we have provided an example of one of the stories developed in writer–mentor editing workshops. These workshops took place over a weekend during which Modupi Phalane initially worked with Patricia Watson and Fred Vonani Bila, with Leora Cruddas. However, the group worked together in revision of the third draft of Phalane's story.

The following extract, from Modupi Phalane's story *Vusi and the Brickyard*, is page 3 of a 9-page story. This page is representative of what kept happening in the writer's first draft:

In a nearby village called Khopo, there was a healing man by the name of Maponyane. Thabo took his daughter there for healing. Maponyane thrown his bones down and said the daughter is being caught by demons (Malopo) of her grandfather who died 34 years ago. He told Thabo that unless he take the child to her granny's grave, she can not be better and that the disease will continue to grow like that until she dies. Granny was a traditional healer and very famous one, his name was Matepe. He was buried at Dinoko's grave yard.

In the same village of Marula there was a well productive brickyard. The boss of the brickyard Mr Valley came to Lephepane nine years ago. He asked land from Makolobe the chief at Lephepane. Makolobe told Valley that the land is already occupied by farmers like: Leeways farm, Masimo, Cooper and Letsoalo farm. The only land available is at Dinoko's grave-yard and that is in Marula's village.

In this extract, the content of the 9-page story is outlined on this page: the crisis of Vusi's illness; the visit to the traditional healer, Maponyane; the solution of Vusi's visit to the graveyard and the climatic moment in which the reader discovers that the graveyard has been turned into a brickyard by the opportunistic brickmaker, Mr Valley. The sequencing of events and the structuring of the narrative is illogical, in that the reader discovers that Vusi's grandfather was a famous traditional healer only after the solution of the visit to his grave is offered.

This extract also shows that the inexperienced writer is prone to giving the whole story in sentence clusters: Every sentence on this page opens into a paragraph that is potentially a page of text. The writer was caught in unpacking these sentences in repetitive loops of story on subsequent pages of the first draft. Thus, this particular page became the starting point for the rewrite in the writer–mentor editing workshops.

Before the workshop, we took it on ourselves to transcribe the writer's first draft into the computer given that the writer was not computer literate. The reasons for typing the story on the computer were to facilitate screen focused editing and to free the writer to "talk in" the changes to his story. In this way, the writer's oral strengths were accommodated. It is important, however, to recognize that the features of oral storytelling that were used in the process of story generation, were substantially backgrounded in the final product, in which features of the oral story, like elaborated name-calling, repetition of action, were edited out as unconventional and contrary to the conventions of the written genre.

THE WRITING AND MENTORING PROCESS

The writer and mentor began negotiating through dialog the sequencing and ordering of events in the story. The writer and mentor used the aforementioned extract to collaboratively develop a skeletal structure. The writer then took existing content from his first draft and mapped it onto the skeletal structure. The mentor's role was to signpost the cultural assumptions of the writer in order to support a wider audience's reading of the social practices related, for example, to traditional healing and ancestral worship. The writer then took time out to fill in the gaps in cohesion relating to character and plot. Part of the writer's development of character involved writing in dialog for his characters. An interesting development was that the traditional healer and the chief's voices are more authentically constructed in Sepedi rather than English. A consequence of this change is that pivotal movements in plot are encoded in Sepedi. In this way the language resources of the writer and by extension his community, were moved from the margins of the narrative to its very center. The workshop process allowed the sedimented knowledge of the writer to expand in the development of the story and the reconstruction of his story remained his property.

The writer then brought the emerging third draft of the story to a roundtable conference with the group. The roundtable allowed the group to share their different expertise. The writer's voice remained central to decision making because he directed the changes to his story and controlled the editorial interventions. According to Modupi Phalane, the process was rewarding and empowering:

> The editor gave me a chance to comment on her contributions. The editor's contribution was not final. She did not change my story but helped me to put it on paper. It helped me to find the beginning of the story and understand that the story should be written chronologically and also where to put the cream of the story. Initially, my story looked more like rough work before this editing process.

The writer–mentor editing workshop was about manipulating the story: critiquing, resisting and advancing in the creative process and afforded the team the opportunity to share their cultural capital. The writers brought their expert knowledge of story, of Sepedi and of their rural communities, whereas we brought our expert knowledge of literary marketplace values, of English and of technology. The dialogue partnership allowed the top-down schemata of the writer to control the definition of meaning as well as our bottom–up interventions.

This collaborative editing process enabled historically deskilled writers to maintain ownership of the final version of their stories and to find a way of entering the community of practice. Writer–mentor editing is a form of what Lave and Wenger (1991) termed *legitimate peripheral participation*. Legitimate peripheral participation is a descriptor of engagement in social practice that entails learning as an integral constituent. For Lave and Wenger, legitimacy is a way of belonging to a community of practice, and peripherality suggests that there are more or less engaged and inclusive ways of being located in the fields of participation defined by a community. The dialogic space construed as the sharing of editing between writer and mentor is at risk when the mentor prevents the writer's full participation in the process of story reconstruction. Lave and Wenger stated that learning can be prevented when the mentor acts like a master or a pedagogical authoritarian, viewing apprentices as novices who should be instructed. Thus mastery resides not in the editors, the writers, or the text, but rather in the community of practice developed in the dialogic space of the workshop.

Legitimate peripheral participation provides a way of describing and challenging the practices by which Black rural writers have been systematically excluded and alienated from participation in the world of publishing (a White, middle-class, male-dominated, institutional site). The workshop process has provided a way for novice writers to gain access to and become members of the community of practice. Both writers and mentors were involved in a learning trajectory that has the potential to transform the community of practice, especially in a society in which certain cherished assumptions about standard English, acceptable modes of expression, and the forms and conventions of writing are being contested. Lave and Wenger's theory therefore provides a way of thinking and talking about the historical production and possible transformations of writers and writing practices, and by extension editors and editing practices.

ON REFLECTION: RECLAIMING OPTIMISM IN A CLIMATE OF POSSIBILITIES

It is important to reflect on how the project was caught in the limitations of its own institutional position. A set of questions that need to be asked concern the collaborative editing process: To what extent has the culture of production already determined the subject positions of writers and mentors? How do the respective positions of the writers and mentors affect the drafting process? In Collins' (1993) words, to what extent is there an absent text—a "lack of shared understanding and textual orientation" (p. 76)—in the collaborative editing process?

The writers' identities are constituted by the fact that they are Black, male, rural, and of lower economic status, whereas the mentor-editors are constituted by our positions as White, female, urban, and middle class. The subject positions of the writers and the mentor–editors seemed therefore to be antithetical. The mentor–editors occupy a different institutional space from that of the writers, which meant that both parties had to suspend their naturalized common sense, to hold their taken-for-granted assumptions of reality in doubt, until mutual understanding was arrived at. Out of these differences, the group found considerable common ground and shared ideological space. There was consensus around what it meant for the group to resist or read against institutional texts.

It is therefore important to ask to what extent the project has simply moved the writers closer to western forms of storytelling by conforming to literary marketplace expectations and the forms and conventions of written texts? Has incorporating the voices of the writers into the publishing arena co-opted these voices more than it has challenged the industry? To what extent have the literary marketplace values of publishing colonised the writers?

To some extent it can be said that the cultural imperialism associated with the English literary tradition in Africa (Ashcroft, Griffiths, & Tiffin, 1989) was in this instance replaced by the writers' own sense of indigenous cultural capital and construction of history and its impact on their lives. It also meant an impressive refiguring of experience in texts with cultural positions and historical depths (Collins, 1993). Gee (1990) proposed that there are ways of decolonizing the apprentice through the acquisition of *mushfake discourse*. Mushfake is a term from prison culture meaning to make do with something less when the real thing is not available (Gee, 1990). Mushfake discourse means the partial acquisition coupled with metaknowledge of the discourse that allows manipulation and can be used to critique, resist, and write against that discourse while advancing in it. We had to be aware, as mentors, of how we doubled as gatekeepers of literary marketplace values; however, it was also possible for us to make an intervention by foregrounding metaknowledge, helping to develop a metalanguage, and aiding and abetting the writers who wrote against the texts of race, class, and history. In this way the writers were able to use English for their own purposes.

The stories have now entered a new dialogic space in the wider cultures of reception. This collection of stories will take their place in the community of stories and in the social practices in which they are articulated and interpreted, such that, in the words of Bakhtin (1994):

> There is neither a first nor a last word and there are no limits to the dialogic context (it extends into the boundless past and the boundless future). Even past meanings, that is, those born in the dialogue of past centuries can never be stable (finalised, ended once and for all)—they will always change (be renewed) in the process of subsequent development of the dialogue.

ACKNOWLEDGMENT

This chapter was presented at the European Writing Conference held in Barcelona from the 23-25 October 1996.

REFERENCES

Ashcroft, B., Griffiths, G., & Tiffin, H. (1989). *The empire writes back: Theory and practice in post-colonial literature.* London: Routledge & Kegan Paul.

Bakhtin, M. (1994). *The Bakhtin reader.* London: Edward Arnold.   .

Bourdieu, P. (1991). *Language and symbolic power.* (G. Raymond & M. Adamson, Trans.). Cambridge, MA: Cambridge.

Collins, J. (1993). The troubled text: History and language in American university basic writing programmes. In P. Freebody & A. R. Welch (Eds.), *Knowledge, culture and power: International perspectives on literacy as policy and practice* (pp. 162–186). London: Falmer.

Gee, J. (1990). *Social linguistics and literacies: Ideologies in discourse.* London: Falmer.

Heller, C. (1994). Writing as foundation for a transformation In A. H. Dyson & C. Genishi (Eds.), *The need for story: Cultural diversity in classroom and community* (pp. 221–236). Urbana, IL: National Council of Teachers of English.

Jones, N. (1990). Readers writers texts. In R. Carter (Ed.), *Knowledge about language and the curriculum* (pp. 154–165). London: Hodder & Stoughton.

Kromburg, S., Govender, M., Birrel, N., & Sibanyoni, M. (Eds.). (1993). *Publishing for democratic education in South Africa.* Johannesburg: SACHED Books.

Lave, J., & Wenger, E. (1991). *Situated learning: Legitimate peripheral participation.* London: Cambridge.

MacDonald, C. (1990). *School based learning experiences: A final report of the Threshold Project (Report SOLING-19).* Johannesburg: HSRC.

Watson, P., & Cruddas, L. (1996). *Dynamising authorship: Creating readers with readers (a Project Literacy Report).* Pretoria: PROLIT.

APPENDIX: SYNOPSIS OF STORIES IN THE SERIES

The Girl With the Golden Tooth by Fred Vonani Bila

This story was written by Fred Bila, a writer living in a rural area in the Northern Province. It is a love story that has strong links with the African oral tradition in storytelling.

Waiting for Lerato by Monique Fagan and Cathy Winter

Two women are framed by the balustrade of an old building in a city, overlooking a taxi rank. They discuss the relationships between men and women, drawing on their own painful experiences. The artwork is experimental, using the comic genre. The scenes from the taxi rank below form a visual subtext that enacts a second narrative—a love story—from which the title of the Reader is taken. The humor of the subtext is set off against the serious and important gender issues raised in the text.

The Spaza by Ethelwyn Rebelo

The Spaza is the story of a young boy who has to deal with his parents' regular and violent arguments.

Magweya by Fred Vonani Bila

This story, which has strong links with the African oral tradition in storytelling, was developed collaboratively at Akanani Rural Development Center during a Zanendaba storytelling workshop. It is about a mean, exploitative giant, named Magweya, who eats the short people of the village.

People Call us Bosslaapers by Gabi Coetzee-Andrew

This story was workshopped with Bosslaapers (or street people) in the Eastern Cape. It talks about their lives, dreams, and aspirations.

We Wait for Elandskloof by Bridget Pitt

Alleta Titus tells the story of her community's forced removal from the farmland in the Western Cape that they had purchased from the Crown. This land claim is presently being addressed in the Land Claims Court.

The Adventures of a Bus Driver by Nkatazo Sitsha

This is an amusing, urban story about a bus driver named Joe, who is mistakenly identified as a thief.

Time to Sit in the Sun by Finuala Dowling

This reader was inspired by the stories and memories of the Masiphumelele literacy class in the Western Cape. It was workshopped with a group of learners and tells the story of Wellington Gqibithole's move from a rural area to the city, his search for work, and his decision to become literate.

The Ring by Monique Fagan

The Ring is a love story created out of a discussion about marriage and the laws (state, traditional, and religious) governing marriage in South Africa. This discussion took place at a workshop held in Soweto in which people from different walks of life came together to discuss belief systems. Like *Waiting for Lerato*, the images experiment with the comic genre.

Vusi and the Brickyard by Modupi Phalane

This story is based on a real incident from rural Lesedi: The village grave-yard was used as a brickmaker's quarry. The story deals with traditional healing, ancestors, and the initiation of the nyaka (traditional healer).

We Remember District Six by Lisa Thorne

District Six was a multiracial community that grew up with music, dance, and carnival on the slopes of Devil's Peak, next to Table Mountain. In 1968, the Apartheid Group Areas Act was applied to District Six. The people were forcibly removed and it was razed during the years 1970 to 1980. The story is told by Vincent Kolbe who grew up in District Six and was instrumental in setting up a museum to preserve its cultural legacy.

The Missing Goats by Fred Vonani Bila

Like *Vusi and the Brickyard*, this story was inspired by a real incident in which some village goats were poisoned by a malicious farmer. It is also a rural story that deals with corruption and the inadequacy of infrastructures in rural areas in South Africa.

The Building by Cathy Winter

The narrator of *The Building* tells the stories of the people who live in an old block of flats in the inner city. The building is a microcosm of the many peoples who make up the urban community.

Amadlozi by Cathy Winter

A suite of 12 drypoint prints, called *Portrait of the Ancestors*, created by art-ists at the Artist Proof Studio in Johannesburg, inspired the story *Amadlozi* (which means ancestors). This is an innovative open-ended Reader that uses images to generate text rather than images to illustrate text.

Sizamile: The Story of Desmond Davis recorded by Richard Jordi

The protagonist of this story, Desmond Davis, lives and works in Sizamile in the Eastern Cape. His story is also the story of a community that has worked together and struggled together. It addresses worker and commu-nity issues: the organization and mobilization of the community, their de-termination to improve the conditions of their lives, labor practices, unionization, and party politics.

Hard to Get Life by Lisa Cannon

This story was inspired by the children and youth living on the streets of Cape Town. Some of the events in the story, like the children who are burned by policemen, did actually happen.

Congo Days recorded and transformed by Rob Simmonds

Rob Simmonds worked with a group of immigrants from Zaire at an adult education centre in Johannesburg to workshop this story. The narrator, Chantal Ngalula, tells the story of her life in the Belgian colony, the people's struggle for independence and postindependent Zaire's problems. She also addresses the reasons for her move to South Africa and the xenophobia she experiences as an immigrant. The story sits between prose, historical biography, and comic frames in which Chantal interacts with her colleagues at the centre.

Nhlanhla adapted from the original by Patricia Watson and Cathy Winter

Nhlanhla, which means lucky, draws on the African myth of the umthondo (penis) tree. It is the story of a beautiful woman called Marimba, who is the object of many men's desires. As their desires govern their dreams of Marimba, their umthondos leave their bodies in an attempt to penetrate her but are caught up in the branches of the Nhlanhla tree. The story deals with the construction of women as witches and the consequences of female self-definition.

IV

Tertiary Education as a Site for Critical Literacies

13

Critical Literacy in the Second Language Classroom: Power and Control

Catherine Wallace
University of London

In this chapter I offer an account of a course on critical reading, which I taught to students of different nationalities at one of Britain's new universities. The course took a critical language awareness approach, to be more fully described later. My discussion centers around the issue of power and empowerment in teaching critical literacy, in particular the nature of the power exercised by the teacher in the adjudication of students' interpretations of texts, within what I refer to, with echoes of Fish (1980), as an interpretative community. As I argue previously (Wallace, 1992), "the longer a class is together the more of a community it becomes and the more it begins to exchange communicative resources" (p. 64). I look at some key aspects of the teacher's role in one segment or episode of the class, in which the students report back to the whole group, their small group analyses of specific texts. First, however, I address some of the wider issues that underpinned this classroom study.

WHAT IS CRITICAL LITERACY?

What do we mean by critical literacy? As Lankshear (1994) said, "critical goes into battle without any clear meaning but with a lot of work to do" (p. 5). Thus we need to ask in what ways is critical literacy different from orthodox literacy or mainstream literacy. As Rothery (1996) put it, "is critical literacy the exclusive province of schooling or is it inextricably linked to everyday worlds, commonplace forms of experiences with print and other media that come under the ever-wider umbrella term of literacy?" (p. 118). One aspect we are likely to agree about in principle is that critical literacy is concerned with relations of power and thus with the manner in which power circulates both in the real world and within particular texts. Certainly critical discourse analysis, which has close links with critical language awareness and in turn with critical literacy, is centrally concerned with the exercise of power as it emerges in the discourses of specific texts. Critical discourse analysts, such as Fairclough (1989) and Kress (1985), have drawn on the Foucauldian view of discourse to refer to the taken-for-granted manner in which particular ways of perceiving and talking about the world systematically work to the advantage of those with social and political power, at the same time as marginalizing other groups. It is the ideological implications of this unequal distribution of power, operating for much of the time below the surface of consciousness, which critical discourse analysis aims to bring to awareness.

The critical discourse analysts tend to assume malign effects of power, which begs the question as to circumstances in which we might wish to look favorably at power. Firstly is the assertion of power always unjustified? Do not parents and teachers, for instance, exercise legitimate kinds of power? Just what might constitute legitimate power is discussed later in this chapter in connection with the teacher's role. Moreover, while we deplore the presence of unchallenged power in the hands of dominant groups, we talk freely of empowering our students, although, as a number of writers have pointed out (e.g., Andersen, 1988) it is not always made clear who or what is doing the empowering, or quite what our students will be empowered to do or become. Luke (1996) noted the tendency to reify power: "power is treated as something which can be identified, transmitted and possessed" (p. 321). We tend to assume that power can be handed to students unproblematically rather than being constantly exercised and resisted in all our activities (cf. Andersen, 1988). With overuse, the idea of empowerment may be weakened to become merely an instrumental concept as in, for instance, the power to do a particular task or to get a job. Such a reductive view of power might lead in turn to a view of literacy instruction in terms of sets of competencies or skills, one that sees forms of knowledge not as being constructed collaboratively in classrooms but as delivered to students. Or, as Freire (1972) critiqued, deposited within them in banking style, often in piecemeal and fragmented kinds of ways.

It is clearly possible to address specific needs without taking such a narrow competency oriented view of empowerment. Thus, Auerbach and Wallerstein (1987), in their work with adult migrants in the United States, have a clear and explicit agenda for forms of action that arise out of the classroom work with their materials. This agenda might take shape in quite modest ways, through, for instance, helping parents to be more assertive and confident in talking through a child's school report; or it may relate to the need to take action in the workplace because of poor trade union organization or neglect of worker health. Auerbach and Wallerstein were careful, however, to present the situations in their material as codes, in the Freirean sense. That is, the texts are selected as likely to resonate experientially with their students but not to simply reflect back day-to-day experience. Indeed such a problematizing stance is the essence of a problem posing as opposed to a problem-solving approach.

However, frequently it is not appropriate or feasible to take the empowerment as action view. We then need to develop a wider agenda and it is here that problems are raised with localized accounts of critical literacy that see empowerment within specific settings. We may have overemphasized difference and contingency, exemplified in a view of literacy which is defined by reference to particular social contexts, while neglecting commonalities of experience and values. Although it has become fashionable to challenge the feasibility of grand narratives, understandably in view of the Eurocentric emphasis they tended to embody, there is a strong case, as McCarthy (1994) argued, for reinstating some sense of the wider picture, the need for common ground within multiple perspectives. As Young (1992) put it "in our present global problem of resource limitation and world pollution we must, for the first time, establish this common ground between different cultures. This is universalisation" (p. 3). In a multinational group of students such as that in this study, it was the tension between commonalities and differences that became a fruitful focus of scrutiny. Students may become more aware of culture specific aspects of identity and social practice, including literacy practice, by locating them within a wider understanding of values and practices that resonate universally. Yukako, a Japanese student in the group, expressed it thus, in the course of an interview with me 3 months after the course:

> Y: when you get down to the bottom line it's just the same thing
>   we're saying, like human rights, about racism, things like that. I

thought we shared our opinion I thought. But I can't explain to you, well, but it does—we did have cultural differences I think yes

CW: there was a cultural difference but also there was some kind of shared

Y: Yes, aha, I think so. For example, I think it was the French girl—I can't remember her name—but she was studying British

CW: British National Party*

Y: National Party, yes BNP, BNP, it wasn't about her country, because she was from France, but she was so against it, and then, for example, for me, Japanese, I do understand Nazism and things like that, but it wasn't so, how d'you say, close to me at all so until she showed her consideration and she take it so seriously.

A wish to reclaim a role for the wider picture does not mean abandoning an interest in context: On the contrary, it involves seeing contexts and identities as complex and multilayered. It means offering a richer understanding of contexts and cultures so that both are seen by teacher and students as shifting and overlapping. An overlocalized, situationalized view of learning and behavior risks stereotyping, especially in a world where we cannot hope to predict what our learners' specific futures will be. We need a view of critical literacy that cuts across the grain of the everyday, the localized and the immediate.

In making a case for a critical literacy that embraces a range of specific social settings, we may wish to rethink the use of the now generally preferred plural form; it may be appropriate to reinstate critical literacy as a mass noun. Auerbach (1992) pointed out a potential problem with the contextualized use of the term, signalled by its plurality: The danger is that we may trivialize the concept in a reductive manner, as witnessed by the fact that, much as we have lists or sets of competencies, we now come across lists of literacies, forming in many cases a disparate and incongruous set. I would prefer to see critical literacy, much as Lankshear (1997) talked of powerful literacy, as a use of literacy—what you do with a text. In

---

*A right wing party in Britain which promotes white racial supremacy.

short, one does not so much have critical literacy as one of a set of aptitudes, as perform it.

CRITICAL LITERACY AND SCHOOLING

I argue that critical literacy is a practice that finds its distinctive place within educational as opposed to everyday contexts. In this sense we might want to say that critical literacy is, in Bernstein's (1996) terms, part of vertical discourse in that it is intertextually constructed and scaffolded, across disciplinary areas within schools. Horizontal discourses are segmental and the competencies or literacies which constitute them (Bernstein used the terms *competence* and *literacy* interchangeably here) are "embedded in ongoing practices and directed towards specific goals" (p. 179). The acquisition of "segmental competencies or literacies is likely to be tacit with reduced or condensed linguistic elaboration" (p. 179). Segmental, contextualized literacies are evoked by contexts whose reading is unproblematic. Vertical discourse, with which I associate critical literacy, as typically more characteristic of the school setting, is explicit and elaborated. It is this feature of explicitness and elaboration that I claim as a defining feature of critical literacy. Critical literacy awareness and use is dependent on the exercise of certain kinds of metalevel awareness that are not so much acquired naturalistically in a day-to-day sense, as developed in educational settings. They are abilities that are learned rather than acquired. Lankshear (1997) drew on this distinction in his account of powerful literacy, which is close to my understanding of critical literacy. Although acquisition, said Lankshear, is a fairly unconscious process, learning is a process of "gaining conscious knowledge via explanation, analysis and similar teaching processes" (p. 71). It is this process that Lankshear claimed is empowering.

Gee (1990) talked rather dismissively of schooling as offering opportunities for "expository talk in contrived situations" (p. 42). Classrooms are necessarily and properly contrived settings, and a specific goal within such a contrived setting is the development of critical literacy in explicit kinds of ways to include, I argue, the development of expository talk, one feature of which is the need to make explicit grounds of argument in ways that may be atypical of day-to-day conversation. However, although there is some agreement in principle about the metalinguistic characterisation of critical literacy, there is little consensus about what *kind* of metalinguistic knowledge is facilitative of enhanced critical awareness. A further dilemma relates to the teacher's role in the mediation of knowledge construction. As Luke (1996) pointed out, the recognition of the need to be explicit does not necessarily presuppose a transmission pedagogy, a problem that has arisen with some interpretations of genre, as Luke noted. One assumption behind the genre movement, an assumption that I broadly support, is that explicitness of linguistic description must be matched by explicitness of pedagogy. However it is in principle possible to make both the content of instruction and learning and teaching processes transparent without opting for a transmission pedagogy. Indeed I argue later and more fully in Wallace (1998) that a critical pedagogy, which is required for the development of critical literacy, presupposes construction of knowledge and understanding in which all class members play an active role.

POWER AND CONTROL: THE ROLE OF THE TEACHER

If we accept that students will be empowered in cases in which content is explicit and classroom learning processes transparent, what are the implications for the teacher's role? As a convenience, and at the risk of overpolarizing, we might take as metaphors the terms *power* and *control*, to signal that although control, as a justifiable exercise of authority, empowers students, power represents an abuse of that role. In practice it may be difficult to determine the point at which legitimate control, which scaffolds and facilitates learning, slips into a form of power that dominates and that disenfranchises students from making full entry into the interpretative community. Even then the term *full entry* requires some qualification if we accept that teacher and students, although partners in enquiry, do not have equality of rights, even in a class of adults. Any such supposed or feigned parity may work to the disadvantage of students. Indeed Bernstein (1996) implied that what he called *invisible practice* is more tyrannical than apparently authoritarian visible pedagogy in which the sources of power are strongly in evidence and not readily open to dispute. Invisible practice, associated with progressivist pedagogy, may, more insidiously, disguise the sources of power. Consistency would recommend that just as we make our teaching explicit, sources for authority should be equally so.

In other words teacher–learner interaction is inherently and generically an unequal encounter. However it can be mitigated in particular ways. Optional features of the lesson genre that offer space for students and teacher to behave in atypical ways can point the way forward to more productive exchanges in the building of knowledge and to longer term change in the classroom culture. A key question—central to critical analysis and critical pedagogy—is how might things be different? Although the domain of schooling will necessarily exercise behavioral and linguistic constraints what unaccustomed spaces can be opened up to facilitate critical enquiry around texts? How may we challenge what is taken for granted, what is seen as natural and inevitable?

Critical literacy itself is an unnatural practice. Its distinctiveness lies exactly in this characteristic. We may want to say that in the classroom we are not so much reading texts as using them, in the terms of Eco (1992), using them, that is, for critical resistant purposes, consciously adopting a stance eschewed in day-to-day cooperative reading. The original text, along with its original envisaged reader, is recontextualized in the classroom. Although critical literacy approaches may build on students' experiential knowledge and existing cultural and linguistic resources, these are then reshaped and reevaluated in the light of closer scrutiny of texts in the classroom setting, sometimes in ways that take both teacher and student by surprise. Lankshear's (1994) characterization of critical literacy as consisting of three objects of critique offered a useful way of thinking about the progression of a practical pedagogy. Lankshear described the progression thus. Critical literacy might involve:

1. Knowing literacy (or various literacies) critically, that is having a critical perspective on literacy/literacies generally.

2. Having a critical/evaluative perspective on particular texts.

3. Having a critical perspective on—that is, being able to make critical readings of—wider social practices, arrangements, relations, allocations, procedures etc. which are mediated by, made possible by and partially sustained through the reading of texts. (p. 10)

PRINCIPLES IN COURSE DESIGN

The course took a critical language awareness approach that means aiming for breadth and depth in two major ways. First we can think of awareness in terms of two levels, which I shall call *micro* and *macro*. Secondly, we can see critical literacy and critical talk as twin and complementary aspects of critical language awareness. I deal with each in turn.

Macrolevels and Microlevels of Awareness

Among current and recent exponents of critical language awareness it is possible to identify two strands. The first looks at language practices, that is the way in which language varieties are used in different contexts of use. The second, indebted very much to critical discourse analysis, is process oriented, inviting attention to the processes at play in the production and reception of the meanings embedded within specific texts. Language awareness at the first, macrolevel, has been the concern of scholars in the fields of anthropology and ethnography. One application of critical language awareness at this level is represented by work carried out by Barro, Byram, Grimm, Morgan, and Roberts (1993) at Thames Valley University. First-year university students were asked to carry out home ethnographies prior to doing similar observations of the foreign cultural setting during a period of study abroad. The kind of observations involved any situation mediated by spoken or written language—pretty well any social setting in other words. The aim was that by gaining greater distance on their everyday, taken-for-granted language and literacy practices, the strange and unfamiliar in the foreign language setting would be viewed as less exceptional or exotic. This cross-cultural dimension to critical language awareness work was seen as an important element of the critical reading course.

The macrolevel of awareness can be related to Lankshear's (1994, p. 10) first stage in a literacy awareness program: knowing literacy (or literacies) critically, that is having a critical perspective on literacy or literacies generally. The gaining of this wider sociocultural perspective can be seen as preparatory and complementary to the second level, which involves critical language analysis of particular texts and draws on specific linguistic tools for the purpose. In the case of this class, those selected were drawn from Halliday's (1985) systemic and functional grammar. Such tools are part of the resources that students can put to use in the scrutiny of particular texts, more specifically in making judgments regarding the manner in which and the degree to which linguistic choices in texts, ideationally, interpersonally, or textually, challenge or confirm prevailing ideologies.

Critical Literacy and Critical Talk

Critical literacy comes into play, not just in the awareness and interpretation of written texts but in talk around texts. Such talk may create the opportunities for either multiple, differentiated readings or consensual interpretations of texts. We can check out our own preferred readings against those of others and, in the interpretative community of the classroom, adjust, defend, or abandon them. A view of literacy as critical practice sees talk around texts as a revisiting and reevaluation of an earlier private and individual reading (in the case of this class texts were read at home in preparation for each lesson). So discussion about and around texts can legitimately be seen as part of the reading process in a wider sense. Indeed this wider view of the reading process is largely what I claim as a key aspect of critical literacy.

THE CRITICAL READING COURSE

The course was offered as an optional module to students on a 1-year placement at a British University, Thames Valley University in West London. However it was also open to other students who had intermediate to advanced level of English language proficiency. About half the group of 14 students were first-year university students; the other half were preparing for the Cambridge University proficiency examination.

In addition, several students following a Masters' course in Teaching English to Speakers of Other Languages (TESOL) audited the course. Most of the students were in their late teens and came mainly from European countries such as France, Spain, and Germany but also included students from Japan, China, and Indonesia. The course was a 15-week, one-semester course meeting for 2 hours per week and was the successor to a number of similar courses, all of which shared two basic principles: an interest in everyday community texts (I draw on the term introduced by Luke, O'Brien, & Comber, 1994) as legitimate objects of study and the development of some specific linguistic tools as a means of analysis. The first of this series of courses is described in Wallace (1992).

Aims and Procedures

The course was posited on the following principles:

1. A basic principle of the course design was that it should keep in sight throughout a context–text relation. As Fowler (1996) counseled: "when teaching it is necessary to specify context in some detail, indicating relevant historic economic and institutional circumstances" (p. 10). The course shifted focus from context to text over the 15 weeks of the course, but aimed to keep the contextual and cultural framing of texts always in sight. Specifically, this meant that the study of any particular text was always seen in its relation to other texts and their associated genres and discourses.

2. Consistent with a shift of focus from context to text was a move from practice to process. That is, the course began with discussion of literacy practices, and associated roles and identities, before looking at ideological effects in texts. For instance, in early sessions students were asked to do simple literacy ethnographies similar in spirit to the kind carried out by the students in the study by Barro et al. (1993). This meant any of the following out of class tasks:

- Observation of reading and writing practices, within particular everyday contexts, such as in homes or on public transport.

- Observation of the presence and physical location of texts, for example, hoardings, community leaflets, and the situating of political material and advertisements in public places.

- Preliminary discussion of the sociocultural significance of both the practices observed and the nature and range of the genres observed.

The assumption underpinning these activities is that patterns of literacy behavior and the framing of literacy events carry social and ideological significance.

3. The need for some kind of model of language, to support language awareness development, was judged axiomatic. I opted for a grammatical framework based on systemic functional grammar that was introduced progressively. This involved the introduction of a simple set of terms within Halliday's (1985) broad macrofunctions of Field, Tenor and Mode, such as *participants*, *processes*, *modality*, *cohesion*. Reasons for drawing on Hallidayan grammar related to:

  - The need for a set of grammatical terms, as a metalanguage to articulate—to pin down—perhaps to rethink, responses to texts made in first impression, more intuitive, global ways.

  - The need for a grammar that has breadth and can link micro to macro textual functions.

  - The need for a grammar that allows the possibility of moving progressively to greater depth of analysis, so that students can find their own level, consistent with their existing knowledge about grammar and their needs and interests in following the course. Some students were able and willing to operate a wider spectrum of terms than others who drew on the framework very selectively.

Such a grammatical framework, it was envisaged, would offer explicitness about key concepts. Moreover, it would provide a metalanguage for the description of terms such as *genre, intertextuality* and the term *context* itself, as well as for terms at textual level.

Texts and Tasks

Texts were drawn from a wide range of community sources and both the students and I brought texts to the classroom. Progression was based on genre rather than topic. Particularly with a group of students from diverse cultural backgrounds it is interesting to compare the existence of genres in different cultural contexts and to see how generic conventions are realized in different ways. Thus genre was the organizing principle. However one is still left with choices as to how to order the genres to offer a rational kind of progression. The choice was made to begin with interpersonal texts, as more accessible to foreign language students, moving on to descriptive and report texts and concluding with expository texts. Within these broadly defined text types that are universally identifiable, are located culture specific realizations of these, in the shape of genres, such as advertisements, political manifestos, leaflets, and newspaper editorials.

As well as criteria related to linguistic and cultural content is the issue of ideological content. Although I argue (cf. Wallace, 1995) that ideology is a feature of texts—not merely a matter of interpretation—ideology is not equally salient. However lack of salience does not mean lack of significance. Indeed the reverse is arguably the case. In terms of text selection one might opt to begin with texts in which ideology is worn on its sleeve, so to speak, moving on to those whose ideological loading is more covert.

Just as the texts were introduced so as to pose progressively greater demands on the students, so were the tasks. Another key principle was that the task should match the text type or genre. Clearly, in mainstream reading we do not read a recipe in the way we would a postcard. Admittedly there is a dilemma here if we accept that one aim of critical reading is to read against the grain by resisting the professed purpose of the text, the manner in which it explicitly announces itself. Nonetheless, although our ultimate goal may be to subvert the intention of text producers, by, for instance, not reading an advertisement in order to purchase something or a magazine article as light reading, we need some initial understanding of what kind of job particular texts are trying to do. Moreover, certain grammatical features repay scrutiny in different kinds of texts and I aimed to reflect this in task design.

A Sample Lesson

Here I look in more detail at one lesson, Lesson 4, to consider not just the content but the classroom interaction that followed the group text analysis. The lesson procedure was as follows: teacher presentation of the text (already read at home), discussion of the genre, with introduction of other exemplars from students as well as teacher, analysis in groups, and, finally, sharing of interpretations. It is this final feedback episode, which typically lasted for about 20 minutes, which I want to claim is particularly important for critical literacy study in the classroom. It allows students, through their selected spokesperson, the opportunity to make explicit their grounds for judgements and opinions and to open them up to other pairs and groups. It reveals the manner in which the teacher exercises a judicious control of proceedings, offering support, clarifying, and contributing her own views or, conversely, exercising power in unacceptable ways.

In short, how does the teacher manage critical talk, which, as argued earlier, is part of what I want to understand by critical literacy? With this question in mind, my account of the lesson content, that is the text and the accompanying task, is followed by commentary on some key aspects of the teacher's role in the feedback episode.

One of the key concepts that the course aimed explicitly to introduce was that of readership, in particular, the idea of model readership and this was the focus of this task that involved identifying the readership of an advertisement for a car (see Fig. 13.1). The major part of the text reads: "Almost anyone can achieve power, the trick is staying in control." In the visual, alongside the picture of the car, is a tumbling statue of Lenin, to whom the text makes reference with the words: "As Lenin wrote, the trick is 'not merely a struggle for power but a struggle against power.' A principle that didn't make for a very pleasant political system, but does keep you in control of your car." As noted earlier, the course assumed the need for a working set of terms to talk about both context and text, to emphasize the manner in which texts of all kinds mediate in the business of everyday life and carry cultural meaning. Thus, terms introduced so far included *context*, what we might understand by context of situation and context of culture, and *genre*. At the same time three key questions had been introduced to guide the macrolevel study of texts carried out in the early weeks of the course. These, adapted from Kress (1985) were: Why has this text been written? What is the topic of this text? Who is this text addressed to?

These continued to be used as orientation questions for initial responses to texts throughout the course with the expectation that they would be revisited, as first-glance readings were revised on closer inspection of the text. For this lesson our interest was in question three. What kind of reader is envisaged and what kind of evidence, both textual and contextual, can we draw on to make a judgment? It was made clear that judgments are not definitive or categorical, but provisional.

Fig. 13.1   An advertisement for a Peugeot car alongside a falling statue of Lenin. Reproduced by permission of Euro RSCG.

However such a task allows us to pose a question that is not typically asked in orthodox reading comprehension. At this stage of the course the text is being analyzed at a fairly superficial level with attention directed at lexical word meaning, in particular connotation. The students worked in groups before offering their comments in the whole-class discussion episode.

THE INTERACTION AROUND TEXTS: FOCUS ON THE TEACHER'S ROLE

I focus on the teacher as necessarily the one with greatest power in the classroom, power in its institutionally ascribed sense. It is largely her or his behavior and her or his management of the talk that facilitates or frustrates the development of critical literacy. If we take talk around texts to be part of what we understand by critical literacy, as argued earlier, then it is the teacher's role to scaffold talk both in order to offer equality of opportunity for students' participation in the classroom community and to offer linguistic tools with which to explore in productive ways the nature of ideological meaning within texts. Here we might draw on three terms that Kramsch (1993) adapted from Goffman (1981) in order to account for the roles that are potentially available to the teacher and that involve the assertion of different kinds of power and control, taking, as noted earlier, power to mean a misplaced, unproductive assertion of the teacher's role, and control to be the legitimate exercise of the teacher's professionalism and expertise. Goffman (1981) talked of three potential speaker roles: that of animator, author, and principal. Adapted to the classroom setting, we might, as Kramsch (1993) suggested, see these roles as follows: As principal, the teacher addresses students according to her position in the social structure drawing on the authority institutionally ascribed to her; as animator, the teacher may be displaying utterances, animating the words of others, possibly by reading aloud the classroom materials; as authors, teachers are speaking in their own voice either within the dominant communication of the classroom or as part of what Kramsch called *sideplays*, in which both teacher and students may slip into different identities.

As principal, the teacher is in charge of the class and much of the talk she or he handles is in this role. It takes the form of what we might call *managerial talk*. This is talk as control in that it is used to scaffold the whole proceedings, to shape the genre, to make it recognizable as a lesson rather than, for instance, a party, a meeting, or a conversation. As animator the teacher is a mouthpiece for a prescribed syllabus. We might also extend the term to include the role in which the teacher frequently animates students' utterances, bringing them to the public sphere. Only as author does she or he engage substantively with issues raised ongoingly.

She or he may also shift into a different identity, possibly on the basis of co-membership with her students, in incidents of side-play. I offer an example of side-play in the Power and Control class. One student, Mirja, offers a qualification to Blanca's claim that "men know more about what's going on." This triggers a side sequence of overlapping turns in which Mirja, Blanca, and CW mutually support each other in solidary fashion on the basis of "we know what men are like":

CW: Anything else you want to add? That's good so far ...

B: Well, its (the advertisement is) for men especially, because its like men are in politics, they know more about the war, what's going on, I mean its ...

M: They're supposed to know more.

B: Yes, they're supposed (general laughter)

CW: Yes ... you always ... yes

B: And the language is quite difficult as well I mean ...

CW: And men can understand more difficult language, you think?

B: No, I don't think so but *they* may think so.

This incident is clearly playful, and incidental to the main business of the lesson. However the teacher, as author, can make more substantive and significant contributions to the overall scaffolding of argument. Young (1992) used the term *fellow enquirer* to describe the teacher identity during those moments of classroom interaction in which there is a series of turns that mutually advance knowledge and understanding, without necessarily reaching closure. On these occasions, the teacher's expertise and authority as principal is "tempered by the knowledge that the purpose is not simply to transmit a set curriculum ... but to foster the pupil's participation in enquiry" (p. 103).

Within these broad role orientations or *footings*, in Goffman's (1981) terms, fit familiar classroom moves, such as reformulation, feedback, and praise. Often it is not the occurrence of these moves as such which is significant but the manner in which they are deployed, which relates to the footing adopted by the teacher. For instance a reformulation may simply animate what students have already contributed, adding nothing new of substance, or it may be an authored contribution from the teacher in the sense that she or he is adding her or his own insights and observations.

Drawing on samples from lesson 4, I offer examples of the teacher filling her role as principal, animator and author respectively.

The Teacher as Principal

As might be expected, this role is exercised at the margins of each episode; the following words function to mark the boundary between the previous group work and the feedback episode to come: "This worked quite well last time. Are you ready in each pair or group just to say something because as I went round I heard people ... people were making some very interesting points about this text."

As principal, the teacher also links the current lesson to future ones. The following example shows her attempting to locate the present lesson in the wider rationale of the course as a whole: "This is what we're going to try and do, you know. When we look at the language, we get a feeling about something. What is it in the language that gives us this?"

The Teacher as Animator

The teacher may be animating, that is, acting as mouthpiece or conduit of classroom material that is not of her or his design or selection. This will be the case when the teacher is using a manual or coursebook, the content of which she or he may be relaying to the students with little or no mediating authorship. This role was hardly relevant in this particular class as the material was designed and planned by myself as the teacher, in consultation with the students. However there are different ways in which teachers may act as animators. They may, for instance, animate orthodox practice unreflectingly in the way of giving praise rather than offering substantive, authored responses. This is the drift of one critically astute comment in the final evaluation of an earlier Critical Reading course:

> I'd like to say something typically English, because here everything you say is always right and a good idea. With English people (teachers especially) you always feel you do very good. Why don't they tell you the truth when you're wrong? That would help you and not upset you. That's a shame because sometimes we've not been told enough what we were saying wasn't exactly right. This feeling of English people using euphemism and not saying the truth is a feeling foreign people have when they come to England. And I think a *critical* view of what we say wouldn't be a bad idea.

This student, from Germany, clearly felt exasperated by my failure to engage with her as author rather than merely animating classroom platitudes. "Tell me what you really think," she is saying.

Equally the teacher may act as animator of the students' contributions by simply repeating them. In such cases, interventions are displays of power rather than exercise of control, in the sense that they do not scaffold the interaction, either interpersonally or ideationally in meaningful ways. An example of the second instance is this moment when my attempt to broker the exchange between Virginia and Domingo is disruptive rather than facilitative. Domingo challenges the text, to be in turn directly challenged by Virginia:

D: I believe that the whole advertisement doesn't make sense at all (general laughter) and I think they do that on purpose. I think they do that on purpose because that way …

V: It does. It makes sense.

D: It makes sense? The whole thing?

V: It makes sense. Yes, very clear.

CW: Christine is it?

V: No Virginia.

CW: Virginia. I meant Virginia.

D: I wish everybody could explain to me …

CW: OK Virginia thinks it does make sense.

V: Yes it does.

CW: So would you like to say what the sense is?

My words: "Virginia thinks it does make sense" merely animate her own words and the question: "Would you like to say what the sense is?" is gratuitous, as Virginia is about to support her challenge to Domingo quite spontaneously.

The Teacher as Author

Revealingly, there are few instances in this lesson of the teacher as author, occasions that is, where she engages substantively with a student's contribution by way of promoting clarification or enhancement of argument. One case, arguably, follows Virginia's response to Domingo's earlier question:

> V: It does (make sense) because the car is a super car. It's a powerful car, so its like a big enterprise, like a country. Lenin, applying his principle, was not able to manage the political system in his country and he fell, but you, applying this system, and being responsible, and with control, you can control this super car.

> CW: Who is "you" by the way? When you say: "You can control"?

In comparable episodes later in the course, this questioning stance is occasionally replaced by more spontaneously authored responses which are impromptu reflections on students' contributions. For instance two students offer contrasting interpretations of the discourses in a text to which I respond:

> CW: Thank you. That's interesting. You were taking slightly—well different views: Is he the sort of "victim of events" or is he …? I think both are true in a funny sort of way eh oddly be … because texts can mean two things at the same time.

CONCLUSION

In the interests of empowering students as learners and co-discussants we can argue the case for the teacher's dual role in the classroom as principal and author. As animator there is an attempt to assert power but, ironically, with a concomitant loss of control. The teacher as animator is only apparently powerful because she or he has not taken responsibility as author for either the content or procedure of lessons. Indeed in many settings teachers are denied this responsibility, being expected to merely deliver a teaching programme handed to her or him via a fixed curriculum. Deskilled teachers mean disempowered learners. As Virginia noted in her comment about the control of the car: The exercise of control involves responsibility.

In short, both teacher and students are empowered, not by merely animating preset curricula and materials, but by becoming authors of their respective contributions to the classroom community. Although the teacher cannot lose sight of her or his role as principal—it is this, as argued earlier, which makes the event a lesson as opposed to a friendly chat—it is likely to be the case that, as the class grows and evolves as an interpretative community she will, as author, play a greater role as a coparticipant in the kind of critical enquiry that, I argue, forms part of the negotiation of critical literacy development in the classroom.

ACKNOWLEDGMENT

This chapter is indebted to conversations with the late Professor Basil Bernstein, who generously offered his time to discuss its content with me.

REFERENCES

Andersen, R. (1988). *The power and the word.* London: Paladin.
Auerbach, E. (1992). Literacy and ideology. *Annual Review of Applied Linguistics, 12,* 71–85.
Auerbach, E., & Wallerstein, N. (1987). *ESL for action: Problem posing at work.* Reading, MA: Addison and Wesley Hall.
Barro, A., Byram, M., Grimm, H., Morgan, C., & Roberts, C. (1993). Cultural studies for advanced language learners. *Language and culture.* Clevedon: British Studies in Applied Linguistics 7 in association with Multilingual Matters.
Bernstein, B. (1996). *Pedagogy symbolic control and identity: theory, research, critique.* London: Taylor & Francis.
Eco, U. (1992). Between author and text. In S. Collini (Ed.), *Interpretation and overinterpretation* (pp. 67–88). New York: Cambridge.
Fairclough, N. (1989). *Language and power.* London: Longman.
Fish, S. (1980). *Is there a text in this class?* Cambridge, MA: Harvard.
Fowler, R. (1996). On critical linguistics. In C. Caldas-Coulthard & M. Coulthard (Eds.), *Texts and practices* (pp. 3–14). London: Routledge & Kegan Paul.
Freire, P. (1972). *Pedagogy of the oppressed.* London: Penguin.
Gee, J. (1990). *Social linguistics and literacies: Ideologies in discourse.* London: Falmer.
Goffman, E. (1981). *Forms of talk.* Oxford: Blackwell.
Halliday, M. A. K. (1985). *An introduction to functional grammar.* London: Edward Arnold.
Kramsch, C. (1993). *Context and culture in language teaching.* Oxford: Oxford.
Kress, G. (1985). *Linguistic processes in sociocultural practice.* Waurn Ponds, Victoria, Australia: Deakin University Press.
Lankshear, C. (1994). *Critical literacy (Occasional paper no. 3).* Canberra, Australia: Australian Curriculum Studies Association.
Lankshear, C. (1997). *Changing literacies.* Buckingham: Open University.
Luke, A. (1996). Genres of power? Literacy education and the production of capital. In R. Hasan & G. Williams (Eds.), *Literacy in society* (pp. 308–338). London: Longman.

Luke, A., O'Brien, J., & Comber, B. (1994). Making community texts objects of study. *Australian Journal of Language and Literacy, 17*(2), 139–149.

McCarthy, T. (1994). On the idea of a critical theory and its relation to philosophy. In D. Hoy & T. McCarthy (Eds.), *Critical theory* (pp. 5–22). Oxford: Blackwell.

Rothery, J. (1996). Making changes: Developing an educational linguistics. In R. Hasan & G. Williams (Eds.), *Literacy in society* (pp. 86–123). London: Longman.

Wallace, C. (1992). Critical literacy awareness in the EFL classroom. In N. Fairclough (Ed.), *Critical language awareness* (pp. 59–92). London: Longman.

Wallace, C. (1995). Reading with a suspicious eye: Critical reading in the foreign language classroom. In G. Cook & B. Seidlhofer (Eds.), *Principle and practice in applied linguistics: Studies in honour of H.G. Widdowson* (pp. 335–348). Oxford: Oxford.

Wallace, C. (1998). *Critical language awareness in the foreign language classroom.* Unpublished PhD thesis, University of London, London.

Young, R. (1992). *Critical theory and classroom talk.* Clevedon: Multilingual Matters.

14

Building Bridges/Making Meanings: Texts of Popular Culture and Critical Pedagogy in Theory and Practice

James W. Bell
Australian Institute of Education, Murdoch
University Campus, Western Australia

This chapter is addressed to teachers who are interested in critical education theory, but for whom much of this theory seems abstract and unrelated to their daily classroom practices. Critical theory[1] is often complex,
sometimes contradictory, and frequently seen as that which is done by ac-
ademics at the university instead of an accessible discourse that invites
the involvement of everyone connected to education. Far too often students and their teachers have difficulty in finding their way into these con-

---

[1]Critical theory is not a cohesive body of theoretical work. Generally it addresses issues of
the ways power and knowledge are related to each other and are structured in society. A
common goal of many critical theorists is first to understand how unnecessary human suffering in the world has been socially constructed and second to act in ways which might begin
to undo some of this unnecessary suffering. As such it is concerned with both concepts and
practices pertaining to social justice.

versations that unfortunately, exclude them from the benefits of critical theory practice.

Critical pedagogy has been cited by a number of thinkers as remaining relatively remote and inaccessible to many of those in whose interests it is written (Kanpal, 1994; Shapiro, 1990; Shor, 1987). Kanpol noted that perhaps the major obstacle he faces in his own critical practice is what his students argue is "critical pedagogy's obscure language [which] makes radical educational ideas almost impossible to grasp" (p. 159). He continued: " This becomes, they argue, a contradiction to the very argument critical pedagogists make: simply, that critical pedagogy is a means and method to undercut oppressive social relations and an attempt to end alienation and subordination" (p. 159).

If the language of critical pedagogy cannot be made more accessible then critical practices cannot emerge in the culture of everyday school life. If critical pedagogical theory cannot be brought into the daily conversations and lives of teachers and their students then it is failing those people in whose interests it has been created.

It is my contention that using texts of popular culture that have a specifically ideological nature is an important way of opening a more critical discourse in primary and secondary classrooms. Texts of popular culture exist everywhere around us and are being used more frequently as classroom resources. Although we are generally aware of the effects these texts may have on the psyche and consciousness of our students and ourselves, we seldom appropriate such texts for a more critical understanding of our world.

RESEARCH SETTING

There were three specific but overlapping goals of my research work with student teachers at the University of North Carolina at Greensboro. First I was interested in probing the critical rationality of student teachers after viewing a popular film, *Pump Up the Volume*. Second I was interested in presenting to these students the ways in which a carefully chosen popular film might resonate with their own lives as future teachers as well as with the lives of their future students. Third I wanted to demonstrate that popular films might be used in critical ways in a number of settings and not only in English Literature or Social Studies curricula, that popular films, in whole or excerpt, might be useful in a critical way in Mathematics classes (i.e., *Stand and Deliver*) or other unexpected classroom settings.

I wanted to understand how dialogs with students may be facilitated through the use of popular film texts. I reasoned that by understanding students' subjective experiences new dialogs about their personal, ethical, and political activities would be possible.

Ryan and Kellner (1988) in their introduction to *Camera Politica* describe the representational power of films in this way:

> Films transcode the discourses (the forms, figures, and representations) of social life into cinematic narratives. Rather than reflect a reality external to the film medium, films execute a transfer from one discursive field to another. As a result, films themselves become part of the broader cultural system of representations that construct social reality. That construction occurs in part through the internalisation of representations. (pp. 12–13)

Here Ryan and Kellner offered a rationale for bringing popular film texts into classroom practice. They argued that films execute a transfer from one discursive field to another. It is this quality of popular film which led me to investigate the power popular film might have in certain university classroom situations. My specific interest was to see how popular film, as a body of generally accessible cultural representations, might be used as a bridge between student experience and the more generally inaccessible body of critical theory. I also wanted to offer an alternative type of assessment that valued students' experiences from outside the classroom.

Many of the students in the teacher education program were young and from traditional educational backgrounds. The course, The Institution of Education, was required of all students who pass through the program and was perhaps the only course in which these students were asked to address a range of topics including issues of social justice and inequality, the social construction of reality, and the moral and political implications of schooling. Many students in each class became overwhelmed and found that they were unable to connect their own voices and experiences with these often challenging issues.

Given this context, popular films were a compelling choice for me. I have always liked films and have often found myself in ongoing dialogs with myself and with others during and after viewing films. I have also been concerned that too little has been done with film. As powerful and as penetrating as film is, little has been done to tap into this power and incorporate it into a reflective public sphere. Most importantly for these classes, popular films are accessible to most all class members. Furthermore, popular films are not in the specific domain of academic material and knowledge: High school and college students are the largest consumers of popular film. Because of this popular films can cross the domain between student "popular" knowledge and academic "high" knowledge. Popular films can be powerful bridging devices between everyday experiences and critically meaningful understandings of these experiences.

In such course contexts in which a wide range of issues are dealt with I have used a number of popular films that have a powerful critical and educational text or subtext. These are subjective choices, but I believe that most popular film has critical significance that can be read in relation to critical practice in education. Films I have offered for students in these class situations are *Rumble Fish, The Year My Voice Broke, Roger & Me, Dead Poets Society, Cool Hand Luke, Shirley Valentine, Matewan, Miss Jane Pitman, Ironweed, Tommy,* and *Sex, Lies & Videotape.* In this chapter I chose to use the film *Pump Up the Volume* because of the way it explicitly raises issues of student voice and voicelessness, democratic possibility, and forms of alienation in a school setting.

POPULAR CULTURE IN THE CLASSROOM

Popular culture can be seen as having an important place in the lives of students. Giroux and Simon (1989) maintained that popular cultural studies are pedagogically important. They extend our critical pedagogical activity into the realm of students' own subjectivities. They allow us to build bridges to their moral and political practices as they come into the school world.

Before going on to explore some of the issues concerning the use of popular culture in the classroom it is important that we become sensitive to the ways in which popular culture impacts the lives of students. Aronowitz (1989) wrote:

> If Althusser claims that the school is the chief ideological state apparatus, this may hold for the production of the symbolic system, the constellation of signs and codes of which what counts as reliable knowledge is constructed; but the mass media construct the social imaginary, the place where kids situate themselves in their emotional life, where the future appears as a narration of possibilities as well as limits. (p. 199)

As Aronowitz (1989) wrote about the social imaginary of students being constructed through various forms of the mass media, he invites us to understand the relationship between students and popular culture texts as a negotiation of possibilities and limits in their lives. It is the psychological space in between the student and the text that is of utmost importance. This is the negotiated space, the space that is marked by both the past experiences of the student and the particular presentation of the text, both the content of the text and what has been left out of the text. Such a perspective demands that we rethink educational activity as not merely the reading of texts or the command of a canon of real and trans-historical knowledge. Within such a rethinking of educational activity we can take seriously educational settings as sites for understanding the relationships between texts and the real lives of students. From this perspective new kinds of pedagogical hope might emerge and grow.

STUDENT EDUCATORS CONVERSE WITH PUMP UP THE VOLUME

In this section I present elements of a conversation among a group of four student educators and me after an informal viewing of the film *Pump Up The Volume*. I probe the kinds of critical issues and thinking that emerged in this conversation, the challenges that these students raised, the excitement they experienced after viewing the film, and the possibilities they desired for more just educational practices. Also I explore some of the dilemmas and powerlessness these students articulated in using *Pump Up The Volume* as a critical teaching resource.

The four student teachers were between the ages of 20 and 26 and had all received at least a general introduction to critical thinking as it relates to educational processes and pedagogy. All four, two women and two men, had some years of living and working experience between their leaving high school and coming to the university. All four students reported that they felt in some ways called to the teaching profession. They wanted to be teachers not merely for professional efficacy, but also for the ways in which they might provide meaningful differences and support in their students' lives. These student teachers, all White and from reportedly stable working-class backgrounds, are not dissimilar to a great proportion of student teachers from this university as well as in universities throughout the United States or in many other countries.

These student teachers were not used as a representative sample. The assumption I made was that these student teachers were as deeply embedded in cultural forms and contradictions as the rest of us. At the same time these student teachers were keen to apply their rudimentary introduction to critical pedagogy. In the following conversation about using a popular film text as a teaching resource, I was interested in the kinds of critical consciousness that emerged.

Pump Up the Volume, written and directed by Allen Moyle (1990) is a film about alienation, powerlessness and despair as it occurs in the lives of a number of fictitious characters who live in the mythical town of Paradise Hills, Arizona. It is also about these characters finding space and opportunity to express their own voices, voices that have otherwise been silenced in their school and home lives. It can justifiably be said that this film is another teenage angst movie created as upper B-grade cinema fodder for a carefully researched and marketed target audience. (Indeed, it is hard to find any film created for general release that is not specifically created for some carefully targeted audience.) In some ways the film is perfect for investigating the possibilities and limitations of using popular film texts for making issues of alienation and social voicelessness more accessible to viewing audiences. Furthermore, the presentation of these themes is far from being unproblematic. The moral representations in this film are often at odds and the power and quality of the contradictions that emerge are more marked than are the resolutions provided for the audience by the end of the film.

This film tells the story of Mark, up-rooted from New York City in his last years of high school, and how he combats the loneliness and isolation of that move by presenting a nightly unregistered and anonymous talk-radio show of ribald dissent, angst, and remarkably perceptive social critique. Mark learns that not all is well at his school as increasing numbers of poorly performing students are expelled. Fellow student, Nora, discovers Mark's identity and the two become involved in pushing the possibilities of the radio show to finally uncover what is going on at the school. They push the message to the listening audience, largely made up of local students, to "seize the air" and refuse the isolation and meaninglessness that is both promoted and accepted by their school and larger environment.

The four contradictory themes in this film can be simply identified as: cynicism and despair versus hope and possibility; traditional role models versus radical role models; alienation and the culture of individualism versus solidarity and community responsibility; liberal conservative reform versus radical and revolutionary change. By discussing the contradictions of the film we might begin to develop a more critically meaningful dialog. As it emerged with these students, however, such conversational spaces are both unfamiliar and difficult. Although these student teachers were able to speak and recreate some of the contradictions and tensions presented within such a popular culture text, it was much more difficult for them to become aware that they were speaking within, and indeed living within, these popular texts.

ON CYNICISM AND DESPAIR VERSUS HOPE AND POSSIBILITY

One of the most powerful responses of the student teachers was their description of hope. Hope for these student teachers was contradictory. On the one hand, they all highly valued hopefulness in their lives. Their desire for a more hopeful living and being was evident throughout their conversations. On the other hand, however, ideas and possibilities of hope were most always closely followed by concerns and experiences of despair.

Pump Up the Volume excited and offered hope for these students. And they were aware of the pleasure involved in seeing a film that is explicitly about activities of hope and transformation. Said one after commenting on the disparity between the good intentions of everyday people and the staid and disempowering everdayness of their lived reality: "But it's nice to be able to live that [the hope of the film] for two hours. It's almost like you're living in him [Mark, the main character] and you're saying 'Yeah, yeah, we can do this, we can do this!'"

The hope expressed, however, was stated with a realization that this is only a film, this is a place for me to live my fantasies before I return to the everyday world.

Another student teacher responded in a way that demonstrated a similar appreciation for the power of the film and an experience of the difficulty of turning the hope within the film into action: "But you're not going to go out and do what he did. At least you can go out and live that [the experience] of facing and addressing alienation, voiceless and despair in a liberational and transformative way for a couple of hours."

This person highlights what I understand to be one of the most limiting dimensions of popular culture texts. The film, or any other popular text, has seductive and erotic features that lead the viewer into particular forms of pleasure. In this case, which is typical of film experience, the film brackets the experience so that the desire for a different reality is felt only within the time bracket of the film experience. Furthermore, films are presented in ways so that the tensions and contradictions that excite are also difficult for the viewer to articulate.

A significant problem with the "good feel" of this film is that this euphoric hopefulness is short-lived. When I asked what a person should do when they lose the hope that the film helped engender, a student responded that you go and see the film again. In such a way, however, the film stands as a pleasure commodity with little or no lasting social resonance. If our hopefulness is dependent on our being within the immediate experience of the consumption of the popular film, we are unable to live any real-life hope after the film. The hopefulness becomes an illusory and transitory experience that we pay for but do not expect or believe that we might take into other parts of our life. This seems to me to be a pseudo and nihilistic kind of hopefulness. The critical nature of hope, as presented in the film, exists only as illusion so long as it remains safely within the boundaries of that film.

Hope is essentially desired by these student teachers and they were quick to remind me of this. One participant identified with the main character, Mark, and, after apologizing for possible egotism in such an identification, commented on the contradictions of the character: "I think I identify with the dualism in his character of hope and desperation at the same time. Why? Why did he hope things would be better? Because basically if he lost that hope, then he's lost everything."

This participant was reluctant to despair and was ready to identify with a character who acted with hope in the face of overwhelming odds and with marked asymmetries of power between the school establishment and himself. Like Mark in the film, this student participant finds that there is not particularly much to hope for, but there is some significant power in developing a vision of a more just and compassionate world.

ON ROLE MODELS AND SOCIAL VISION: CONSERVATIVE, LIBERAL, AND RADICAL PRESENTATIONS

One of the more powerful dimensions of this conversation dealt with the action and qualities of a "good teacher." One participant found the teacher, Ms. Emerson, the good teacher of the film, to be the conduit for hopeful transformation in the narrative: "I liked her role. I liked the fact that eventually she did speak out and that she was the kind of connector to the students and hope in that system."

All of the participants saw the role of teacher as being one of communicator and bringer of hope in a world where hope is often elusive if not already snuffed out. Their vision of a good teacher, however, is a liberal one. They do not yet see the teacher as a professional who must be committed to an ongoing critical appraisal of pedagogical practice in the schools.

The student teachers praised this teacher in the film for her courage (she is fired from her job for her outspokenness and for challenging authority). They admired her compassion for her students and her ability to identify with the lives of her students. This teacher was young and had not outlived her idealism. Perhaps most important to these participants was this teacher's commitment to encouraging student voices in her classroom. As one participant commented: "She was, you know, trying to encourage him [Mark] to have that voice in the classroom and I feel that's really the important role of a teacher."

These student teachers expressed a valid goal of encouraging students' voices and usefully see that as an activity of the good teacher. Voice of itself, however, is insufficient in overcoming issues of powerlessness and alienation. What seems missing from these student teachers' analysis of Ms. Emerson is some kind of critique of her value-neutral stance as she encourages students to find their "heart's voice." There is no indication in these conversations that the participants are asking for critical understandings and moral challenges within their students. It seems that finding and promoting student voices, no matter what these voices might be saying, is enough. The student teachers have not yet seen themselves as people responsibly involved in guiding difficult moral and political conversations within their classrooms. Instead they are concerned with the challenges, which are considerable, of getting their students to say anything at all that is personally meaningful or significant to them.

The participants were generally suspicious of the role of teacher as conveyor of information. This is probably not surprising given that all the participants were nearing the end of their term in the undergraduate course in sociology of education and critical pedagogy. In the following passage a student simultaneously rejects the banking method of education in which information is simply deposited while advocating a teacher attitude that begins to take into account the real concerns, interests and needs of students:

> [For a student] it would be easy to take a piece of paper and write down a lot of stuff about Beowulf, but the paper doesn't feel and the paper doesn't think and the paper doesn't have other things like in the life of a student. So [as a teacher] it's just important to remember that you're not dealing with a bucket that you can pour stuff into. You're dealing with somebody that has feelings, and fears, and anxieties, and desires that are exclusive to whatever you have to say. And that [as a teacher] you're not doing the most important thing in the world [for all of the students].

Remarkable about this statement is that it begs teachers to be aware of their possibilities and limitations within a classroom situation. All too frequently, young teachers believe that they must somehow be all things to all people in the classroom situation. This is a belief reinforced by burgeoning government imperatives of what a teacher should be. These student teachers were aware that the things that go on in the classroom are not going to be the most important things in their students' lives. They actively reject a banking concept of education, at least on theoretical grounds, and respect their students as more than so much passive flesh needing to be filled with so much formal school knowledge.

It may very well be that teachers who take into account their own limitations with regard to what they are able to accomplish with people may be in a much better position to succeed. The students addressed challenges of speaking out about injustices in their school environment in the following and other statements: "The dilemma for someone in that situation is 'Do I quiet myself just enough to stay in the system, or what?' I mean, she stood up and lost her job.... As a teacher do you shut up just long enough to stay in there, you know. I imagine it's a real dilemma."

Understandably these student teachers seemed to be caught between wanting to speak out in difficult and unjust situations and wanting to obtain and keep their jobs, not only for the financial implications, but also because they foresaw losing their jobs under such circumstances and thereby also losing the potential effectiveness they would have with their students in their classrooms.

ON ALIENATION AND THE CULT OF INDIVIDUALISM VERSUS GROUP COMMITMENT AND COMMUNITY SOLIDARITY

These student teachers are deeply committed to seeing themselves as individuals. Their previous educational journeys have been ones of individual challenges and activities. They live in a culture that values the individual most highly. And the challenges they face in their professional lives are marked by attitudes of individualism and isolation. They see their battles as ones that must be fought in a kind of social and professional vacuum. The only kind of community consciousness I detected in their conversations was related to the coarse body language and profanity in the film.

Perhaps the greatest concern for the participants was indeed the fairly extreme use of coarse and profane language in the film although they seemed to believe that this was essential for the film. Said one student teacher:

> It's like a wake-up call.... It's because a lot of voices are so stifled that they have to go a little bit overboard to be heard. Like when you have a group that is speaking out against something ... they have to do things like break windows and make noises and do things that they would probably not do under normal circumstances because it is the only way that people are going to stand up and listen to them. That's the only way that they are going to be heard.

There is an attitude among this group that the coarse language helped to break the silence for the characters within the film as well as for the audience:

> It seems to me that there are a large cluster of taboo topics. Things you don't say.... It seems to me that profanity and talking about existential turmoil are taboo. Once you get inside the school and say 'Listen, get buck naked and fuck', then you've broken that barrier and you can start [talking about] the existential turmoils of schools.... So I think within the context of this movie [the profanity] was like chipping the rock from the bottom of the dam so that the entire thing could just collapse and all the water could run through and we could talk about suicide, and we could talk about mastur-

bation, and we could talk about alienation, we could talk about how the school sucks etc., etc.

This tells me that these students find it difficult to see people coming together in socially meaningful ways except in a kind of violent or wildly disorganized protest. Indeed, western industrial cultures present very few favorable or popular images or stories of people joining in communities of solidarity. Although there is a belief in using rough language to open up an important critical sphere and potentially reduce isolation, one participant told the story of a particular freshman student who was in a biology class that he deplored:

> There's this guy in my Biology class who is a freshman, 18 years old and he's hating this Biology class with all his heart. And he sits beside me in class and every once in a while he'll just scream. I mean he'll just be very loud with some kind of odd remark or odd sound. And it's like he's looking, he's frustrated, he's sick of it, he's voicing it but it's not an effective voice, unfortunately. It's effective for him in that little moment.

The student in the biology class is simultaneously admired for his coming to his own voice and is disliked for the disturbing and disruptive influence he has on the rest of the class. Undoubtedly other students in the biology class are experiencing similar kinds of despair and struggle. But the student relating this tale does not see this voice as something that might be amplified through the despair of others in the class or beyond. Again, the individual is alone and isolated. There is no vision of a group consciousness that can express particular voices in amplified and communal ways.

DISCUSSION

During our discussion of the issues related to the film's use of a large amount of profanity and coarse body language the matter of the body at school was raised. I found it interesting that these student teachers wavered between speaking quite candidly among themselves and with me on their ideas and reflections on the film and speaking in a more guarded and formal university-speak. This latter more formal discussion seemed to obscure their more candid experiences with the film. I was aware of the tilt in the power asymmetry in my direction in relation to the group: although not their lecturer, I was a lecturer in the course they were completing. The conversations we had, however, were not as rich as I had hoped. Although the students were not reluctant to speak, their discourse was limited both by their language and the lack of experience they have had in articulating critical cultural experiences.

Although all the students believed that the PG rated film was quite powerful and raised many important issues related to education, most said that they would be unwilling to show the film in a high school class setting. I wondered why. One student responded that they would not show the film if they wanted to keep their job with the provision: "Oh yeah, unless I'm going to run up to the TV and cut down the volume every time there's a four-letter word." There was general agreement among the participants on this issue.

A contradiction arises in the value that these student teachers placed on the role of coarse language and explicit body and sexual references. The group was in strong agreement that such expressions were absolutely essential to the film in breaking down the barriers for the audience to look at and listen to the real and personally important concerns of students in schools. Disturbingly, these student teachers are going into schools with a strong belief that they are not allowed to talk about the things that really matter to their students and in ways that are accessible and comfortable to their students. However, if they are still committed to these activities, they will certainly suffer a number of tensions given this dilemma.

The educational outlook for these student teachers is not good. These student teachers see themselves as alone and isolated, and they will bring this attitude with them into their professional school lives. This belief will only encourage and normalize this isolation. These student teachers do not talk about teachers coming together in political ways to work for the kinds of justice in the schools that they affirm. Alone and without an understanding or belief that a public forum may present them with new possibilities for support and power in their professional contexts, the outlook for these people's work in education is bleak, indeed.

They long for a professional life of meaning and significance. They have a developing moral sensibility in relation to what is really important in the lives of students and what really hurts students. Much of this understanding is related to their own school experiences. They need skills in talking about these issues, in seeing and discussing the contradictions in which they are suspended as teachers in the educational system. Their vision of the world is so dominated by individualism that it will be difficult for them to engage with other colleagues in beginning to create the kinds of pedagogy they can best envisage. They will hope, but will not hope for anything in particular, because, as one related, without hope "you have nothing left."

A difficult dilemma in these student educators' lives is the kind of Freirian (Freire, 1970) interplay between their moral consciences and their social and intellectual consciousnesses and how the development of this interplay relates to their critical pedagogical activity. These student educators, like a great many of their peers, are intensely well-meaning. They desire emancipatory classrooms to the extent that they can articulate injustices within educational settings. They are aware that current modes of educational practice are frequently unjust from their root constructions and are more often about silencing the critical and moral thinking of their students than they are about encouraging them. And to varying degrees they are also aware that current educational practices stand as a great sorting station whose ends are fundamentally about deciding which students are able and will achieve some version of "the good life" and which most probably will not. Furthermore, these student teachers are generally aware that the kinds of social practices taught in schools, both explicitly and implicitly, do much more to inhibit any critical rationality in their students than to promote such activity.

What has become increasingly clear to me from these students' conversations about the film *Pump Up The Volume* is the lack of awareness of the contradictions which are embedded in their own ways of describing possibilities within their professional educational practice as related to critical issues presented within the film. I believe, however, that it is by wrestling with these contradictory tensions that the greatest terrain of ideological and practical struggle might occur in their professional lives. Furthermore, I hold that it is within these contradictory tensions that students may begin to meet the challenges of the ongoing construction of their political subjectivities.

Such work demands, among other things, an acceptance that we are all, students and teachers alike, politically responsible world citizens. Further, we must accept that schools are a place to develop political understandings and action. An essential part of awakening political consciousness is developing a vision of a world we would like to create.

Giroux & Simon (1989), value the use of popular culture for the very reason that it helps educators to understand how their students are morally and politically involved in their everyday lives. Teachers can hope that the gulf between everyday life and school life may be bridged in some significant ways, and that through this bridging a more emancipatory educational practice may find genesis.

The value of including popular culture in the development of a critical pedagogy is that it provides the opportunity to further our understanding of how students make investments in particular social forms and practices. In other words, the study of popular culture offers the possibility of understanding how a politics of pleasure addresses students in a way that shapes and sometimes secures the often-contradictory relations they have to both schooling and the politics of everyday life (Giroux & Simon, 1989).

We must see this educational vision as liberal at possibly its most extreme and related to what the Polish philosopher Lesjek Kolokowski as quoted by Jones (1992), describes as *Democratic Socialism*:

> Democratic Socialism requires, in addition to commitment to a number of basic values, hard knowledge and rational calculation ... It is an obstinant will to erode by inches the conditions which produce avoidable suffering, oppression, hunger, wars, racial and national hatred, insatiable greed and vindictive envy. (p. 20)

Toward such democratic activity, social critique is absolutely crucial in the realization of any such inch-by-inch erosion of oppressive conditions. And, as expressions of popular culture are part of the dynamic of our contemporary understanding of reality, they must be critically evaluated in relation to goals of social justice.

CONCLUSION

What emerges from this conversation is not a clear litmus test for using this film as a source for improving critical literacy in the classroom. Rather, it is an illustration of the difficulties related to bringing any text of popular culture into a classroom to develop critical literacy. What becomes increasingly clear in this conversation are the conflicting sensibilities of the student teachers' experiences with this film text. Not surprisingly, many of their responses fit within the conflicting constructs Antonio Gramsci (cited in Femia, 1987) terms *good sense* and *bad sense*. This is a kind of dual sensibility in which critical clear sightedness coexists with an acritical close mindedness.

I do not wish to minimize the potential power of the critical sensibilities of these student teachers. The contradiction exists, however, that in some significant ways critical sensibility is all there and is not there at all. On the one hand, they know everything. They have all experienced the kinds of alienation and despair that is represented in the film. They know first hand how degrading it is to live a school life filled with largely meaningless and repetitious work, a life in which some of the most meaningful and important things are silenced and devalued. On the other hand, they know very little in a critical sense. They are seeking teaching positions in the schools and, although suspicious and critical of some of our current practices of schooling, they are invested in believing uncritically in the inherent goodness of schools. The mixture of both critical and acritical experiences with these student teachers and this film underscore the difficulties involved in developing critical literacy in the classroom through popular films.

The goal of understanding the moral and political subjectivities of students seems to be an essential element of a critical pedagogy. As individuals and as a larger community we have grown to desire certainty and resolution more than anything. In our increasingly despairing and randomly dangerous world we seek psychological and physical security more than ever. More than anything we want things that offer us safety, experiences and thoughts that help set our minds and bodies at ease.

Within the teaching professions there can hardly be a more certain and secure kind of pedagogy than that embodied in a banking concept of education or that which is based on an updated social learning model in which for any input X into the system some desirable and predictable output Y will occur. If there are problems with the output it is not that there is anything fundamentally wrong with the system. It is merely that the system needs some adjusting and fine tuning. IQ tests and standard curves all help to underscore our belief in a version of the world that is predictable, controllable, and without any significant unresolvable contradictions. Educational change within such a view must always be conservative. At best, such conservative reform will provide us with more of the same in our institutions of education. And, as is clear from most of the current debates relating to educational funding, there is relatively little support for even this kind of educational change and reform.

While longing for certain emancipatory changes within school life, these student teachers are reluctant to accept the kinds of upheaval and professional vulnerability that will occur in their own lives in the wake of such changes. Although they may not directly challenge the present school system, I hear these student teachers lifting their voices for a more just and compassionate world. They see themselves as educators with a kind of vision that reaches beyond current processes of educational practice and they have certain germinal understandings that educational practices are in need of radical transformation. Furthermore, they have begun to see that carefully chosen popular culture texts may well provide the bridging mechanisms between potent social theory and the problems and challenges faced by their students.

REFERENCES

Aronowitz, S. (1989). Working-class identity and celluloid fantasies in the electronic age. In H. A. Giroux & R. Simon (Eds.), *Popular culture: Schooling and everyday life* (pp. 197–218). New York: Bergin & Garvey.

Femia, J. F. (1987). *Gramsci's political thought: Hegemony, consciousness, and the revolutionary process.* Oxford: Clarendon.

Freire, P. (1970). *Cultural action for freedom.* Cambridge, MA: Harvard.

Giroux, H. A., & Simon, R. (1989). *Popular culture: Schooling and everyday life.* New York: Bergin & Garvey.

Jones, G. (1992). Redefining socialism. In D. Kerr (Ed.), *Reinventing socialism*. (pp. 11–26). Melbourne, Australia: Pluto.

Kanpol, B. (1994). *Critical pedagogy: An introduction.* London: Bergin & Garvey.

Moyle, A. (Writer and Director). (1990). *Pump up the volume* [Film]. (Available from New Line Cinema and RCA/Columbia Pictures Home Video, Burbank, CA)

Ryan, M., & Kellner, D. (1988). *Camera politica.* Bloomington, IN: Indiana University.

Shapiro, S. (1990). *Between capitalism and democracy: Educational policy and the crisis of the welfare state.* New York: Bergin & Garvey.

Shor, I. (1987). *Critical teaching and everyday life.* Chicago, IL: University of Chicago.

15

Responding to Academic Discourse: Developing Critical Literacy at a South African University

Jenny Clarence-Fincham
Natal University, South Africa

What is the impact of a South African university environment on first-year students as they enter the institution for the first time? In the South African context, the answer to this question is diverse and complex, with many intersecting, sometimes contradictory factors contributing to the experience as a whole.

For English-speaking students, both Black and White, who have had the benefits of a privileged education, initial university experience is challenging, often somewhat daunting, but it is not entirely unfamiliar. Many come from homes that incorporate educational experiences into early, primary discourse (Gee, 1996). So, although they are confronted by the demands of more independent life styles and the need to acquire aspects of academic literacy, their transition between school and university is relatively smooth. By sharp contrast, for the majority of Black, African students who are not native speakers of English, and who have experienced the deprivations of apartheid education, the university is an environment that represents both an extraordinary achievement and a totally unfamiliar set of experiences. They are inserted into a context in which learning in English is only the beginning and most obvious of an array of demands that can be alien and alienating.

Since the early 1980s, under increasing pressure and with growing rigor and commitment since the unbanning of the African National Congress (ANC) in 1990, South African educational institutions have begun to implement processes of transformation designed to redress the inequities and injustices of the past. This chapter considers one strand of such a process: It describes how Critical Language Awareness (CLA) was introduced into a university course in academic literacy entitled *Learning, Language and Logic*. This course, which was introduced at the University of Natal in Pietermaritzburg in 1984 has been developed for first-year, second language speakers of English. Its broad purpose is twofold. Firstly, it aims to respond to the academic and communicative needs of these students with a view to increasing their confidence and competence to communicate fully and effectively within the university context. This means that a large part of the course involves the acquisition of the academic literacies required for success at university. Secondly, and integrally linked to the first aim, the course attempts to provide a context in which students can begin to understand and to critique the less visible dynamics of the university; to explicitly consider the power relations that shape the institution and to reflect on how they are positioned within it.

This second aim is linked to the development of the critical dimension of the course and to an 8-week program in CLA that was designed to facilitate this. In this regard, the observations of a Black female student responding to one of her early university experiences has become a touchstone of our thinking. Her insights provide an indication of the many factors that intermesh to contribute to the total experience of an unfamiliar social and academic environment, and have assisted us in attempting to address some of these issues in our curriculum.

This student had enrolled for *Learning, Language and Logic* and during the first quarter, her tutorial group, consisting of 10 students, was asked to investigate any aspect of the university community that interested them. They decided to interview Deans of Faculties about the university's admission policy, especially as it pertained to Black students. The purpose of this activity was to develop the linguistic and personal confidence of new students by placing them in contexts that would challenge them to use all their linguistic, sociolinguistic, and strategic resources and in which they would experience, as interviewers, some control of the encounter.

In preparation for the interviews, students worked in small groups defining their purpose, making the necessary appointments, role playing potentially difficult situations, and discussing interviewing strategies. Once the interviews had been completed, they were required to present their findings as formal written discourse and then to pool information by reporting orally to the whole class. The final section of the written report consisted of a personal evaluation of the interviewing experience. The student mentioned previously said this:

> What I learnt from the interview was that things didn't occur as I expected them. I was so tensed since it was the first time that I had to interview a white man. What I discovered was that he appeared to be a kind somebody. While I was fighting with my monitor trying to construct sentences for introducing ourselves, the man asked if we would like to have a cup of coffee. I was surprised by the question to the extent that I hardly trusted my ears that he really meant it. I responded with yes but still felt hesitation so I said no. He himself provided me with coffee. Still asking myself why he was lowering himself like that, the man bumpered us with answers of the unasked questions. He talked a non-stop speech of about one and a half hours. By the time he stopped, he expected questions from us. I was amazed and it was difficult to know which questions were answered and which were not.... Being bewildered, I asked fumbling questions just to console myself that I can ask a question. Still the man responded to them nicely.
>
> To me the interview was absolutely wonderful. It changed my conclusions about the whites whom I regard as superior. I was brought to the conclusion that some are just like myself, willing to help and to socialise.

This response highlights several intersecting, sometimes conflictual facets of the social and educational context that contribute to the experience of the university environment. As a young Black woman, this student had to manage and to some extent overcome, a wide range of life experiences that interacted to constitute her 'tensed' and 'bewildered' response to the situation. Firstly, the racial divisions and stereotypes that characterize this country are clearly evident. Secondly, and crucially interacting with the racial dimension, are the traditional and unequal gender relations, which are so stringently defined within many Black communities (Ramphele & Boozaier, 1988). The fact that she was both Black and female, in addition to being a first-year, second language student, simply served to make her task all the more taxing.

Her responses give some evidence of this complexity. Most interesting are the contradictions that permeate her discourse. Two broad, apparently conflicting strands of the experience emerge.

On the one hand, she discovered that, contrary to her tensed, socialized fear about interviewing a White male, the "white man ... appeared to be a kind somebody" who she was amazed to find lowering himself to make her coffee and who was prepared to respond nicely to her "fumbling" questions. Importantly, like her, he was also "willing to help and to social-ize" and his friendly, informal manner was certainly an unexpected aspect of the experience that, at this level, was a pleasant realization for her.

In contrast to the positive aspects of her experience, are the consider-able confusion, the element of mistrust and lack of control of the interview that emerge in her discourse. The fact that "things," as she said, "did not occur as I had expected them," served to almost totally disempower her in this context. An interview is usually an interaction between two people in which the interviewer initiates and controls the encounter. Here, it is clear that this student was not engaged in an interview at all. No amount of fore-thought and anticipation could have prepared her for being "bumpered ... with the answers to the unasked questions" and no interview is ever de-fined as "a non-stop speech of about one and a half hours." At different points during the interview she describes herself as "fighting with her monitor," feeling "bewildered" and, in the end, being able to ask only "fumbling questions" in order to "console" herself that she was capable of asking a question at all. The positive and pivotal aspects of this encounter appear to be based on an unexpected, courteous, and informal welcome from a White male and his making her a cup of coffee. There is no evi-dence that she had, at any level, control of the situation or the means, after setting up the meeting, to take even a little of the initiative.

What is of note here are the various ways in which this student was con-structed and positioned in the situation—by the Dean, by the institution, and, indeed, by herself. The competing interpretations of the encounter (the difference between her construction of meaning and mine) espe-cially in the light of the current discussions around the idea of otherness (Ellsworth, 1989; Weiler, 1991) are also significant. The difference be-tween her subjectivities, as a Black, first-year, female, Zulu speaker, and mine as a White, female, feminist, academic, English speaker are clearly evident, and, in any further discussion, the creation of a forum in which these differences could be constructively articulated would be essential. Most crucial, however, is that her feelings and experience should be seri-ously acknowledged (Ellsworth, 1989; Weiler, 1991). Her overriding im-pression, at this time in her life, is extremely positive. She found that she could interact with him and that she could, despite her confusion, ask some of the necessary questions. The fact that, for her, "the interview was absolutely wonderful" and that "it changed [her] conclusions about whites" indicates that she felt that she had experienced important percep-tual shifts and these are likely to have increased her confidence in other, later encounters.

The situation described is one example of the multifaceted nature of the experiences facing students, particularly Black students, coming to the university for the first time. It helped us to generate some of our key pedagogical questions. How, for example, can we facilitate in students a deeper understanding of the power relationships that shape our educational institutions and that would arguably provide access to other ways of understanding the encounter described previously? What are the implications of making the power relationships more transparent for the teacher and the learner? How do we accommodate in our classrooms competing interpretations of the same situation? How can we better understand why the same student is passive and silent in some situations and yet confident, verbal, and challenging in others?

The attempt to facilitate the development of this critical perspective overtly has important pedagogical implications. It has resulted in a far more rigorous and critical reflection on our own practice and a movement away from an emphasis on appropriacy per se as, for the past 5 years, we have tried to integrate a critical dimension into the course. In 1991, for example, we began with an 8-week component in CLA designed to facilitate the development of academic reading skills while (by analyzing texts drawn from university discourse) encouraging a critical understanding of the university environment. Implicit in this shift of emphasis is a conscious commitment to a methodology that incorporates but moves beyond the idea of communicative competence and an acknowledgment that our previous focus on it might in fact have denied students opportunities to operate as powerfully as they could within the institution (Fairclough, 1992; Peirce, 1989). Before describing this component in more detail, a brief consideration of our theoretical framework is necessary.

THEORETICAL FRAMEWORK

Two central, interrelated ideas informed the development of the program. These are the idea of language as social discourse (Chouliaraki & Fairclough, 1999; Fairclough, 1995) and that of multiple subjectivity (Weedon, 1997). Language viewed as social discourse implies that language is a socially constructed phenomenon which is political in nature. Rather than providing an innocent reflection of social conditions, language both shapes and is shaped by social change. Within this framework, subjects are constituted in and by language. Subjectivity is multiple and changing rather than static and unified; it is produced in discourse within particular historical circumstances and its forms can change in shifting discursive contexts (Weedon, 1997).

The implications of these claims are significant for the development of a course in critical academic literacy. A Black, first-year female student, for example, may be a submissive daughter in the context of a rural Black family and a student activist in the university context. A White male student may be dominant in the context of his family and his personal relationships, yet submissive and disempowered in the context of a university residence. In the construction of student behavior or responses within university discourses, these are crucial considerations. Student silence, for example, could well be the result of a choice not to speak in particular contexts rather than the outcome of authoritarian educational structures that have silenced the students. It also impacts on the way in which oppression is constructed because it is possible for one individual to be oppressed in some contexts but not in all (Janks & Ivanic, 1992). A Black, first-year female student may be disempowered in most situations, in relation to her father, lover, and the church, for example, as well as in the society at large. She may, however, be the acknowledged leader in a specific university society or club or adopt a central and shaping role in her rural home where male members are absent and women take up powerful domestic and social positions. She is constituted and constitutes herself in different ways depending on her particular discursive conditions. And crucially, her subjectivities are constituted in language.

A linguistic theory compatible with the theoretical framework sketched earlier is CLA. This is primarily concerned with formulating a principled account of the relation between language, power, and ideology and with the way in which texts, through the selection of specific linguistic structures and lexical items, encode these relations and reflect the interests of particular groups of people, most especially the dominant and powerful. It seeks to demystify social processes, to show how and why reality is structured in a particular way and to make hidden meanings explicit. By uncovering hidden ideological assumptions it encourages a conscious and critical debate about them and implies that if the construction and intention of dominant conventions and practices can be better understood, they can also be critiqued and either accepted or rejected.

CLA provides a critique of the idea of communicative competence and appropriacy. Through the development of an understanding of the way in which language encodes power relationships, it is an approach that can assist students, not only to understand the generally accepted conventions and practices of a given institution or society, but crucially, to ask questions that provide a framework for understanding the historical conditions of those conventions. Focus is not only on what is stated but also on what is left unsaid and there is an explicit interest in the way in which powerful social groups benefit from traditional, common sense practice. CLA has the potential to equip people to make better informed choices about if and when to contest dominant practice, and encourages the development of the self-assurance to do this.

THE CLA PROGRAM

What follows is an account of how we attempted to translate these considerations into the *Learning, Language and Logic* curriculum. I begin with a brief overview of the whole program, focus on one or two activities in more detail and finally consider some of the student evaluations of the process.

The CLA program was taught during the first 8 weeks of the term to a 100 students who were divided into tutorial groups of 15. Its aim was to open up possibilities for students to develop a critical response to the university as an educational institution while beginning to address some of the academic strategies required for successful study. They began by writing a short account of how they perceived their roles as members of the institution. The purpose of this task was to have some record of how students initially positioned themselves within the university and to try and assess the range of activities they thought of as being options for them. This was followed by recollection of past school experience, focusing on the most positive and negative incidents and then a short written piece in which they wrote about what, for them, constitutes a good student. Important discussion followed this. revolving around such questions as:

- Who made the rules in your school?

- Who benefitted from the rules?

- What happened if anyone challenged them?

- How much say did students have in any decision making processes?

- Whose ideas are contained in the good student texts? Ours? Our parents'? Teachers'? The society's?

- How much choice do we really have in the decisions we take or the ideas we formulate?

Through this discussion, students were introduced to several central concepts. Although not technically named, questions relating to subject positioning, interpellation, dominant group interest, power relationships and ideas of determinacy and agency were briefly touched on. Some of these were developed later in other parts of the program.

From this point, the focus moved from the school to the university context. Students began discussing the various ways in which the institution divides its social space and how it represents itself, particularly through text. They then worked with a questionnaire designed to elicit their responses to the initial range of texts they had received from the university as incoming students. Then, concentrating on one text, they considered authorship, purpose, and attitude and were also asked to suggest any changes they thought necessary.

During the third week, students listened to a lecture, delivered by a member of staff, entitled "The Challenges of Critical Language Awareness." This had a dual purpose: to make explicit some of the theoretical principles underpinning the program and also to facilitate the development of students' note-making strategies. The next task involved a comparison of two texts advertising reading courses on the campus. The first of these had been circulated in 1989 and, as a direct result of student comment and criticism during *Learning, Language and Logic* tutorials, had been substantially rewritten. The outcome was a very different construction, one that excluded many of the original negative structures, made different nondeficit model lexical choices and generally positioned students much more positively. Students responded enthusiastically to this task, perhaps partly because the second version had been a result of student criticism.

The second part of the program consisted of a series of tutorials during which students discussed and wrote about ways in which a selection of discrete linguistic structures are used in a range of university texts. Two important and interrelated features provided the context for this work.

The first was that students themselves provided the texts on which exercises were based. They drew from a wide range of sources that included residence rules, the code of conduct, extracts from student newspapers, and the mission statement, political slogans, and advertisements off notice boards and the Vice Chancellor's opening address to first-year students. Logistically, this process made preplanning difficult and preparation somewhat pressured but this was outweighed by the benefits of incorporating students, if only to a small degree, into the development of the curriculum and the belief that student-selected texts are likely to have a more immediate bearing on their lives, and, by extension, their level of motivation. This was borne out by a tutor later when she evaluated the program:

> Students were very motivated and engaged when doing the critical language exercises. Using material which has real consequences in their lives certainly enabled them to see why certain structures are used in particular linguistic contexts, in a way that using just any material would not. I think it also motivated students to understand and be motivated to master linguistic structures in a way that traditional grammar teaching seldom achieves.

The second feature was the use of a large collage—a combination of, and further selection from, the students' choices. This especially constructed text from text, entitled *Voices of a University*, had two functions. First, it was used in an attempt to keep the broader context in mind (and literally in sight) while concentrating on discrete structures. Second, it was a means of introducing students to the idea of intertextuality, the intersection of meaning between texts and the impact of each on the meaning of others (Fairclough, 1992). A later student evaluation of the program indicated that, at least for some, this had been effective:

> It has helped students to realise the importance of the total context in the production and interpretation of texts, considering the way in which meaning of texts is influenced by other texts and to see that different texts position readers in different ways.

The linguistic constructions selected for the language tutorials were modality, the active and passive voice, the article, and the use of pronouns. The significance of lexical choice was also considered, often in conjunction with one or more of the other structures. Students began by dealing with each construction separately and were engaged in a wide range of tasks (reading, discussing, analyzing, and writing). For example, in discussion of modality, students considered the implications of the use of the present tense in such sentences as: "It is a privilege to have been selected to live at Malherbe Residence?" or "Everyone is calling for the resignation of Magnus Malan."

They then related this to the often questionable use of the present tense in their own academic essays. They analyzed a text commemorating Sharpeville Day in which police were described as having opened fire "in a moment of over-reaction." They also tried to identify who *the community* referred to in the Vice Chancellor's opening address to first years and asked similar questions about "the customary society norms" to which he referred.

One of the extracts that caused particularly animated discussion was drawn from the Malherbe Residence Rules:

HELPFUL INFORMATION.

1. Security

1.1 Doors

WOMEN STUDENTS: Doors to the Women's Residence are locked promptly at 11.30 p.m. Monday to Saturday and at 11.00 p.m. on Sunday. A late leave key is issued to women to let themselves in after hours, but this privilege may be withdrawn if used irresponsibly.

MEN STUDENTS: The front door is locked at 10.30 p.m. but unrestricted entrance is available through the basement door.

IF YOU ARE OUT AND ANY DIFFICULTIES ARISE PLEASE DO NOT HESITATE TO TELEPHONE EITHER THE WARDEN OR ONE OF THE SUBWARDENS.

Students first considered this text in terms of the lexical choices only (e.g., why keys for women were a privilege, why women were likely to abuse this, and the implications of the unrestricted entrance available to the men). Later, when asked to use any insights gained from the CLA program, this was one of two texts students analyzed in detail. Many students were aware of the unequal gender relationships, as the following extracts show:

In the text from Malherbe Rules the women and men students are positioned differently. To position women students strong words are used like doors locked promptly, withdrawn etc. With male students the doors are just locked so making the issue ... much softer. For women students it seems to be a privilege to have their doors open ... for male students there is no such privilege ... the writer puts this as if it's their right.

The idea behind the text is inferiority of women and superiority of men. This has been encoded in the text so as to retain the status quo ... nothing may be withdrawn from men and there is no irresponsibility which may be dealt with as is the case with women ... girls are subtly but strongly discouraged from being out later than 11 p.m.

One student considered the implications of the agentless passives:

We don't know who is responsible for the action. So it is difficult to ask some further information about the Malherbe situation.

In some cases the rules were interpreted as a protective measure. This applied to responses from both male and female students. The following response is from a woman: "I think rules are tough to women because protection is needed to them, whereas men are able to protect themselves. If there was an unrestricted door even for women I think even rapists would enter while students are asleep."

The emergence of what Ellsworth (1989) called "affinity groups" (p. 317), which are small groups within the larger class who discover common experiences and values different from those of other students is significant here. The wide diversity of opinion over the interpretation of this text evidences the varied interests and investments of different groups. Both the written responses and debate in tutorials left us in no doubt that some students, men and women, were extremely keen, not to reach consensus, but to legitimate their own views at the expense of others. One of our future tasks is to find ways of incorporating these differences and possible conflict into the curriculum rather than attempting to avoid difficult issues and hoping that students will reach consensus (in some instances an impossible task).

It is impossible to estimate the extent to which students will develop and integrate an increased awareness of the more subtle uses of language into the ways in which they read and how they define themselves within the university and other contexts. Certainly, tutors reported responses in tutorial discussions that at times evidenced a sharper and more critical focus than we have encountered previously. This comment was included in one tutor assessment:

> I had some students who internalised and expressed the empowering nature of this approach quite clearly. When I asked for examples of how a command could be expressed in a masked form, using some modal structures, I had a student quite accurately refer to a statement I had made ... at the beginning of the tutorial. I was most impressed at the student's willingness to turn new knowledge so neatly on the language of her teacher.

Student evaluations of the program were extremely positive. Although they inevitably differed in approach and emphasis, they all felt that the program had been of considerable benefit and many linked it directly to their approach to reading more critically. These are a few typical responses:

> "CLA has taught me not to accept the text as it is written but to find out who the writer is. To be critical about the language he (sic) has used and to find out where I am positioned as a reader ... I can now challenge writers in what they are saying."

> "Before, I did not even bother about the words used by an author and their effect on readers. I now do that ... I also question an author's use of words now and I even consider the words that might have been used instead of those used."

> "It means we can derive meaning from text, not just general meaning but hidden ones, if any."

CONCLUSION

Since 1991, the critical linguistic component of Learning, Language and Logic has been included later in the year, this because the urgency of familiarizing students with academic essay-writing skills has necessitated a reallocation of time. The change represents both gains and losses. On the one hand, we lose the impact of the totally unfamiliar context that students need to interpret and explore. On the positive side, the fact that students are more embedded in the university environment means that they have the capacity of be more reflective and, crucially, the personal experiences to use as a basis for analysis and discussion. There is also, in general, a more critical slant to the course as a whole that implies greater integration of the CLA into the curriculum. Ideally, the critical linguistics should form an integral strand of every aspect of the course and should not be taught as a discrete component.

However it is contextualized, critical language awareness can provide students with valuable insights into some of the complex and perplexing relationships that make up the university environment. It has the potential to empower them within the university context and it offers possibilities for the construction of alternative discourses. In this, CLA has a crucial role to play in the process of transforming universities in South Africa. One of the students, in her evaluation of the program said: "The CLA tutorials also make me feel as one who can play a great part at university."

A comment like this one is the starting point from which more detailed analysis can begin.

REFERENCES

Boozaier, E., & Sharp, J. (Eds.). (1988). *South African keywords: The uses and abuses of political concepts.* Cape Town: David Phillip.

Chonliavaki, L., & Fairclough, N. (1999). *Discourse in late modernity: Rethinking critical discourse analysis.* Edinburgh: Edinburgh University.

Ellsworth, E. (1989). Why doesn't this feel empowering? Working through repressive myths of critical pedagogy. *Harvard Educational Review, 59*(3), 297–324.

Fairclough, N. (Ed.). (1992). *Critical language awareness.* London: Longman.

Gee, J. (1996). *Social linguistics and literacies: Ideologies in discourse* (second edition). London: Falmer.

Janks, H., & Ivanic, R. (1992). Critical language awareness and emancipatory discourse. In N. Fairclough (Ed.), *Critical language awareness* (pp. 305–331). London: Longman.

Peirce, B. N. (1989). Towards a pedagogy of possibility in the teaching of English internationally: People's English in South Africa, *TESOL Quarterly, 23,* 401–420.

Ramphele, M., & Boonzaier, E. (1988). The position of African women: Race and gender in South Africa. In E. Boonzaier & J. Sharp (Eds.), *South African keywords: The uses and abuses of political concepts.* Cape Town: David Phillip.

Weedon, C. (1997). *Feminist practice and poststructuralist theory* (second edition). Oxford: Basil Blackwell.

Weiler, K. (1991). Freire and a feminist pedagogy of difference. *Harvard Educational Review, 61*(4), 449–474.

16

Tensions and Ambiguities in Critical Literacy

Nathalie Wooldridge
Marryatville High School, South Australia

I became interested in critical literacy when I was working in a training and development project that aimed to support junior secondary teachers in South Australian schools (both government and independent) with a high proportion of students living in poverty. For me, recognition that literacy is not neutral and that every literacy event involves social and cultural values led to different ways of seeing and accounting for the educational outcomes (as judged by such signs as tertiary entrance and school literacy tests) of these students.

But what does teaching for critical literacy look like in practice? This is the question a group of secondary teachers, and I investigated in an action research project (Wooldridge, 1995). The project, which included presenting and critiquing units of work, took place over five sessions totalling about 25 hours, spread over the final term of a school year. Each of the teachers involved worked in government schools with high numbers of students who lived in poverty.

Critical literacy is an orientation to literacy: It is not something separate from literacy in general, or a particular part of literacy; it goes with decoding and encoding practices, not after. Critical literacy is not a technique or set of strategies, but rather, part of a pedagogy underpinning a whole approach or classroom practice. A critical approach to literacy is about decoding and encoding the social, political, and ideological situatedness of literacy. I include encoding here because literacy is about producing texts as well as reading them. A critical approach provides—and, as shown here, frequently leads to—questions rather than answers.

This chapter describes some of our work and the questions it raised for us. The first section describes some of the textual practices we worked with, and the questions they raised for us. Although most of the work I describe here is more about critical reading or decoding (as indeed much of the published discussion about critical literacy seems to be), encoding is a recurring theme. The second section briefly describes an approach to curriculum in general, applying some of the textual practices to the bigger picture of curriculum planning. The final section describes a framework for critically reading our teaching practice and noting the difficulties we experienced in this work.

All but one of the units of work described here were used with senior secondary students involved in studies for Stage 2 of the South Australian Certificate of Education (SACE), a certificate that accredits work done in the final years of secondary school. Stage two is most often undertaken in the twelfth year of schooling. Subjects completed for Stage 2 of SACE must follow a set syllabus; their assessment involves either external moderation or public examination. Nevertheless, within these syllabus statements and frameworks, my colleagues and I found spaces to explore critical literacy.

TEXTUAL PRACTICES

My co-researchers and I recognized a critical orientation to literacy as one which focuses on the constructedness of readings (indeed, on the constructedness of knowledge). We explored textual practices like critical questioning, intertextuality and framing for their potential to show how readings encode particular social and cultural contexts, including power relationships—hence the potential they may offer for challenging or at least resisting these power relations. While we found these approaches useful to varying degrees, we also found there are limitations in the extent to which these practices assist in reading the social and political dimensions of texts. Further, their application was not easy and often led to ambiguities.

Many teachers in South Australia have begun to explore critical literacy using questions such as those found in the work of Comber (1992), Kress (1985), and Smyth (1995). My coresearchers and I used questions such as the following to direct readers to look at what is taken for granted in texts:

- What (or whose) view of the world, or kinds of behaviors are presented as normal by the text?

- Why is the text written that way? How else could it have been written?

- What assumptions does the text make about age, gender, and culture (including the age, gender, and culture of its readers)?

- Who is silenced/heard here?

- Whose interests might best be served by the text?

- What ideological positions can you identify?

- What are the possible readings of this situation/event/character? How did you get to that reading?

- What moral or political position does a reading support? How do particular cultural and social contexts make particular readings available? (e.g., who could you not say that to?) How might it be challenged?

Although we found the questions useful, applying them was rarely straightforward, as the following two examples show.

One co-researcher described a senior Women's Studies unit that aimed to help students understand the construction of gender. The unit involved a considerable amount of shared reading of magazine advertisements, to work out the explicit and implicit messages they were presenting and how masculinity and femininity were constructed in the advertisements. The unit took students beyond decoding to encoding, in asking them to work out strategies for (re-)constructing other images of females.

At first we found it difficult to critique this unit ("you would have trouble making it more critically literate, I think." Transcript Day 3). However, asking "who is silenced/heard here?" led us to some interesting discussion about the need to be protective of students (e.g., what effect did this have on the woman in the class who wanted to be a model?) and about essentializing or treating all women as having the same needs, experiences, or desires. In particular, we saw it as important not to present women as victims, and to find positive images of women: There are different stories. We also noted that just as the students could critique the media images using the critical questions, the questions could be applied to the students' own reconstructions, which could also be seen to essentialize women.

In another unit in which students were encouraged to identify ideological positions and interests, it became apparent that applying the questions could sometimes lead to dilemmas, often exacerbated by the teacher's own background knowledge (or lack thereof). The unit was used in a Women's Studies class with many adult students of non-English speaking backgrounds. It involved students investigating how aspects of women's lives are depicted in film. The teacher described a small part of the unit in which, in "trying to be inclusive, however artificially," (Transcript 3:20) she selected a film about Vietnamese women because she had a Vietnamese student. The student became most upset on viewing the film, because of what she saw as false representations. What was depicted as being in South Vietnam was in fact North Vietnam, with the same woman speaking over both scenes. The student's knowledge of the feminists who were extolled in the film led her to believe that they had done little to improve conditions for women in Vietnam, contrary to what was shown in the film. The film was an antiwar film that took the side of the communist north, whereas the student was from the south. The student showed her class the film, pointing out the propaganda and "things that there's no way an audience living in Australia would know." This was one of several occasions during our research when we questioned the notion of inclusivity, or practices adopted in the cause of inclusivity. The main issue here for the teacher, however, concerned background knowledge (Wooldridge, 1995): "how do we develop in students these skills of critical literacy without that background knowledge to have the framework to be able to ask the questions" (p.86)

The teacher saw from this example how our lack of knowledge about something could lead us to inadvertently do what this film maker had done. The question was especially important for her because she felt she could not assist students with analysis for their individual research because she had little knowledge about many of the issues students selected, and she also did not have a set framework of questions that she could share with students.

Our critique focused on the idea that there are multiple readings, depending on the frame and the context, and that texts and readings are constructed from different positions: "She's constructed a particular story, the Australian constructed a story—there are different stories rather than one ultimate and final definitive tale.... The interesting thing is to ask what purpose was served for her to look at events in that way.... What were the devices [the film maker] was using to create a particular view?" (p.87)

We saw that we could support critical literacy by helping students to recognize different readings of texts, but this was not enough. Again, we wanted to support students to develop practices for encoding and producing texts as well as reading them, so we wanted to support students to see how texts are constructed (the devices that are used) and to be able to construct texts themselves.

Many South Australian teachers also have begun exploring the possibilities for critical literacy provided by putting different texts or different versions of the same story alongside each other, interrupting texts or framing them differently to foreground possible different readings, following the work of researchers such as Mellor, O'Neill, and Patterson (1987, 1992), and Morgan (1992). However, we felt that much of the work that had been done focused more on gender than on other power relationships, and there were few examples outside English classrooms.

One coresearcher pursued these ideas in two senior history units that foregrounded the construction of different readings. The first was about Scott, a British explorer in India (for a full description of this unit, see Sidoryn, 1995a). Sidoryn found two very different extracts about the explorer's expeditions. He developed a task that asked students to "identify evidence that would seem most important to support the following interpretations." He provided 11 conflicting interpretations, ranging from "Scott is a sadist" and "Scott is a hero" to "the king's officers were as brutal as Scott" (p. 29) and "the king's officers showed a humanity lacking in Scott." This was followed by some "What if?" (p. 30) related scenarios, a research activity, a question about how readers produce interpretations, and ultimately, "Explain how you produced your account about Scott and his victim" (p. 31).

We saw that this kind of activity brought into question the construction of knowledge, supporting students to see how history is a construction. The ways different texts had been juxtaposed and the kinds of questions asked seemed to be powerful strategies for supporting students to read differently and to see how texts position readers.

The second unit (described in Sidoryn, 1995b) aimed to explore different readings or versions of the past that could be made of photographs from World War I, and how each of these readings is constructed in particular interests. Sidoryn wanted to support students to look critically at sources, "to see that there is a selection process involved in whatever you do." To do this, he used several different versions of the same photograph, including one version that provided only part of the picture and another that was included as the cover photo of a magazine in 1993. He wanted students to see that a photograph is a frame that selects information from a particular point of view; the frame, and the framing context (e.g., the difference between looking at the photograph in 1920 and in 1993), creates a particular way of looking at things. This was particularly interesting given that the framing context for one version of the photograph was a public examination paper, where it had been used in a question using 'original source' material.

These history units led us to think about the power of teachers as selectors and framers of knowledge and tasks, and raised again questions about teachers' background knowledge: "What I've found in doing this is that in a sense you've got a really powerful intervening role because you are setting up the particular sources, and a lot depends on your own knowledge and ability to come up with them." (quoted in Wooldridge, 1995, p. 704)

Exploring these textual practices helped us recognize how the curriculum decisions we make in selecting particular resources and in framing them in particular ways reflect our own perceptions and biases.

These units focused more on the constructedness of readings than on the interests they represented, or the social constructions and power relationships that make particular readings available to particular audiences. The description of the units led us to discussions about truth and the idea that different truths are highlighted by different frames. Although our critique briefly raised the question of "whose truth?" and the idea that nothing is innocent, these questions were not taken up at this stage, and there was no questioning from any of us about what makes particular readings available to particular groups of people. In a sense, then, these units could therefore be seen as promoting a technical skill, rather than a socially situated reading practice. However, it is understanding reading as a social practice that led to this exploration, and questions about what makes particular readings available cannot arise until those readings are in fact available. Perhaps our lack of questioning here was a result of our lack of familiarity with the technique: We needed to try out this kind of textual practice and to think about the possibilities of using the idea of framing.

Exploring the kind of language used in the text can be another useful way of decoding its sociopolitical position. Although knowledge of complete systems, such as Halliday's (1985) functional grammar, offers many tools for linguistic analysis, even a limited knowledge can be put to use. For example, article, voice, and agent are relatively easy concepts to learn and use without further technical knowledge. I was exploring elsewhere the possibilities provided by using just a few simple grammatical concepts (Hattam, Kerkham, & Wooldridge, 1994), and I shared the work I had been doing with my coresearchers, along with another article that illustrated the application of several simple elements of linguistic analysis (Janks, 1991), and we briefly tried the tools in looking at an advertisement. However, linguistic analysis was new to five of the seven researchers, and, although we agreed it could be useful, we did not return to it again in any substantial way during our work together. It is interesting to conjecture why we did not make more use of this practice.

AN ISSUES BASED, PROBLEM-POSING APPROACH

Although we felt that particular textual practices offered many possibilities for implementing a critical orientation to literacy, questions arose for us about situating those practices more generally in curriculum. We agreed with Singh (1989) and Shor (1988) that it was important for pedagogy to be "situated in the language, statements, issues and knowledge students bring to class" (p. 106). For this reason, we thought it necessary to negotiate aspects of curriculum with students, to use what Shor called a "problem posing" (p. 109) approach that foregrounds the students' own experiences and in which the teacher asks questions, and helps students to ask questions, rather than tries to transmit their own subject expertise. We found that an issues-based approach to topics or to unit planning seemed to offer most possibilities in this respect. However, as with the textual practices, our exploration once again led to grey areas, as the following two examples show.

Many of the senior secondary subjects undertaken for the SACE involve a major independent research unit. These research units must comply with guidelines set in the relevant syllabus statements; nevertheless, there is usually considerable potential for negotiating aspects of the work with students. We looked at a research unit for senior drama students, in which students had to research an issue and present a report in some way. Although the teacher had not used a critical pedagogy orientation in planning the unit, what some students had done could be seen as exercising critical literacy. For example, in response to a play that involved domestic violence, one girl's project was about social structures and domination: The problems she posed led her to carry out an investigation in the school about domestic violence, and to present the resulting information to her peers.

Our critique of this unit raised issues about a social action component that we felt needed to be part of curriculum developed from a critical orientation. The student who had investigated domestic violence had adopted a problem-posing approach; her work involved a socially significant task; the social and political dimensions of it were clear; and the presentation to her peers gave it transformative potential. However, we were concerned that project work as required by the syllabi of several Year 12 subjects frequently resulted in students collecting and presenting information as if it is just there, rather than being connected to a social system. We noted that students who set out to research Elizabethan theaters in response to viewing Shakespeare's plays could become passive recipients of information unless they were encouraged to question the information, for example, to think about the social implications of the theater being constructed as it was, and which places were reserved for which groups of people. Although we saw that independent research work could become critical through negotiation between student and teacher, we also talked about how to set up projects in such a way that students were led to problem pose, rather than simply inform. We suggested it might be possible to build in questions that related the research to social structures.

Another coresearcher presented a Year 10 science unit about forensic science, a unit that called into question the construction of science as a school subject. The unit had been developed for girls who had chosen not to proceed with physics and chemistry, and they had been involved in negotiating the content of the unit. The researcher wanted the girls to be able to relate to their work, and to investigate issues that were connected with their own lives. The literacy supported in this class was not technical skills but the ability to 'read the word and the world' (Shor & Freire, 1987). The unit involved the students in discussing videos and in practical activities such as fiber analysis and designing and solving each other's mock crimes. It was a highly engaging unit in which the students used a wide range of texts and were involved in a range of activities. The researcher was aware that some of the girls or members of their families had been involved in crime. However, she now felt that for some girls who had been victims of particular crimes, it was too close to their lived experiences.

In our critique, we recognized many ways in which this unit illustrated a critical orientation to literacy curriculum. We raised the possibility of using the difference between this unit and more traditional science units as a way to help students question the construction of science and in whose interests that construction of science operates. We also suggested that the unit presented an opportunity for asking questions about the construction of gender, race, and class, in relation to crime. Here our critique pointed to ways to further support students to connect social structures with positions of individuals and groups of students, in the way stressed in the work of Freire (1972) and Shor (1987).

In trying to develop curriculum that was issues based, engaged students' lives and used problem-posing pedagogy, we felt that the teacher's own background knowledge is again an issue. The bigger problem for us here was how we ran the risk of being intrusive rather than inclusive as we tried to engage the lives of the students and involve them in meaningful, authentic action.

CRITICALLY READING OUR TEACHING

For us, a logical extension of a critical orientation to literacy was critically reading our teaching: seeing the teaching itself, as well as the texts and tasks we used, as socially situated political activity. This is why we continually tried to critique the units we presented, as described earlier. We found potential for critically reading our teaching in two frameworks.

The first came from the draft of an article some colleagues and I (Hattam et al., 1994) were writing. This article proposed (and used as its organizing framework) the following four characteristics of a critical literacy approach:

- knowledge is considered to be socially constructed and represents particular interests;

- students develop concepts and methods for critically reading the word and the world;

- the curriculum engages the lives and language of students; and

- the curriculum engages students in meaningful authentic action.

After one coresearcher showed how she had used this as a framework to critique her work, as well as a reference point in planning, as a group we used it in some shared unit planning.

The second framework we found useful in critically reading our teaching was the following set of questions.

- What view of knowledge do we present? (e.g., who has it? where is it found? what counts as knowledge? what/whose knowledge is seen as valuable?).

- How else might the lesson have been taught/the aims achieved?

- How do we construct ourselves as teacher in the lesson (e.g., as source of knowledge, as person who controls?) How are the students constructed (e.g., as passive recipients, as having something done to them?) What/whose view do we present, and therefore, whose views are not represented or being seen?

- What are the students learning besides particular content? (e.g., about learning, the uses of literacy, what it is to be a student, what it is to be poor/female?).

My initial research question had been about teachers as curriculum decision makers. It seemed to me that we needed to recognize ourselves as curriculum decision makers before we could recognize the interestedness of our curriculum decisions. However, in our earliest discussions we had not seen ourselves as curriculum decision makers in any real sense. When we did recognize some of the decisions we made, we tended to attribute the reason for them to syllabus statements and departmental policies, seeing ourselves and our work as positioned and controlled by syllabus statements and department expectations. Things were taught because they met the objectives of a syllabus set out by someone else. The goal was accreditation for students, development of skills, knowledge, and understanding in order for accreditation, rather than accreditation being simply the recognition of development of skills, knowledge, and understanding. Maximizing the results in the accreditation system was the significant goal for some of us, no matter the cost (quoted in Wooldridge, 1995, pp. 111–112):

> When I look at that ESF (Extended Subject Framework for the SACE, in this case, drama) and objectives, they are not mysterious, they make sense ... (I don't have any trouble saying to students—if you want to meet this objective you have to do this; you either have to be this sort of person or act like this, and in acting like this you sometimes become like them.

This can be read as an example of imposing a way of being, an ideology—a hegemonic curriculum in which the students have to abandon their own culture and way of being in order to obtain accreditation.

The accreditation system was one reason we might not encourage students to read critically because the students might be penalized by the markers (quoted in Wooldridge, 1995, p. 111):

> A possible block [to encouraging critical reading] could be the established assessment criteria: whether or not a critical understanding is part of that assessment criteria. This picks up [coresearcher's] point about the PES (Public Examination Subject) marker.

However, we agreed that if critical reading involves recognizing and being able to read from several different positions, students who are critically literate will be able to recognize and adopt the position necessary to meet their ends in a given situation such as a SACE assessment.

Apart from the syllabus and the system, the paramount influences on our curriculum decisions were the needs of students, but we did not question how we judged the needs of the students. For a long while, we skirted around the politics of what we were doing, loathe to attribute our actions to our own ideological stances, an instance of Edelsky's (1989) assertion that teachers "want things to be nice" (p. 64). We quickly realized that pedagogical constructs and beliefs about learning were also a major influence, but it took much discussion for us to critically read our teaching and see that those beliefs and constructs were based on a view of the world, an ideology.

The work described in this chapter helped us to denaturalize our practice, to challenge our "ways of knowing and being in the world" (Gee, 1990, p. 142), to explore the work that they do and how they might operate as regimes of truth. However, as Janks (1991) found with her students, "the process of denaturalization creates ... [in those who to begin with are less socially aware] a profound sense of unease.... Some become angry, others become frightened as they resist the process" (p. 199).

Although we found the frameworks described previously useful, we found critically reading our teaching to be an extremely difficult task, recognizing that it meant seeing ourselves as complicit in a situation that perpetuates and constructs injustice. For almost all of us, this was highly confrontational because it involved challenging our 'ways of being in the world': The transcript is littered with expressions that reveal our discomfort. It involved fundamental questioning of our everyday taken for granted practices: We saw it (Wooldridge, 1995, p. 94) as like 'standing on shifting sand', a place of chaos and much discomfort.

One major discomfort was caused by the realization that a critical orientation can become a regime of truth. As Ellsworth (1989) put it, a critical orientation can become "Have we got a theory for you!" (p. 306) an approach that imposes one view rather than an acknowledgment of the complexity of the situation and the unknowable. We concluded that every set of values should be questioned because it reveals and constructs power relationships; there is not a place that is beyond any critical evaluation and that we could involve students in that evaluation rather than imposing our own.

At our final session, we brainstormed a list of principles that we felt were important for implementing a critical literacy approach:

- There are certain aspects of the way society is that we think students ought to be equipped to question (not destroy).

- The tasks we set need to reinforce the idea that there are multiple readings and realities.

- The tasks need to get students to actively engage with the learning, then do something with that learning, supporting students to work toward an informed personal meaning.

- This is not a didactic approach: Meaning does not lie in the text; this is not about transmitting an alternative meaning.

- The way you give students access to texts is an important part of this (which two pieces you select, in which order, emphasizes the selective nature of knowledge and information).

We also asked, "How do we make sure this isn't just another way of maintaining old power relationships of teacher?"

Despite the difficulties, we felt that the value of the approaches we worked on lay in the ambiguities and tensions we encountered: The questions were real but not paralyzing.

REFERENCES

Comber, B. (1992). Critical literacy: A selective review and discussion of recent literature. *South Australian Educational Leader, 3*(1), 1–10.

Edelsky, C. (1989). Literacy education: Reading the word and the world. *English in Australia, 89,* 61–71.

Ellsworth, E. (1989). Why doesn't this feel empowering? Working through repressive myths of critical pedagogy. *Harvard Educational Review, 59*(3), 297–324.

Freire, P. (1972). *Pedagogy of the oppressed.* London: Penguin.

Gee, J. (1990). *Social linguistics and literacies: Ideologies in discourse.* London: Falmer.

Halliday, M. A. K. (1985). *An introduction to functional grammar.* London: Edward Arnold.

Hattam, R., Kerkham, L., Wooldridge, N. (1994). Critical literacy: Against consent. *Critical Pedagogy Networker, 7*(1), 1–11.

Janks, H. (1991). A critical approach to the teaching of language. *Educational Review, 43*(2), 191–199.

Kress, G. (1985). *Linguistic processes in sociocultural practice.* Waurn Ponds, Victoria, Australia: Deakin University.

Mellor, B., O' Neill, M., & Patterson, A. (1987). *Reading stories.* Perth, Australia: Chalkface.

Mellor, B., O'Neill, M., & Patterson, A. (1992). Re-reading literature teaching. In J. Thomson (Ed.), *Reconstructing literature teaching* (pp. 40–55). Adelaide, Australia: AATE.

Morgan, W. (1992). *A poststructuralist English classroom: The example of Ned Kelly.* Melbourne, Australia: Victorian Association for the Teaching of English.

Shor, I. (1987). *Critical teaching and everyday life.* Chicago, IL: University of Chicago.

Shor, I. (1988). Working hands and critical minds: A Paulo Freire model for job training. *Journal of Education, 170*(2), 102–121.

Sidoryn, N. (1995a). Interrogating Scott. *Literacy Learning: Secondary Thoughts, 3*(1), 27–31.

Sidoryn, N. (1995b). Remembering our finest hour. *Literacy Learning: Secondary Thoughts, 3*(2), 25–30.

Singh, M. (1989). A counter hegemonic orientation to literacy in Australia. *Journal of Education, 171*(2), 35–56.

Smyth, J. (1995, June). *Developing schools as collaborative communities.* Paper presented at the Social Justice Curriculum Seminar, Adelaide, Australia.

Wooldridge, N. (1995). *A collaborative exploration of critical literacy pedagogy: Private detective work?* Unpublished MEd thesis, University of South Australia, Adelaide, Australia.

17

Critical Literacies and Local Action: Teacher Knowledge and a "New" Research Agenda

Barbara Comber
University of South Australia

Given the debates about what counts as literacy right now, as Western postindustrialized nations review their educational achievements, the addition of the word *critical* to *literacy* serves to complicate matters even further. And complicating things is one of the important features of a repertoire of practices that might be named *critical literacy*. When teachers and students are engaged in critical literacy, they will be asking complicated questions about language and power, about people and lifestyle, about morality and ethics, about who is advantaged by the ways things are and who is disadvantaged. Critical literacy resists any simplistic or generic definitions because its agenda is to examine the relationships between language practices, power relations, and identities—and this analysis involves grappling with specific local conditions.

Although we resist a formula or definition for critical literacy, we do believe that it is useful to consider what critical literacy is not. In our view, it is not being negative and cynical about everything. It is not political correctness. It is not about censoring the bad books and only reading the good books. It is not indoctrination. It is not developmental. It is not about identifying racism, sexism, prejudice, and homophobia somewhere else or in texts that have little relevance for the readers. It is not whole language with social justice themes. Such assertions and criticisms about critical literacy circulate in literacy educators' communities in ways that block innovative teaching and limit what students learn. Such myths produce a fear or distaste for critical literacy and reinforce the conservatism that pervades educational institutions and research. Our object is to illustrate the potential of critical literacies as positive and locally negotiated practices.

BUILDING TEACHER KNOWLEDGE AND ASSEMBLING NEW PRACTICES

We accept, however, that to work toward a socially critical literacy is not unproblematic. It requires that we look at the ways we read the world, which is much easier to say than to do. It requires examining what we take for granted, which is a difficult thing to do, given the very nature of its being "taken for granted." How does one immersed in and constructed by a particular culture manage to stand out of it and examine some of its integral and implicit tenets? And it is not always obvious what the payoffs might be. Critical analysis requires interrogating what texts tell us about the way things are and why. This is not straightforward, as most of us have learned to defer to the authority of the text. Indeed in some cultures it is heretical to question sacred texts, and the regard demanded by such texts is often carried over to other texts. Cultures that do not yet have a proliferation of "junk" mail and popular texts may have few obvious targets for criticism. An analysis—a socially and materially situated analysis—of relations of power is central to critical literacy.

We have found that it is important to build teacher knowledge and analytical capacities, including our own, in:

- Undertaking demographic analyses of school populations
    Who are these children?
    Who are their families?
    What are their incomes?
    What are their educational histories?

- Learning how to see communities anthropologically
    How do these young people lead their various lives?
    What are their "funds of knowledge"?

- Developing linguistic knowledge
    What are the language practices and representational resources these students have?

What kinds of genres, registers, fields of knowledge do students need to learn? Do teachers already have this knowledge?

How do persuasive and authoritative texts work linguistically? What can we replicate for our own ends? What needs to be interrogated, resisted and contested?

- Revising what we know about pedagogy

  What are the effects of this practice on different groups of students?

  What are we being loyal to in preserving this approach? Does it have the effects we intend? How will we know how it's working and who it works for?

  Where does literacy pedagogy begin and end?

- Re-imagining what counts as literacy in new times and learning new literacies

  What new forms of techno-textual practices do teachers and students need to learn?

In other words, it is not just a matter of deciding to "be critical." Teachers who are engaged in a critical literacy project have assembled and continue to assemble their theoretical, research, and pedagogical repertoires over time and across careers. They respond to changing times and circumstances rather than simply replicating old formulae. They are engaged in self-critical practices as educators and remain open to other ways of doing things. For these reasons, we believe there is a need for more documentation and analysis of the work that is going on, which richly contextualizes the wider circumstances within which the pedagogy is designed and enacted.

Because critical literacy has as its object the study of relations of power, the political contexts and educational systems where such work is done matter greatly. The contexts of teachers' work always impact on local iterations of curriculum, pedagogy, and theory. Indeed the "local" may be central to the actual design of the curriculum (Comber, Thomson, & Wells, 2001). Clearly, the negotiation of critical literacies needs to be local, strategic, and prudent, taking on the constraints that impinge on curriculum design and practice. At the same time, our purpose in assembling accounts of pedagogical work in such different contexts (some of which may seem unlikely situations for the construction of critical literacies) is to demonstrate that we are "freer than we feel" (Foucault, 1988, p. 10). These cases show that there is room to move even in policy environments and political situations that may at first appear closed to contestation and questioning, or in contexts where teachers have minimal resources to support literacy programs. It is in the local action with/in particular communities that we can draw some common lessons and principles for re-imagining practice.

Hence Pippa Stein (chap. 10, this volume), a university researcher, is able to report such work in a Black township school outside Johannesburg, where teenagers write stories about political leaders to perform orally and with translation for their multilingual classmates. Incorporating local oral traditions with contemporary mass media, they contest the political realities of post-Apartheid South Africa. In another long-term project in Johannesburg, Hilary Janks (1993; chap. 9, this volume) and her colleagues write and trial workbooks for and with secondary school students. These workbooks interrogate everyday media and school texts. They question whose interests are served by specific linguistic usage and image making in advertisements, newspaper stories, cartoons, and so on. Such texts, although "everyday" in some places, may be relatively new in other communities. However, the Coke advertisements, Nike images, and other signs of multinational corporations are becoming increasingly familiar global icons that have currency for young people across the world.

Vivian Vasquez (chap. 4, this volume), working in multicultural suburban Toronto, assists kindergartners to practice articulating their arguments at the classroom Speakers' Corner and to petition for their rights at school. In rural India, Urvashi Sahni (chap. 2, this volume) works with primary school children to appropriate and make use of the written symbol system in imagining and composing different, more optimistic futures. In Portland, Oregon, Bill Bigelow (1999; chap. 7, this volume) has long investigated the hidden curriculum of public schooling with his high school students. Bigelow, along with some other educators, continues to produce a radical newspaper for teachers, *Rethinking Schools*, where teacher writers conduct ongoing policy analysis and critique of mainstream reforms, not only through hard-hitting editorials and essays, but with cartoons, jokes, and poetry. In this volume, Bigelow points to the need to look critically at new pedagogical texts, including CD-Rom, to check racialized versions of history reproduced in these new sources of information. In urban San Francisco, Anne Haas Dyson (1993, 1997; chap. 1, this volume) witnesses, narrates and analyzes the ways in which young children use their knowledge of popular culture to make social and academic meanings in the early years of their school lives—meanings that contest limited and limiting lifeworlds and future trajectories.

Educators in Australia grapple with uncertainty to analyze what makes a critical literacy curriculum and then critically analyze the effects of their teaching practices (see Wooldridge, chap. 16, this volume). Wayne Martino (chap. 11, this volume) confronts adolescent boys with images of masculinity that are embedded in Western culture and offers them opportunities to read that culture, and their place in it, differently. Second language learners in Catherine Wallace's (chap. 13, this volume) classroom in the United Kingdom provide the impetus for her reexamination of the teacher's role in a critical language awareness course. In these accounts, it is clear that critical literacies are provisional practices, where the teacher is subject to self-interrogation and continuing change.

Most of these projects are ongoing. These glimpses give a sense of different ways literacy educators in different places work with young people and other educators toward socially just practices and the acquisition of critical literacies (see also Edelsky, 1999; Muspratt, Luke, & Freebody, 1997). In negotiating critical literacies, there are no photocopiable blueprints, no scripts to follow, no generic lesson plans, and it would be dangerous if there were (Kamler & Comber, 1996; Luke, 2000). But, internationally, teachers at all levels of education do learn from other teachers' accounts of practice, listening selectively and analytically for what they might appropriate and what they might change. Dressman (1999) claims that narratives of "good practice" are important in persuading other teachers to *"believe in it"* so that they might implement a version in their classrooms and also so that student teachers might imagine themselves "being there" and "doing that." (p. 501)

However, Dressman (1999) points out that their generativeness is reduced when teachers work in "suboptimal" or in very different situations from those in the original study. The stories in this volume are told with this caution in mind, in the spirit of making available theorized accounts of practice that might be useful and illuminating to educators in other places and in the hope that within the extraordinarily wide range of contexts described here, teachers may be able to relate to some of the different pedagogies and analyses provided. A key element of the stories of teachers' practice necessarily involves an examination of the political, cultural, social, and economic conditions in which the pedagogy is created and situated. The politics of curriculum, pedagogy, assessment design, and delivery, although increasingly subject to global discourses, remain local in their particular manifestations and affect what might be the most effective and appropriate strategies for practitioners.

History has shown that different pedagogical orientations, even those that make claims for emancipatory effects, have different consequences for different groups of students in different locations (Cochran-Smith, 1995; Edelsky, 1991; Ellsworth, 1992). With regard to literacy education, critical researchers have demonstrated that assumptions held by White middle-class progressivists about the empowering effects of naturalistic approaches are unfounded (Delpit, 1988; Freebody et al., 1995; Lensmire, 1994; Luke, 1993; Walton, 1993; Willis, 1995). Evidence suggests that race, ethnicity, language, poverty, location, and gender impact on students' educational success and the ways in which they participate in the authorized discursive practices available in educational institutions. It is not possible to work with any simple formula, and each group of students' specific cultural and political histories impact on what is needed and what is possible.

Our main agenda is to sketch some ways in which critical literacies are being put together in very different classrooms in very different locations. These practices represent each teacher's commitment to ethical and pedagogical standpoints that respect students' ways of knowing and speaking. The stories of practice described here are not merely "set" in very different classrooms or contexts around the world; they are informed explicitly and very deliberately by, and make central use of, local cultural and political agenda. In this final section, we draw out some common pedagogical principles and also make a case for further research and teacher education work that is needed to sustain and extend a social justice agenda through literacy curriculum.

CRITICAL LITERACIES AS PRINCIPLED PRACTICE

These projects involve students and/or their teachers exploring relationships between language and power. They attempt to disrupt "taken-for-granted normality" to consider how things might be otherwise. What is being done in these very different situations has some core dynamic principles and repertoires of practices that can usefully be teased out as indicative pedagogical moves that include teachers and students. These might be characterized as:

- Engaging with local realities,

- Researching and analyzing language–power relationships, practices, and effects,

- Mobilizing students' knowledges and practices,

- (Re)designing texts with political and social intent and real-world use,

- Subverting taken for granted "school" texts,

- Focusing on students' use of local cultural texts, and

- Examining how power is exercised and by whom.

In the pedagogical work reported here, the students' interests and purposes are taken up by teachers as the foundation for what evolves in the classroom. Many of the students are culturally anchored in places where English is only one of several languages and where school literacies compete with other language and literate traditions. Critical literacies must, therefore, be negotiated amidst conflicting and changing cultural practices and expectations. This work is often done not only in multilingual and multicultural classrooms, but also in some instances in sites of poverty with minimal educational and material resources.

The way that critical literacies might be developed is also contingent upon the wider historical and political milieu. The teacher is very differently positioned in Hong Kong and Singapore with regard to the authoritative nature of the pedagogue and indeed the text. Where the teacher and/or the text are seen as deliverers of knowledge, clearly the work to be done in exploring the constituted nature of knowledge and power proceeds differently (see Cheah, chap. 5; Lin, chap. 6; Sahni, chap. 2, this volume). Inevitably then what counts as critical literacy varies in relation to competing ideologies, discourses, and cultural practices.

How the principles and practices just highlighted are realized looks very different, depending on the educational histories and contemporary practices of particular sites. Hence teachers may allow space for students to learn autonomy and selfhood (Sahni, chap. 2, this volume); help students take risks (Cheah, chap. 5, this volume); explore the possibility of questioning texts and forms of knowledge (Clarence-Fincham, chap. 15, this volume); and to permit students to use set texts for their own purposes (Lin, chap. 6, this volume). These educators demonstrate that awareness of language as a tool for critiquing the status quo allows students the space to become autonomous learners who can create and critique texts (including their own).

Common threads can be found as teachers use students' concerns and interests (or what teachers understand as their interests) to build a critical curriculum, to make spaces where social justice questions can be raised (Vasquez, chap. 4, this volume). The different chapters illustrate how social justice issues and questions about class, race, and gender are manifest in different places and across boundaries. For example, gender and sex roles became central or at least a key issue in the work of Dyson and Bigelow in the United States, for O'Brien, Mellor and Patterson, and Martino in Australia, and for Clarence-Fincham and Janks in South Africa. Sahni, Vasquez, Bigelow, Wallace, Stein, and Cruddas and Watson tackle questions about race, power, and cultural differences in India, Canada, the United States, the United Kingdom, and South Africa. In many cases, these educators have started with texts and practices invested with meaning for their students, whether it be a popular teenage movie (Bell, chap. 14, this volume), social events of the day (Vasquez, chap. 4, this volume); important cultural events, such as Mothers' Day (O'Brien, chap. 3, this volume) and Chinese New Year (Cheah, chap. 5, this volume), children's cartoon characters (Dyson, chap. 1, this volume), new interactive technology (Bigelow, chap. 7, this volume), or personal histories and oral stories (Cruddas and Watson, chap. 12; Stein, chap. 10; Janks, chap. 9, this volume). In situations where curriculum constraints restrict the teacher's flexibility, students themselves may negotiate set texts for their own purposes (Lin, chap. 6, this volume).

Reviewing these accounts of practice, one cannot fail to be impressed by the ways in which these teachers have grounded their work in the immediate concerns of their students. Although enacted very differently and seen through various lenses, the common themes are strikingly similar. Indeed it could be argued that the very real and often starkly contrastive local contexts described serve to underline shared concerns of educators worldwide and the fundamental importance of developing pedagogies that engage with matters of substance and offer students new discursive resources.

CRITICAL LITERACIES AND A "NEW" RESEARCH AGENDA

Recent work in the New Literacy Studies (Barton, Hamilton, & Ivanic, 2000; Gee, 2000; Prinsloo & Breier, 1996; Street, 1995) has increasingly emphasized and demonstrated that literacy practices are situated; that is, they are negotiated in everyday contexts, involving social, symbolic, and institutional relationships. It is no accident that such research has brought the local nature of literate practices into the foreground. Indeed ethnographic, anthropological, ethnomethodological, and linguistic analyses focus on the specific everyday worlds of participants in unfolding discursive practices. There is an emphasis on context, standpoint, and researcher position. This kind of research has illuminated what counts as literacy in practice, often importantly and deliberately focusing on the mundane lived experience of people in communities (Barton & Hamilton, 1998). Ironically, such research has made school practices look even stranger; that is, the rationalities (social and goal-driven) underlying literacy practices in the community contrast sharply with those typical of schools (individualized and assessed). Researchers taking critical ethomethodogical, anthropological, ethnographic, and/or sociological perspectives on mundane literacy events in classrooms have made it clear that the logic of school institutional practice, classroom routine, curriculum discourse, and pedagogy often produces "interactive trouble" (Freebody et al., 1995), identity conflicts (Luke, 1992; Willis, 1995), and ultimately academic failure for many students whose lifeworlds are most different from those of school (Comber, 2000).

This volume offers detailed practitioner accounts of the emergence of critical literacies as local and historically contingent practices. Such descriptions are crucial to building a significant corpus of theorized critical stories of young people and radical educators working for social justice. We get a sense of the assignments they tackled, the language of their analyses, the writing they produced, and the way school work became reconnected with community action. Yet there is a great deal more to be told if critical literacies are to remain dynamic and responsive to changing lifeworlds and institutions. Such accounts can inspire others to action (Dressman, 1999), but they can also be easily written off as simply the narratives of some rare heroic educators and as irrelevant or impractical elsewhere. Research is needed, therefore, to explore classroom and school communities where critical literacies and innovative pedagogies are being created. As educational researchers where do we put the camera to capture critical literacies, where and when do we turn on the sound? We believe that if we are to contribute to the production of curriculum where young people are engaged in curricula of depth and consequence, working on the construction of equitable relations and designing ethical, possible, and productive social futures (Gee, 2000; The New London Group, 1996), then more analysis of the discursive practices, productive routines, institutional ethos, and curricula of classrooms where teachers are engaged in negotiating critical literacies is needed. Such research is crucial in informing ongoing teacher education, both pre-service and in-service.

Documenting and analyzing community, school, and classroom practices that make a visible and positive difference in the life chances and experiences of young people, particularly those who may otherwise be disadvantaged by their material and cultural locations and circumstances, is necessary to sustain an aging and in some places demoralized education workforce. Such documentation could explore questions like: What are the repertoires of discursive practices we want young people to acquire? What do teachers and students in these classrooms say to each other? What are they able to say and write in the wider community? What relationships do they negotiate in school and with their communities? What are the social and pedagogical effects of their assignments, performances, artifacts? Who are these young people becoming? How can their teachers be sustained? What are the optimal conditions for such work? What knowledges, discourses, or representational resources do young people in these classrooms acquire, and what difference does that make now and in the future? How can we best assess and demonstrate the learning outcomes that are produced through these practices? Such research, in our view, is best done with teachers and university researchers working together, with both involved in genuinely reciprocal inquiry and learning relationships. University faculty and researchers need to learn about the actual contemporary conditions of teachers' work in real communities. We need to engage intellectually with the pedagogical hybridity that educators invent in order to pursue particular goals with particular students. Such reciprocal alliances might also involve filmmakers and journalists working together to produce different and new stories about work in schools and universities. Rather than recycling old agendas, we are calling for new kinds of research and documentation to get new kinds of work done. The outcomes and artifacts associated with such inquiry would include not simply books and papers, but also film (see, e.g., Comber et al, 1994; Comber & Nixon, 1999), newspapers (see *Rethinking Schools*), online clearing houses and so on.

We have many detailed and insightful studies of how schools fail some groups of students. There are blow-by-blow descriptions of how this unfolds in classroom talk and literacy events. Although there are accounts of course of effective schools and best practice in classrooms, there are few microanalyses undertaken of critical practices under construction—the classroom discourse that builds powerful and worthwhile learning and that works for students who are traditionally at risk of academic failure. We propose, therefore, that an urgent task for those committed to critical literacies in educational communities is to build more detailed accounts of such practices as they are negotiated (see also Knobel & Healy, 1998). This would involve ethnography, ethnomethodology, anthropology; it would involve audiotapes, photographs, documentaries, soundtracks, web sites—whatever ways the sites of productive pedagogy might best be represented. It would probably involve collaborations from critical educators coming from different perspectives and standpoints. Gunther Kress (1999) recently argued that, "Theoretical debate is essential: yet in the end, it is judged by its effects on practice" (p. 461). Finding better ways to thoroughly study the effects of theories of critical literacy on the enacted practices of teachers and students in classrooms must be a priority.

REFERENCES

Barton, D., & Hamilton, M. (Eds.). (1998). *Local literacies: Reading and writing in the community*. London and New York: Routledge.

Barton, D., Hamilton, M., & Ivanic, R. (Eds.). (2000). *Situated literacies: Reading and writing in context*. London and New York: Routledge and Taylor & Francis.

Bigelow, B. (1999). Probing the invisible life of schools. In C. Edelsky (Ed.), *Making justice our project*. Urbana: IL: National Council of Teachers of English.

Cochran-Smith, M. (1995). Uncertain allies: Understanding the boundaries of race and teaching. *Harvard Educational Review, 65*(4), 541–570.

Comber, B. (2000) What *really* counts in early literacy lessons. *Language Arts, 78*(1), 39–49.

Comber, B., Badger, L., Hill. S., & Nixon, H. (1994). *Literacy, diversity and schooling.* Centre for Advancement University Teaching, University of South Australia, Melbourne, Australia: Eleanor Curtain Publishing.

Comber, B., & Nixon, H. (1999). Literacy education as a site for social justice: What do our practices do? In C. Edelsky (Ed.), *Making justice our project: Critical whole language teachers talk about their work.* Urbana, IL: National Council of Teachers of English.

Comber, B., Thomson, P., & Wells, M. (2001). Critical literacy finds a "place": Writing and social action in a neighborhood school. *Elementary School Journal. 101*(4),451-464.

Delpit, L. (1988). The silenced dialogue: Power and pedagogy in educating other people's children. *Harvard Educational Review, 58*(3), 280–298.

Dressman, M. (1999). Mrs. Wilson's university: A case study in the ironies of good practice. *Language Arts, 76*(6), 500–509.

Dyson, A. (1993). *Social worlds of children learning to write in an urban primary school.* New York: Teachers College Press.

Dyson, A. (1997). *Writing superheroes: Contemporary childhood, popular culture, and classroom literacy.* New York: Teachers College Press.

Edelsky, C. (1991). *With literacy and justice for all: Rethinking the social in language and education.* New York : Falmer.

Edelsky, E. (Ed.). (1999). *Making justice our project.* Urbana, IL: National Council of Teachers of English.

Ellsworth, E. (1992). Why doesn't this feel empowering? Working through the repressive myths of critical pedagogy. In C. Luke & J. Gore (Eds.), *Feminisms and critical pedagogy.* New York: Routledge.

Foucault, M. (1988). The political technology of individuals. In L. Martin, H. Gutman, & P. Hutton (Eds.), *Technologies of the self: A seminar with Michel Foucault.* Amherst: University of Massachusetts Press.

Freebody, P., Ludwig, C., Gunn, S., Dwyer, S., Freiberg, J., Forrest, T., Gray, S., Hellsten, M., Herchell, P., Luke, H., Rose, J., & Wheeler, J. (1995). *Everyday literacy practices in and out of schools in low socio-economic urban communities: A descriptive and interpretive research program: Executive summary.* Department of Employment, Education, and Training. Carlton, Victoria: Curriculum Corporation.

Gee, J. P. (2000). The new literacy studies. In D. Barton, M. Hamilton, & R. Ivanic (Eds.), *Situated literacies: Reading and writing in context.* London and New York: Routledge and Taylor & Francis.

Janks, H. (Ed.). (1993). *Critical language awareness series.* Johannesburg, South Africa: Witswatersrand University Press and Hodder & Stoughton Educational.

Kamler, B., & Comber, B. (1996). Critical literacy: Not generic—not developmental—not another orthodoxy. *Changing Education: A Journal for Teachers and Administrators, 3*(1), 1–2, 4, 9.

Knobel, M., & Healy, A. (Eds.) (1998). *Critical literacies in the primary classroom.* Rozelle, New South Wales: Primary English Teaching Association.

Kress, G. (1999). Genre and the changing contexts for English Language Arts. *Language Arts, 76*(6), 461–469.

Lensmire, T. (1994). Writing workshop as carnival: Reflections on an alternative learning environment. *Harvard Educational Review, 64*(4), 371–391.

Luke, A. (1992). The body literate: Discourse and inscription in early literacy training. *Linguistics and Education, 4*(1), 107–129.

Luke, A. (1993). 'The social construction of literacy in the primary school. In L. Unsworth (Ed.), *Literacy learning and teaching: Language as social practice in the primary school.* Melbourne, Australia: Macmillan.

Luke, A. (2000). Critical literacy in Australia, *Journal of Adolescent and Adult Literacy, 43*(5), 448–461.

Muspratt, S., Luke, A., & Freebody, P. (Eds.). (1997). *Constructing critical literacies: Teaching and learning textual practice.* Cresskill, NJ: Hampton.

The New London Group. (1996). A pedagogy of multiliteracies: Designing social futures. *Harvard Educational Review, 66*(1), 60–92.

Prinsloo, M., & Breier, M. (Eds.). (1996). *The social uses of literacy: Theory and practice in contemporary South Africa.* Cape Town, South Africa: Sached Books. Amsterdam, The Netherlands: John Benjamins.

Street, B. (1995). *Social literacies: Critical approaches to literacy in development, ethnography and education.* London and New York: Longman.

Walton, C. (1993). Literacy in aboriginal contexts: Re-examining pedagogy. In A. Luke & P. Gilbert (Eds.), *Literacy in contexts: Australian issues and perspectives.* St. Leonards, New South Wales: Allen & Unwin.

Willis, A. (1995). School literacy experiences: How culturally narrow are they? *Discourse: Studies in the Cultural Politics of Education, 16*(2), 219–235.

Author Index

Subject Index